Marketing in Evolution

Essays in Honour of Michael J. Baker

D1824079

Edited by

Susan A. Shaw

and

Neil Hood

MACMILLAN

Selection, editorial matter and Chapter 1 © Susan A. Shaw
and Neil Hood 1996

Individual chapters (in order) © Christian Grönroos,
Robin Wensley, Susan A. Shaw and John A. Dawson,
Patricia W. Meyers and Gerard A. Athaide, Susan J. Hart,
Arch G. Woodside, Neil Hood and Stephen Young,
Michael J. Thomas, John Saunders 1996

First published 1996 by
MACMILLAN PRESS LTD
Houndmills, Basingstoke, Hampshire RG21 6XS
and London
Companies and representatives
throughout the world

ISBN 0–333–66264–4

A catalogue record for this book is available
from the British Library.

10   9   8   7   6   5   4   3   2   1
05   04   03   02   01   00   99   98   97   96

Copy-edited and typeset by Povey–Edmondson
Okehampton and Rochdale, England

Printed in Great Britain by
Antony Rowe Ltd, Chippenham, Wiltshire

Contents

v

List of Figures and Tables

Figures

Tables

Notes on the Contributors

Gerard A. Athaide is Assistant Professor of Marketing in the Joseph A. Sellinger, S. J., School of Business and Management at Loyola College in Maryland. His research focuses on new product development and innovation management in high-technology industries. He is particularly interested in the use of relationship marketing strategies to seek competitive advantage in technological settings. His research also includes identifying factors which influence a firm's decision to engage in exporting. He has published in the American Marketing Association's Summer and Winter Educators' *Proceedings* and the *Journal of Product Innovation Management*. He is a member of the American Marketing Association and the Academy of Marketing Science.

John A. Dawson is Professor of Marketing at the University of Edinburgh. His research interests are across retailing where he has been actively studying European retail activity since the mid-1960s. Current research is on retailer–supplier relationships, information use by retailers, the measurement of the retail sector, and retailer internationalisation. A recently initiated project is into retailer entry mechanisms into Poland and is funded by the EU. John Dawson is a Visiting Professor at ESADE in Barcelona, where he teaches on regular management programmes. He has also held visiting positions in the USA, Australia and Japan.

Christian Grönroos is Professor of Marketing at the Swedish School of Economics, Finland, where he also is Head of the Department of Marketing and Corporate Geography. He has since the 1970s been pursuing the development of services marketing and service management theory. Since the late 1980s he has been studying the ongoing paradigm shift in marketing towards a relationship marketing orientation. He has published numerous articles on service and relationship marketing and management topics. His 1983 book on the marketing of services has become a classic for students as well as for practitioners in four Scandinavian languages. In English he has published *Strategic Management, Marketing in the Service Sector* and *Service Management and Marketing*.

Susan J. Hart is Professor in the Department of Marketing at the University of Stirling. After working in industry in France and the UK she joined the University of Strathclyde as a researcher. She completed her doctoral degree on the subject of product management and worked on research projects examining the contribution of marketing to competitive success and new product design and development in manufacturing industry funded by the Economic and Social Research Council, the Chartered Institute of Marketing and the Design Council. She has held academic positions at Strathclyde and Heriot-Watt Universities, has worked with several industrial companies in teaching company schemes and holds visiting professorships in Denmark, Spain, The Netherlands and the USA. Her current research interests are in the development of new products and innovation, the contribution of marketing to company success and tourism marketing.

Neil Hood is Professor of Business Policy and Director of the Strathclyde International Business Unit in the Department of Marketing, University of Strathclyde. He is a former Dean of the Strathclyde Business School and former Deputy Principal of the University. His previous career includes a period as Director of Locate in Scotland and of Employment and Special Initiatives with the Scottish Development Agency. He combines academic life with the holding of a number of directorships in public and private companies. He has published widely on international business, business strategy and industrial development.

Patricia W. Meyers is Associate Professor of Marketing and Innovation Management at the School of Management, Syracuse University, Syracuse, New York, where she is also Associate Dean for Master's Programs and a research associate of the Earl V. Snyder Innovation Management Research Center. She holds degrees from the University of Michigan, Ann Arbor, and Syracuse University. Her research focuses on the development and commercialisation of technological innovations. Her articles have appeared in several books and journals, including *Research Policy, Journal of the Academy of Marketing Science, Journal of Macromarketing, Logistics Information Management* and the *Journal of High Technology Management Research*. She is a member of the American Marketing Association and the Product Development and Management Association.

John Saunders is Director of Loughborough University Business School and National Westminster Bank Professor of Marketing.

Previously he worked for the Universities of Warwick, Bradford, Huddersfield and Hawaii, the Hawker Siddeley Group and British Aerospace. He edits the *International Journal of Research in Marketing*, is assistant editor of the *British Journal of Management*, is on the European Marketing Academy's Executive, the British Academy of Management's Fellowship Committee, and the Chartered Institute of Marketing's Senate. His publications include *Principles of Marketing: The European Edition*, with Philip Kotler, Gary Armstrong and Veronica Wong, and *Competitive Positioning*, with Graham Hooley, and over sixty journal articles. As a consultant and trainer he has worked with many multinational organisations.

Susan A. Shaw is Professor and Deputy Principal at Strathclyde University. She entered academic life at the University of Stirling after a period working as a market analyst with ICI. Her academic interests lie in the areas of distribution channel management and inter-business relationships, particularly in the food industry, and she has involvement in food industry policy through membership of the Council of Food from Britain and the Food Advisory Committee and through work for international organisations. She has published widely on retailing and channel management and on food industry issues.

Michael J. Thomas was Chairman of the Chartered Institute of Marketing in 1995, Chairman of the Marketing Education Group 1983–7, has built a new business school in Gdansk, Poland, 1991–, and was awarded the Order of Merit (Commander's Cross) of Poland in November 1994. He travels (Visiting Professor, Universities of Georgetown, Indiana, Syracuse and Tennessee (USA), Karlstad (Sweden), Malta) and is an active publisher (*Gower Handbook of Marketing*, 4th edition) and editor (*Marketing Intelligence and Planning*).

Robin Wensley is Professor of Strategic Management and Marketing at the Warwick Business School and was Chair of the School from 1989 to 1994. He was previously with RHM Foods, Tube Investments and London Business School, and Visiting Professor at the University of California (Los Angeles) and the University of Florida. He is a Council member of the Tavistock Institute, a member of the ESRC Research Grants Board, and of the Senate of the Chartered Institute of Marketing. He has been involved with consultancy and management development with many major companies. His research and consultancy interests include marketing strategy and planning, investment decision-making and the assessment of competitive advantage. In this regard he has published a number of books and articles in the *Harvard Business Review*, the *Journal of Marketing* and the *Strategic Management Journal*, and worked closely with other academics and practitioners both in Europe and the USA. He is on the Editorial Board of the *International Journal of Research in Marketing* and has twice won the annual Alpha Kappa Psi award for the most influential article in the US *Journal of Marketing*.

Arch G. Woodside is the Malcolm S. Woldenberg Professor of Marketing, Freeman School of Business, Tulane University, New Orleans. He serves as editor of the *Journal of Business Research* and *Advances in Business Marketing and Purchasing*. Professor Woodside is a Fellow of the American Psychological Association, the American Psychological Society and the Southern Marketing Association.

Stephen Young is a Professor at Strathclyde University. He has spent his entire career in the fields of marketing, exporting and international business. He entered academic life after a period working as an economist with the Government of Tanzania and then as Head of International Economics with a UK food organisation and has maintained strong industrial links. His academic career has involved periods in the USA, visiting appointments in a number of continental European schools, and research and teaching assignments in numerous countries in Asia and Africa. He has published widely in the international business field.

1 Introduction

Susan A. Shaw and Neil Hood

This edited collection of original essays in honour of Michael John Baker continues the academic tradition of acknowledgement of distinguished contributions made by individuals to academic thought and life, in this case to the subject, marketing. Since marketing is a relatively new academic discipline, it is particularly appropriate that we pay tribute to the academic pioneers of our subject, of whom Michael is most assuredly one. The occasion of this acknowledgement is one of celebration since 1996 marks the twenty-fifth anniversary of the establishment of the first chair of Marketing at the University of Strathclyde to which Michael was appointed and which he still holds. It also marks the twenty-fifth anniversary of the founding by Michael of the Department of Marketing at the University of Strathclyde which Michael headed from 1971 to 1985. This department has grown and flourished over 25 years. It is a department which holds the highest British ratings for the quality of its research and of its teaching and which we like to consider one of the leading European university departments of marketing.

After graduation from the University of Durham, military service and periods in the private sector and in further education, Michael began his career in academic life as a Management Education Fellow at the Harvard Business School from 1968 to 1971. While there, he was awarded the Certificate of the International Teachers Program and a Doctorate in Business Administration for research on industrial innovation. This was the start of an academic career which has led to over 20 books which Michael either authored or edited about marketing and which have helped to define the subject, educate new generations of academics, educate practitioners and extend the awareness of the importance of the marketing function and philosophy in successful business management. His books include:

Marketing: Theory and Practice (first edition 1971), *Marketing New Industrial Products* (1975), *Offshore Inspection and Maintenance* (with S. T. Parkinson and M. A. Saren, 1975), *Industrial Innovation* (editor, 1979), *Market Development* (1983), *Successful Exporting* (1983), *Dictionary of Marketing and Advertising* (first edition 1985), *Marketing*

1

Strategy and Management (first edition 1985), *Organisational Buying Behaviour* (with S. T. Parkinson, 1986), *The Marketing Book* (first edition 1987), *The Role of Design in International Competitiveness* (with D. O. Ughanwa, 1989), *Marketing and Competitive Success* (with S. J. Hart, 1989), *Research for Marketing* (1991), *Perspectives on Marketing Management* (editor, four volumes 1991–4) and *Encyclopaedia of Marketing* (editor, 1991).

In the process of developing his subject he has further progressed as author of a large number of research articles and through the *Journal of Marketing Management* which he founded in 1985 and of which he remains editor. This journal is one of the most important European marketing journals and is one which receives distinguished contributions from around the world. It has provided a forum for discussion of marketing theory and application across a wider area, from central contributions on the nature of marketing thought to contributions from newer areas of marketing application such as social marketing and services marketing. More recently, successive volumes of *Perspectives on Marketing Management*, with their invited contributions, have provided a forum for presentation of leading edge thought in marketing. In addition he has been a member of ten other journal editorial boards.

Michael's contributions to marketing, of course, extend far beyond his writings and his role as a marketing educator can have few parallels. Several contributions must be highlighted. The first is the creation of the Department of Marketing at Strathclyde, already mentioned, which today teaches over 2000 undergraduates, offers single and joint honours degrees in marketing, two full-time postgraduate marketing programmes with over 100 students, a doctoral programme and two open learning masters programmes. He has successfully supervised 38 doctorates, of students who are now themselves educators in many countries around the world. Indeed, 13 (a Baker's dozen) of these former students now themselves hold university chairs.

He is a former chairman of SCOTBEC (Scottish Business Education Council), a governor of the CAM (Communication, Advertising and Marketing Education) Foundation and serves on the Economic and Social Research Council. He has been a visiting professor at ten universities in five continents. Of considerable importance to the general development of marketing education in the United Kingdom, he has had many years of active involvement in the Chartered Institute of Marketing. He was National Chairman of the Institute, 1986–7 and in 1994 became the founding chairman of the Senate of the College of

Marketing of the Institute. He was chairman of the Marketing Education Group (MEG) from 1973 to 1986 and became its president in 1986. Given his major role in the creation and development of MEG it is entirely appropriate that Strathclyde University's Department of Marketing should be hosting its annual conference in 1996 on his and our twenty-fifth anniversary and that this provides the occasion for us to present him formally with this present volume. We are of course not the first to honour him. He became a Fellow of the CAM Foundation in 1983, an Honorary Fellow of the Institute of Marketing in 1988, a Fellow of the Royal Society of Arts in 1986, a Fellow of the Scottish Vocational Educational Council in recognition of outstanding service to Scottish education in 1988 and a Fellow of the Royal Society of Edinburgh in 1995.

The University of Strathclyde is greatly in his debt for contributions which are wider than those to the Department of Marketing and its students. He acted as Dean of the Strathclyde Business School from 1978 to 1984. He was appointed as Deputy Principal of the University in 1984, Deputy Principal Management in 1988 and Senior Adviser to the Principal in 1991. His period as Deputy Principal was a period of rapid and successful development for the university to which he made a major contribution with his role in facilitating the transition from an administered to a managed system.

In this anniversary year, these many contributions will also be acknowledged elsewhere, but the purpose of this volume of essays is to honour Michael's contributions to marketing thought and as an educator and to this theme we now return. Michael's writings cover many aspects of marketing, since he has always emphasised the importance of a holistic approach to the subject and breadth as well as depth of understanding at both academic and practitioner levels. Common themes underpin his writings embracing his belief that marketing education should rest on a profound understanding of the core principles of the subject. The first of these is the role of demand and his writings emphasise the centrality of the need to understand customers, whether final consumers or business customers. Quality of response by businesses can only be understood in the context of consumer needs and wants. In *Marketing*, his introductory textbook, he quotes Adam Smith (*The Wealth of Nations*, 1776) who says that the 'consumption is the sole end and purpose of production'. Thus he emphasises the importance of understanding that competitive success is a process by which businesses make the same product at a lower price or a better product at the same price. This is the core around which analysis, whether it be of corporate strategy or, more broadly, the sources of competitiveness, must be built. This reductionist approach, he has argued, academics and practitioners ignore at their peril. He emphasises the complexity of the decision making processes of customers but shows through his presentation of decision making structures (*Marketing*, 1991; *Organisational Buying Behaviour*, 1986) the way in which logical analysis can provide understanding.

A second core theme is the prevalence of change. We must understand how to analyse the ways in which wants and needs change as a result of external factors and as a response to the activities of the business itself. Those businesses which combine an awareness of change and the ability to be flexible in response with the centrality of the customer are most likely to achieve competitive success (*Marketing and Competitive Success*, 1989).

The concern with core principles is linked to a belief that the principles of marketing are universal ones. Whether the emphasis is on processes of innovation (*Market Development*, 1983) or export marketing (*Successful Exporting*, 1983) or industrial marketing (*Organisational Buyer Behaviour*, 1986) or subsets of the subject (*The Role of Design in International Competitiveness*, 1989), his aim has been to demonstrate that each area must manage its specific characteristics within a framework which is generalisable and internally consistent.

More recently, he encourages us to revisit these basic principles. His contributions remind us in a timely way that the issues which currently preoccupy writers, such as concern with social processes in marketing, a concern with value chains and concerns with the management of change are not new but deeply embedded in the Western traditions of business thought, now stretching back several centuries. As he observes in the *Journal of Marketing Management* (1993), 'while fashions and theory ebb and flow there is a strong central current so that most arguments are very similar but appear in different guises, reflecting the original distinctions introduced by Aristotle and Plato'.

The clarity of thought which underlies Michael's contributions explains the success of the two textbooks, *Marketing: Theory and Practice* and *Marketing: Strategy and Management*. The number of editions and reprints of these books is testimony to the value which teachers and students attach to them. The philosophy underlying these texts is an uncompromising one: a view that students should not overcompartmentalise their thinking. They must understand that 'demand is the controlling factor and understanding of it must underlie all marketing functions' (*Marketing: Theory and Practice*, 4th edn, 1985).

These are not textbooks which can be learned by rote but ones which both require and promote analysis as a prerequisite to comprehension and leave the student with an effective understanding of their subject, making them in due course better practitioners. This meets his overriding concern that 'scholarly endeavour in the field of marketing should be directed towards, and seen as relevant and useful to, marketing practitioners' (*Perspectives on Marketing Management*, 1991) since 'theory and practice are inextricably linked' (*Perspectives on Marketing Management*, 1993).

Our volume of essays in his honour covers three overall themes. Firstly, Chapters 2 and 3 reflect some of the major conceptual debates which have been taking place within the marketing discipline over recent years. These range from the nature and future of modern marketing itself (Grönroos) to a reappraisal of the distinctive competencies of marketing (Wensley). Secondly, Chapters 4 to 8 examine a number of specialist and cognate areas which are broadly related to some of the interests represented in Michael Baker's work. These are wide-ranging and focus on the contributions which the individuals have made to their respective fields over many years in most cases. In view of Michael's own output, it is perhaps not surprising that innovation and change are both dominant themes, especially in Chapters 4, 5 and 7. In detail, Chapters 4 to 8 include the evolution of distribution channel theory (Shaw and Dawson); the role of relationship marketing and organisational learning in new product development (Meyers and Athaide); a theory of customer rejection of superior manufacturing technologies and product-service innovations (Woodside); new product success (Hart); and the evolution of international business and international marketing thought (Hood and Young). Thirdly, the two concluding chapters return to more general and overarching considerations related to the marketing profession and appropriate education within it (Thomas) and to a pithy reprise of the nature of marketing knowledge and marketing stars in the international academic firmament (Saunders). Both of the latter are areas in which Michael Baker has taken a keen interest. He, like us, will smile at some of the observations made, although he might not always agree with all the conclusions that are drawn. He might recall that Horace was ambitious enough to encourage his readers 'to seek the truth in the groves of Academe', but did not guarantee that they would always find it there.

The essays commence in Chapter 2 with a contribution from Christian Grönroos which seeks to evaluate what modern marketing is, and what it is not. Appropriately for a book of this type, it advocates that the fundamental cornerstones of so-called 'modern marketing' have to be rethought, not least because mainstream marketing based on the marketing mix management perspective is regarded as having little to offer service industries and manufacturers of industrial goods and equipment. Based on the changing marketing situations in the Western economies, it contends that either marketing as a discipline and as practised in companies must change radically or it will become a marginal phenomenon without much credibility. This analysis leads to the view that a paradigm shift in marketing is needed if it is to survive as a discipline. By way of offering a solution, it is suggested that the emerging theme of relationship marketing is just such a new paradigm but one which goes back to the very roots of the marketing phenomenon. The final section of the essay offers six propositions about the traditional cornerstones of mainstream marketing in the light of the way in which thinking has developed on relationship marketing. The last of these propositions suggests that, in order to develop understanding and a culture where it is possible to implement relationship marketing, it may be necessary 'to replace the term "marketing" with a neutral and psychologically more easily accepted term to describe the task of managing the firm's market relationships'. Although he is always interested in what marketing is, this might just be a step too far for Michael Baker!

In Chapter 3, Robin Wensley is equally keen to suggest that marketing requires to return to its roots, but in this case by encouraging it to be less concerned with what is in the domain of strategy and the fluctuating fads and fashions within the discipline itself. In his closely argued essay, Wensley considers that the (temporary and coincidental) link between marketing and strategy is becoming more and more tenuous for reasons of fashion and more refined analysis. The former has led to a shift from analysis to process and from formulation to implementation. The latter has resulted in a better understanding of the inapplicability of simple decision rules for all types of commercial success. This leads Wensley to argue with conviction that marketing needs to recognise its own sphere of distinctive competence, which in his view has two components, namely theory and research, related to buyer behaviour; and the functional focus on the nature and activities of marketing management. He makes a strong appeal for renewed intellectual effort in both of these areas in order to enhance the contribution which marketing makes to society.

The essay by Susan Shaw and John Dawson (Chapter 4) addresses channel evolution and channel management theory, an area of study which Michael Baker has in the past identified as deserving more attention. The particular scope of the chapter relates to the European experience and to consumer goods channels dominated by large retail businesses, a topic of special interest to the authors. They review the evolution of distribution channels for consumer goods in terms of structural change, the growth of retailer power, and the changes in channel characteristics, especially in the processes of channel management. In their subsequent critique of the contribution which distribution channel theory has made to explaining and placing these changes in context, Shaw and Dawson identify a number of gaps. These include the treatment of both channel functions and their location in areas such as new product development. In general they find a failure in channel research to address the relationship between the channel and the internal functioning of the business. Equally, more work needs to be directed to the functioning of the entire distribution chain before its operations can be fully understood. Among other implications of such a suggestion would be the necessity to consider the networks of other relationships which facilitate the functioning of the channel. They consider that the network approach has been rather neglected in the marketing literature on channels. One consequence of this critique is that the authors believe that approaches to channel research have been partial and therefore do not help understanding as to how channels evolve over time. In order to aid the process of integration they offer both a conceptual framework to assist in the understanding of channel evolution and an extensive agenda for research which would fill some of the knowledge gaps which they have identified.

Both Chapters 5 and 6 relate to new product development, a topic of long term interest to Michael Baker, dating back to his doctoral research in industrial innovation. The essay by Patricia Meyers and Gerard Athaide (Chapter 5) is the more narrowly based of the two. It reports on a specific clinical research project designed to investigate organisational seller–buyer relationships during new product development in a health care related applications software company, code named Medco. Their interest is in how the management of such relationships by the selling organisation involves effective organisational learning and generates competitiveness. The specific findings from the clinical study highlight the way in which the company used information from its relationships to respond to buyers' needs in real time. They also show that the cumulative information from these relationships helped the organisation to learn how to manage more effectively both its product and its relationships. A substantial part of the chapter relates the detailed findings to the wider literature on this topic, thus generating propositions for future research in high-technology innovation. As in the Grönroos chapter, relationship marketing is strongly featured. In this instance it is viewed as a form of market orientation which generates information which is acted upon by the seller to clarify the product's advantages, modify products and facilitate implementation.

The Susan Hart essay (Chapter 6) sets out to offer a conceptually based model for measuring new product success against a background of continuing debate about the determinants of success in this area. It makes frequent reference to related work by Michael Baker. The contribution commences with a discussion of the literature on the nature of new product success. This is based on a recognition of the many difficulties which confront research designed to separate the factors determining new product success and failure. Financial and non-financial measures of new product performance are assessed, and the need for these to be viewed in a more rounded and conceptually based manner is emphasised. Hart concludes that there are serious limitations surrounding the use of either type of measure, not least because of the lack of theoretical development in both, the inability to apportion relative weightings to the two different types of measures and the validity of the measures which are actually used to capture success in either category. The latter topic lays the basis for the second section of the chapter, which critically evaluates the major methodologies employed by researchers to measure new product success and failure. The argument is founded on the view that the observed shortcomings in the literature are partly related to the provenance of the measures chosen, the data collection method and the analytical techniques used in this type of research. Regarding the first of these points, Hart concludes that the evidence suggests that there has been insufficient managerial input into the components of measurement scales and that practitioners appear to demonstrate greater sensitivity to the role of the customer in determining success than do marketing academics.

The penultimate section of the Hart chapter turns to the interrelationships among success dimensions, concentrating on the associations between the level of analysis, cause, time and effect. This lays the foundations for the subsequent examination of two potential frameworks for measuring new product success based on two dimensions which are regarded as particularly critical, namely the level of analysis and time. It is suggested that the adoption of this approach could be a first step to a more rigorous and balanced approach to future research in this important area.

In Chapter 7, Arch Woodside sets out to describe and examine empirically several propositions on the causes and realised strategies that are likely to be found in different industrial marketing–purchasing situations involving rejecting versus accepting superior technological innovations. The empirical application in this case is to fibre glass light poles, as an example of a high performing and low lifetime-cost product which apparently continues to be rejected by US light pole buyers. Having set the scene, Woodside proceeds to extract the core propositions relating to both marketing and adopting superior technological innovations which have emerged from the academic and business literature. He draws attention to six main propositions, though the first of them has five micro elements to it. Together these emphasise the controlled chaos aspect of adoption, the need for new channels, lack of buyer familiarity, defensive marketing tactics by installed base technology and so on. Woodside usefully pulls some of these propositions together, links them to his own empirical research and thereby generates a rudimentary expert system of the acceptance/rejection of new superior technologies. He subsequently discusses its various elements and its applicability to his own and other work at some length. The penultimate section of the chapter tests the model empirically with reference to fibre glass reinforced poles, namely lamp posts. He finds that many of the theoretical propositions were supported by this particular field study. It was evident that overcoming resistance in the marketing channel and among heavy users of the installed base technology was a much greater task than realised by the manufacturers of superior technologies. Equally, both the finding and serving of customers responsive to the benefits of adopting the superior technologies are likely to require the development of hybrid marketing channel relationships.

In Chapter 8, Hood and Young turn to international aspects of marketing and international business, areas of enquiry which have developed with particular rapidity over the past 25 years. Linking back to Michael Baker's earlier work on export marketing, the authors review the evolution of theories and concepts in international business and international marketing. Four separate but interrelated themes are discussed: international production, the internationalisation of the firm, managing across borders and marketing across borders. In each of these, central research questions are posed and addressed. The authors trace the theory of international production through its various stages, including those linked to established traditions such as those of industrial organisation, markets and hierarchies, internationalisation and transactions costs, product cycle theories and the various attempts to synthesise these into integrated frameworks. Although from many common roots and showing signs of convergence, the literature on the internationalisation of the firm has developed at times rather separately from that on explanations for multinationality. More concerned with international market entry and market development activities, much of this research has been influenced by behavioural conceptualisations. These are reflected in the deployment of concepts such as establishment chain, innovation–adaption cycle and psychic distance. A further aspect has been derived from international industrial marketing research, focusing upon interactions, relationships and networks. The interaction and network approaches confirm the complexity of the processes of internationalisation. As elsewhere in this volume, the authors note that there is no shortage of knowledge in this field, but a continued need for explanations.

In their examination of international management, where the emphasis is placed on general and strategic management, Hood and Young conclude that many of the early theories and frameworks have limited applicability today. Some early typologies of management orientations still have currency, as does the classic environment–structure–strategy paradigm, and others conceptualising transnational organisations, heterarchies, hybrids and so on. Among the many gaps to be filled as theory struggles to keep pace with the scale, complexity and diversity of the phenomenon are the implications of non-equity modalities, the role of culture. To date, and regrettably, the authors observe, the common core of culture has not been utilised to provide a unifying framework in the international management field. The fourth section of the essay turns selectively to consider the direction of research into marketing across borders. It acknowledges much of the criticism which has been directed to one part of this area of study, especially to export marketing as regards the dearth of conceptual work, the weaknesses in methodology and so on. But the area of international management is a broad one although, as recent reviews have shown, several of its research streams have been given limited attention. Hood and Young conclude by emphasising the differential development of conceptual work within the four themes which they considered, finding that the international management and international marketing fields have both lagged behind over the period of review. Contingency and multidisciplinary approaches are offered as providing potential foundations for future subject development.

Chapters 9 (Thomas) and 10 (Saunders) comprise the final section of this volume. From his distinctive position within the marketing profession, Michael Thomas brings his own perspective to bear on the world of marketing and business. With echoes back to Robin Wensley's chapter, he draws out the elements of the intense debate about the future of marketing and the marketing profession, not least as regards the continued existence of marketing as a specialist function in a more customer oriented business environment. Thomas establishes an agenda for discussion by posing key questions about customers, markets, technology, communications and marketing organisations, all of which suggest that marketing as a function is going through a period of challenge and change. It leads the author to advocate the replacement of the manipulation of the four Ps (product, promotion, price, place) with relationship marketing in view of the rising countervailing power of demand and the limited ability of the supplier to engage in such manipulation. He calls for caveat vendor to replace caveat emptor. Pursuing this line of thought (see also Chapter 2) Thomas argues that, as regards the marketing professional, marketing has to be an organisational orientation which transcends narrow functional activities. The transition is from the functional to the attitudinal. In this vein, Thomas then considers different attitudes to capitalism across the business world and the impact which both the role change and the environment change must have on marketing education. He contends that this requires the development of an advanced marketing capability which is operationally closely linked to R&D management and incorporates newly relevant skills in finance, information technology, quality management and strategy. There is much to think about in this chapter and, if its prescriptions were followed, radical reform would occur in much of marketing education.

In Chapter 10, John Saunders turns his mind in another direction in his wistful musing on what it is which makes a star in our academic firmament. He notes the paucity of precedent for such research and, warming to his topic, he outlines his imaginative methodology. Astronomical metaphor abounds as he sets the framework for his task. No reference is made to the eighteenth-century work of Edward Young, but it might have been . . . 'Devotion! daughter of astronomy! An undevout astronomer is mad.' With no lack of devotion and with much historical reference in similar tone, Saunders proceeds to review the stars in the academic marketing firmament, deploying some acid tests to the product of their minds and word processors: clear or weighty? focused or opportunistic? intellectual or pragmatic? team players or individualists?, and so on. He subsequently positions the stars within their galaxies. Some, of course, are their own galaxy, while others aspire to being their own universe! Following his reprise on star qualities, and in the true professional spirit of a volume of this type, Saunders identifies Michael Baker as the star's star. This chapter may make the movies!

In spite of the diversity of the contributions to this volume, a number of recurring themes emerge, albeit often viewed from different perspectives. One is the influential role which network concepts are making in the shaping of marketing thought, analysis and practice. Another is the sense that marketing as a discipline is at yet another of its watersheds, this time prompted in part by its eclectic nature and in part because of the everyday commercial challenges to the entrenchment of its functional focus. It has been long argued by Michael Baker and others that marketing is a state of mind. Business has been showing clear signs of both believing this and therefore being less willing to leave it to the (marketing) professionals. One of the many consequences of this relates to the unanswered questions in research in marketing. As these essays show, there are many of them, and another common theme is the call for them to be addressed, and addressed with more rigour to ensure credibility in an ever more sceptical environment.

References

Baker, M.J. (1971, 1974, 1979, 1985, 1991) *Marketing: Theory and Practice*, 1st – 4th eds (London: Macmillan).

Baker, M.J. (1983) *Market Development* (Harmondsworth: Penguin).

Baker, M.J. (1983) *Successful Exporting* (Helensburgh: Westbourne Publishers).

Baker, M.J. (1985, 1992) *Marketing: Strategy and Management,* 1st and 2nd eds, (London: Macmillan).

Baker, M.J. (1991) *Perspectives on Marketing Management, I* (Chichester: Wiley).

Baker, M.J. (1992) *Perspectives on Marketing Management, II* (Chichester: Wiley).

Baker, M.J. (1993) *Perspectives on Marketing Management, III* (Chichester: Wiley).

Baker, M.J. (1993) 'Editorial', *Journal of Marketing Management*, 9, 16.

Baker, M. J. and S. T. Hart (1989) *Marketing and Competitive Success* (London: Philip Allan).

Baker, M. J. and S. T. Parkinson (1986) *Organisational Buying Behaviour* (London: Macmillan).

Horace, *Epistles*, ii.45.

Smith, A. (1950) *The Wealth of Nations. An Inquiry into the Nature and Cause of the Wealth of Nations* (London: Methuen) (first published 1776).

Ughanwa, D. O. and Baker, M. J. (1989) *The Role of Design in International Competitiveness* (London: Routledge).

2 The Rise and Fall of Modern Marketing – and its Rebirth

Christian Grönroos

INTRODUCTION

In mainstream textbooks modern marketing is regarded as being based on the marketing concept and to include management-oriented activities that revolve around the marketing mix and its four Ps. The needs and wants of the customers are established through market research, and in this way the customer input into the marketing planning and implementation processes that is required according to the marketing concept is achieved. Is this modern marketing today, in view of the current situation in most market-places and the continuing development towards more global competition, maturing markets and more sophisticated customers? The purpose of this chapter is to discuss what modern marketing is, and what it is not. It is suggested that the emerging relationship marketing is a new marketing paradigm that goes back to the roots of the marketing phenomenon. Fundamental cornerstones of what now is considered 'modern marketing' have to be rethought. Therefore, six propositions about relationship marketing are formulated and discussed.

HOW 'MODERN MARKETING' BECAME MODERN

According to the literature, what we call marketing first emerged in the early years of the twentieth century (see, for example, Sheth *et al.*, 1988). It developed into what often is considered modern marketing with the formulation of the marketing concept (compare McKitterick, 1957), the introduction of the notion of the marketing mix (Culliton, 1948; Borden, 1964) and the development of the marketing mix management approach with the 4P model (McCarthy, 1960). This

14

approach to marketing quickly swept away previously introduced notions and models of marketing and achieved the position of the dominating marketing paradigm. It did so with surprising speed. In the pre-Second World War era economists expanded price theory to include more variables to fit what they called oligopolistic competition (cf. Chamberlain, 1933). The functional school of marketing (cf. McGarry, 1950) also created lists of marketing variables, probably under the influence of the theory of oligopolistic competition. These lists were, however, soon absorbed by the short list of the 4Ps. Very soon the connection to microeconomic theory was cut off and subsequently totally forgotten. Although the lists of marketing variables were largely based on empirical induction, 'the marketing mix eventually became just a list of Ps without roots' (Grönroos, 1994, p. 350). Theoretically, there have been serious doubts about the validity of this list (for example, Waterschoot and Van den Bulte, 1992; Kent, 1986).

In the 1950s researchers of the so-called Copenhagen School, many of whom also were economists, developed an approach to managing marketing based on microeconomic theory and theories about *action parameters* (for example, Frisch, 1933; von Stackelberg, 1939; Abbott, 1955) that they called *parameter theory* (Rasmussen, 1955; Mickwitz, 1959, 1966). This marketing management theory has several similarities with the marketing mix. It is, however, more developed and, through market elasticities, has a firm connection with microeconomic theory. However, the pedagogical simplicity and managerially appealing toolbox nature of the 4Ps of the marketing mix soon confined parameter theory to mere footnotes in marketing textbooks. For the sake of marketing, parameter theory deserved a better fate.

The marketing concept as it was developed around 1960 is often seen as the foundation of modern marketing. The importance of the customer to the success of the firm was clearly recognised at that time. The vital role of the customer was not, however, established only then, although the marketing literature likes to imply that. As early as 1916, Romilla, a Norwegian (originally Irish) teacher of market communication, in a book about sales, advertising and other means of market communication formulated the following motto for success: 'Try to look at things from the customer's side of the encounter' (Romilla, 1916, p. 35). Older still, an ancient Chinese proverb says that 'customers are precious, goods are only grass'. As we can see, the approach to doing business that is based on the customer perspective, what today is often termed 'modern marketing', is certainly not new. Its roots go far back in the history of trade and commerce.

Why did the marketing mix management approach to marketing become so successful? One of the key reasons for this is probably that Borden's original idea of a list of a large number of marketing mix ingredients that have to be reconsidered in every given situation (cf. Borden 1964) was shortened. This seems to have been done for pedagogical reasons to fit textbook purposes. However, a more limited number of marketing variables did seem to fit typical situations observed by the initiators of the shortlist of four standardised Ps. These typical situations can be described as involving consumer packaged goods in a North American environment with huge mass markets, a highly competitive distribution system and very commercial mass media. Prerequisites for this marketing approach are mass markets, anonymous customers and to some extent standardised products. In the industrial society, the foundation of which was laid by, for example, Adam Smith (1950) and Frederick Taylor (1947), this marketing perspective was regarded as modern in most situations. However, even in other markets (at that time) the infrastructure was to varying degrees different and the products only partly consumer packaged goods. Nevertheless the 4 Ps of the marketing mix became *the universal marketing theory* and an almost totally dominating paradigm for most academics. They have had a tremendous impact on the practice of marketing as well (cf. Dixon and Blois, 1983; Kent, 1986; Grönroos, 1994).

In the industrial society of the post-Second World War era the marketing mix management approach inevitably was helpful for very many industries in many markets. In that sense it was at that time modern. The rise of this 'modern marketing' coincides with the time when the industrial society was reaching the peak of its life cycle in the Western world. A good enough product and effective sales were no longer sufficient to guarantee success in the market-place. *Marketing mix management turned marketing into a highly effective impact machine.* The markets for most goods and services were still growing. The mass-oriented philosophy and the functionalistic approach of scientific management based on specialisation of labour, standardisation of products and the anonymous nature of customers were still valid as a management perspective.

However, since that time the market environment has changed, especially in the Western economies, and the decline of this type of 'modern marketing' has begun. First, the once dominating mass markets are becoming more and more fragmented. Second, by and large customers do not want to remain anonymous anymore and to be treated as such, and they are becoming more sophisticated. Third, more and more markets are maturing. Fourth, competition is increasing and becomes global. Fifth, the market offerings are becoming less standardised, because in many situations customers want this and new technology makes it possible in a totally different way. Nevertheless, marketing mix management is, no doubt, still a valid marketing approach, for example, for many manufacturers of consumer goods, but it has definitely lost its position as the mainstream and dominating paradigm of modern marketing. The once so effective impact machine has started to fall apart. Only mainstream marketing research and standard marketing textbooks have not noticed it yet.

'MODERN MARKETING' FALLS INTO DECLINE

In fact, marketing mix management did not lead only to positive results. Externally, *consumerism* emerged as a protest movement, and in many societies mechanisms such as the consumer ombudsman were established to keep an eye on the way marketing was practised. The impact machine did not please everyone. Eventually, negative effects occurred internally as well. Marketing mix management includes at least the following *five cornerstones*: the marketing mix itself, the marketing department, marketing planning, market segmentation, and market research and market share statistics. None of them as they are treated in mainstream marketing thought are based on very solid ground in today's marketing environment.

The *marketing mix and its 4P model* define the variables that are considered part of marketing. Although the Ps are not at all useless as marketing variables today, the philosophical foundation of the marketing mix and its Ps are not very well fitted to the competitive situation that has been emerging in most industries in the Western world for some time. The mass marketing and transaction orientation as well as the adversarial approach to customers do not allow the firm to adjust its market performance to the demands of more and more customers today: enhanced value around the core product, reliable service to accompany the product, a trustworthy relationship with customers, suppliers, distributors, and so on. As Dixon and Blois (1983) put it, 'indeed it would not be unfair to suggest that far from being concerned with a customer's interests (ie: somebody *for whom* something is done) the view implicit in the 4 P approach is that the customer is somebody *to whom* something is done!' (p. 4) (emphasis added). To use a marketing metaphor, the marketing mix and its 4 Ps constitute a *production-oriented* definition of marketing, and not a market-oriented or custo-mer-oriented one (see Grönroos, 1989). Today with more sophisticated customers, maturing markets and intensifying global competition this approach to customers will not do a firm much good. Cooperation rather than an adversarial situation is a better foundation for market-ing in today's market situation.

The *marketing department*, including specialists on various subareas of marketing, is the organisational solution for managing, planning and implementing marketing activities. This functionalistic organisa-tional solution is inherent in the marketing mix management approach and follows the general principles of scientific management. Specialists should themselves take care of a task for specialists. However, except for some special cases, such as many consumer packaged goods, marketing is no longer the sole task of marketing specialists anymore. Marketing is spread throughout the organisation, and this goes for a growing number of businesses, in service industries and in the manu-facturing sector alike (cf. Gummesson, 1987; Grönroos, 1990, 1995).

Eventually marketing and the marketers have become isolated in the organisation. As we have observed in another context, 'both from an organisational point of view and from a psychological standpoint the marketing department is *off side*' (emphasis added) (Grönroos, 1994, p. 356). The marketing department cannot influence the people in the rest of the organisation outside the marketing department to take their role as *part-time marketers*, to use a term coined by Gummesson (1987). Part-time marketers are people outside the marketing depart-ment who are not marketing specialists but rather specialists in, for example, maintenance, deliveries of goods, claims handling, operating telephone exchanges, or just about any type of job, where their attitudes and way of doing their job have an impact on the customer's perception of the firm and of the quality of its market offerings. Hence they have dual responsibilities, both for doing their job well and, in doing so, for making a good marketing impact.

Gummesson observes that, in industrial markets and in service businesses, the part-time marketers typically outnumber several times over the full-time marketers, that is the marketing specialists operating within the marketing and sales departments. Furthermore, he con-cludes that 'those marketing and sales departments specialists (the full-time marketers) are not able to handle more than a limited portion of the marketing as its staff cannot be at the right place at the right time with the right customer contacts' (Gummesson, 1990, p. 13). Hence the part-time marketers do not only outnumber the full-time marketers, the specialists; often they are the only marketers around in the very moments of truth (cf. Normann, 1983) when the marketing impact is made and a basis for customer satisfaction is laid. And the marketing department cannot plan the job of the part-time marketers or in any way take responsibility for their attitudes and performance. In the final analysis, a traditional marketing department will always be a barrier to the spreading of a market orientation and an interest in the customer throughout the organisation (compare Piercy, 1985; and Grönroos, 1982, 1990).

Furthermore, the marketing specialists organised in a marketing department may become alienated from the customers. Managing the marketing mix means relying on mass marketing. Customers become numbers for the marketing specialists, whose actions, therefore, typically are based on surface information obtained from market research reports and market share statistics. Frequently such full-time marketers may act without ever really having encountered a real customer. As we observed as early as 1982 in a study about service firms, traditional marketing departments may make a firm less customer oriented and make it more difficult to create an interest in marketing among employees who do not belong to such departments (Grönroos, 1982).

Market planning is the process of planning and developing budgets for the activities of the marketing department. As long as more or less all marketing activities are in the hands of the marketing department traditional marketing planning is fine. However, in a situation where much or even most of the marketing impact is the result of activities that are not the responsibility of the marketing department it does not make sense to plan the activities of that department separately and call this plan a 'marketing plan'. It is of course part of marketing, but so much more that today is planned as parts of other plans should be planned from the same marketing perspective as the activities of the traditional marketing plan. Just preparing a 'marketing plan' within a marketing department does not mean that the firm's total marketing activities as perceived by its customers are planned. It easily becomes a plan that is counteracting what is planned as part of human resource management, production and operations and so on, or counteracted by those plans. *The result is not well-planned marketing.* What is called the 'marketing plan' is more or less only covering external marketing activities, by which the firm *gives promises* to potential and existing customers. Interactive marketing activities and the performance, attitude and behaviour of the part-time marketers are not planned with a customer perspective in mind. Hence how *promises are fulfilled* is not planned from a marketing point of view. If top management, the marketers and people from other departments internally believe in such a 'marketing plan', which they often seem to do, the marketing concept, that is, the notion that the interest of the customer should be kept in mind in the firm's planning processes, is not fulfilled.

Market segmentation (cf. Smith, 1956) is the process of identifying and evaluating subgroups of customers that are internally more homogeneous than the total market. As long as markets can be viewed as masses of anonymous customers, market segmentation has served marketing well. However, when customers do not wish to be treated as numbers anymore but as individuals, the traditional notion of market segmentation becomes less helpful. Identifying groups of numbers that somehow look alike is in many cases still a valid approach to segmentation, but it is often more important for the firm to identify its existing and potential customers as individuals representing households or organisations. From a profitability point of view, getting a larger share of the purchases of such individuals may be better than getting a larger number of customers in a given market segment.

Market research and market share statistics are a way of finding out needs and expectations of customers and monitoring the level of satisfaction among the firm's customers, and of evaluating the relative sales result of a firm as compared to that of the competition. When marketing is based on a notion of masses of anonymous customers, this is a practical way of monitoring how well, on the average, the firm is doing. Far too often, however, market share alone is treated as a way of evaluating the success of the firm in satisfying the needs and expectations of its customers. The better the market share is maintained or increased, the healthier the customer base. Of course, this is not the case, but as frequently no other than at best ad hoc information about customer satisfaction is available it is easily understood that good sales performance is taken as a measure of satisfied customers. This may, however, turn out to be a dangerous misunderstanding. And the closer natural contacts the firm has with its customers, the less defendable it is to mix up market share statistics with satisfaction and the health of the customer base.

Market research is based on surveys, and because such data-gathering methods normally do not allow for obtaining in-depth information about the thoughts and intents of customers, mostly surface data are gathered. Such data may be useful, too, but, for example, information about how satisfied the customers are and about customer needs, desires and expectations that employees who on a daily basis or from time to time interact with customers are accumulating is neglected. The firm knows very little about the specific needs, desires and expectations of every individual customer, although the information technology available today makes it possible to develop customised databases (cf. Vavra, 1994).

WHAT IS THE FUTURE OF MARKETING?

What can marketing offer in the new post-industrial era? Mainstream marketing based on the marketing mix management perspective has little to offer service industries and manufacturers of industrial goods and equipment. Although many of the marketing mix variables are useful for firms within these sectors, the perspective is not geared to the current market situation and is therefore misleading. The short-term, transaction-oriented and adversarial nature of marketing mix management as a function more or less only for specialists does not guarantee that the firm is creating and delivering the total value package or offering that today's customers are looking for. At best this type of marketing has only a marginal effect or is a harmless waste of the firm's money. At worst it becomes dangerous, with a fatal excess of promising, followed by mismanagement of the fulfilment of promises resulting in low customer perceived quality and eventually lost business.

Even in the consumer goods sector firms are starting to look for new approaches, among other things because traditional mass marketing costs too much and is not as effective as it used to be (cf. Rapp and Collins, 1990; McKenna, 1991). So also in this sector new approaches are needed.

WHAT IS NEEDED IN MARKETING?

On the basis of the changing marketing situations in the Western economies it is not too difficult to draw the following conclusion: either marketing as a discipline and as practised in companies changes radically, or it will become a marginal phenomenon without much credibility. Threats can be seen already. As Sheth put it in a commentary at a 1994 relationship marketing conference, the sales function is going towards a renaissance. Because marketing is at risk of increasingly occupying itself with only marginal and second-rate issues for the

development and maintenance of customer relationships, sales become the function that at least has direct, on-line contacts with customers (Sheth and Parvatiyar, 1994). A *new sales orientation* may be emerging. The other threat comes from the *total quality movement*. As Stauss (1994) demonstrates, total quality management (TQM) is at best taking the customer perspective into the development of various business processes. Successfully implemented TQM processes should result in a firm that understands the needs and expectations of its customers and takes this into account when planning and implementing its various processes, and thus delivers the quality and value its customers are looking for; and all this without the cooperation of marketing. 'If Total Quality Management efforts become everybody's duty – customer satisfaction is everybody's business' (Stauss, 1994, p. 14).

At first glance, both these scenarios may look somewhat far-fetched. However, they include contemporary trends in business. If marketing does not demonstrate that it is the discipline that understands the customer and how to handle customer relationships better than others, we may easily find that either of these scenarios, or both in support of each other, make marketing unnecessary. To avoid this, *a paradigm shift in marketing is needed if marketing is to survive as a discipline.*

RELATIONSHIP MARKETING: A MARKETING PARADIGM FOR THE 1990s AND BEYOND[1]

From the 1970s an alternative approach to marketing based on the establishment and management of relationships has emerged within two streams of research emanating from Scandinavia and Northern Europe and eventually spreading to many parts of the Western world. These streams of research are the Nordic School of Service (cf. Grönroos and Gummesson, 1985; see also Berry and Parasuraman, 1993) that looks at management and marketing from a service perspective and the IMP Group (cf. Håkansson, 1982) that takes a network and interaction approach to understanding industrial businesses. A common denominator of these two schools of thought is that marketing is more a management issue than a function, and that managing marketing, or market-oriented management as marketing is frequently called, normally has to be built upon relationships rather than transactions. Building and managing relationships has become a philosophical cornerstone of the Nordic School of Service and the IMP Group since the late 1970s. However, 'relationship marketing' as a term was not used until the latter part of the 1980s. It was first coined in the USA in 1983 by Berry (1983) and the relationship marketing approach is spreading there (Kotler, 1992; Webster, 1992, 1994; Hunt and Morgan, 1994; Sheth and Parvatiyar, 1995) and in an Anglo-Australian context (Christopher *et al.*, 1992) as well. Although the concepts that are used in these various areas of relationship-oriented marketing differ to some extent, and the viewpoints taken are somewhat different, one can probably conclude that an understanding of services and how to manage and market services is a key to understanding the nature of relationship marketing. Understanding how to manage networks and partnerships is another one. When taking a relational approach every firm offers services (cf. Webster, 1994). 'When service competition is the key to success for practically everybody and the product has to be defined as a service, every business is a service business' (Grönroos, 1996).

In the literature there is no agreement on a definition of relationship marketing. Although most definitions have common denominators, there are differences in scope. A comprehensive definition states that: 'Relationship marketing is to identify and establish, maintain, and enhance relationships with customers and other stakeholders, at a profit, so that the objectives of all parties involved are met . . . this is done by a mutual exchange and fulfilment of promises' (Grönroos, 1989, 1990, 1994). This definition is supplemented by a statement that such a marketing approach should lead to a trusting relationship between the parties involved. Key aspects of such an approach to marketing are the importance of not only getting customers and creating transactions (identifying and establishing) but also of maintaining and enhancing continuing relationships. Marketing has both the responsibility of giving promises and the task of fulfilling them. Profitable business relationships rely on the capability of a firm to develop trust in itself and its performance among its customers and other stakeholders. Internal marketing becomes a critical issue in relationship marketing if the organisation is to be well prepared for its new marketing tasks (Grönroos, 1990). In a recent article about relationship marketing, Bitner (1995) emphasises the need for a firm to manage not only the task of giving and fulfilling promises but also the task of enabling the fulfilment of promises if marketing is to be successful.

With some variety in broadness and emphasis, most of the definitions about relationship marketing offered in the literature so far have a similar meaning (cf. Christopher *et al.*, 1992; Blomqvist *et al.*, 1993; Hunt and Morgan, 1994; Sheth and Parvatiyar, 1994; Gummesson,

1995). For example, Sheth and Parvatiyar (1994) state that relationship marketing is 'the understanding, explanation and management of the ongoing collaborative business relationship between suppliers and customers' (p. 2), whereas Gummesson (1995) defines relationship marketing as a marketing approach that 'is based on relationships, interactions and networks'.

In more general terms the Grönroos definition of relationship marketing can be formulated as a generic marketing definition: *Marketing is to manage the firm's market relationships* (Grönroos, 1996). This definition includes the fundamental notion of marketing as a phenomenon basically related to the relationships between a firm and its environment. It points out that marketing includes all necessary efforts required to prepare the organisation for, and implement activities needed to manage the interfaces with, its environment. Markets are of course of several kinds: customers, distributors, suppliers, networks of co-operating partners, and so on. Transaction-oriented activities heavily relying on the 4Ps are but a special case with uncomplicated and mostly non-personal relationships. This generic definition makes it possible to develop marketing strategies according to a relational approach or a transactional approach depending on what suits any given market situation best (cf. Grönroos, 1995).

In none of these definitions is the concept of *exchange* (cf. Baggozzi, 1975) that for about two decades has been considered a foundation of marketing included. Focusing on exchange is considered too narrow a view. A relationship includes much more than exchanges, and if a trusting relationship between two or several business partners exists, exchanges should inevitably occur from time to time. However, there is so much more to a continuing relationship that also has to be taken care of, if exchanges of offerings for money are to take place. Moreover, what actually is exchanged especially in a long-term relationship is not very clear. The relationship is a more fundamental unit of study than the exchanges that from time to time take place in them. Hence the basic concept of marketing is the relationship itself rather than singular exchanges that occur in the relationship. From this it follows that the concept of exchange relationship that is frequently used is a contradiction (cf. Craig-Lees and Caldwell, 1994). 'Exchange is a concept with a short term notion where something is given to someone else, whereas relationship has a long-term notion implying an association of two parties. The combination of the two does not make sense' (Grönroos, 1996).

Marketing from a relational perspective is not a new phenomenon. Rather it is a return to what perhaps can be called the roots of trade and commerce, before scientific management principles were used so extensively, and before the entrance of the middleman in the relationship between suppliers and users that broke up these relationships. Marketing was based on management of relationships. The orientation towards mass production, mass distribution and mass consumption, which at a period in the history of economic development in the Western world served the creation of wealth well, made it difficult to maintain this basic nature of marketing. As we have discussed above, we have already entered a post-industrial society with a new business environment and new marketing challenges. New management principles are needed. This makes it possible for marketing to return to its roots again.

THE PARADIGM SHIFT: CONSEQUENCES FOR MARKETING

In a previous section we briefly discussed how the current understanding of *five cornerstones* in mainstream marketing may cause problems in today's marketing environment. In this final section we put forward five propositions regarding the future directions of these areas, based on the analysis of the shortcomings of the marketing mix management paradigm and on the nature of the emerging new relational paradigm. Finally, a sixth proposition is added.

The Marketing Mix and the 4Ps

The marketing mix clearly includes variables, such as advertising, selling and pricing, that are needed in a relationship-oriented marketing approach. However, the basic perspective that the marketing mix consists of a number of predetermined groups of decision-making areas that together are what should be planned as marketing is wrong. It fits a situation where the customer is anonymous and the market offering is a fairly simple product, such as many consumer packaged goods. When the firm can identify its customers (or distributors or suppliers), when interactions between these parties and their staff occur, and when it is important to make current customers interested in buying again (cf. Reichheld and Sasser, 1990), marketing impact is created by a large number of people, the part-time marketers and other resources in the organisation, in addition to the full-time marketers. Hence marketing variables can neither be predetermined, because they vary from case to case, nor separated from activities that, for example, belong to production and operations or deliveries or a host of other business processes. We can formulate the first proposition about how to understand the nature of marketing and marketing variables in relationship marketing.

Proposition 1

In relationship marketing the firm cannot predetermine a set of marketing variables to use, but has to found its marketing decisions on the stage and nature of the relationship with any given existing or potential customer at any point in time and use the resources and activities that make a desired marketing impact by creating value and enhancing satisfaction, whatever those resources and activities are and regardless of where in the organisational hierarchy they are located.

The Marketing Department

As marketing resources, defined as to include part-time marketers, can be all over the organisation and not only a group of specialists, total marketing cannot be organised in one specialised marketing department. Marketing responsibility must be spread throughout the organisation. Moreover, it is probably not possible for the head of a marketing department to take responsibility for the marketing impact of part-time marketers and to have a decisive influence on investments in equipment and operational and administrative systems that also have a marketing impact on the customers. Only top management or the head of, for example, a regional organisation or a division can take that responsibility. Marketing specialists are of course still needed to take care of full-time marketing activities such as market research, some advertising programmes, and so on. In addition to that, as specialists on the customers they can assist top management as internal marketing facilitators, taking on internal marketing tasks as internal consultants. As Berry (1986) observes, 'service marketing directors not only must persuade customers to buy (for the first time), they must also persuade – and help – employees to perform' (p. 47). Marketing specialists can help in making part-time marketers understand and accept their marketing responsibility through educating employees on managerial and non-managerial levels about the nature, purpose and applications of part-time marketing, they can strive to support invest-ments in tools and systems that make it easier for part-time marketers to perform, and they can be visible supporters of good quality in the organisation (Berry and Parasuraman, 1991). If the group of marketing specialists in a firm becomes too big and takes the form of a traditional department, problems with market orientation and customer con-sciousness will follow. Although these observations were made in service contexts, they are equally valid for all firms that are adopting a relationship marketing approach. Hence we can formulate the second proposition about how to organise marketing.

Proposition 2

In relationship marketing, marketing cannot be organised as a separate organisational unit, but instead a marketing consciousness has to be developed throughout the organisation. However, marketing specia-lists are needed for some traditional marketing activities and as internal consultants to top management in order to help in instilling such a marketing consciousness.

Marketing Planning

As marketing resources can be found all over the organisation and not only in a marketing department, marketing cannot be planned in the form of a traditional, separate marketing plan. Instead the marketing impact of resources and activities that are planned under other head-ings than marketing, such as production and operations, human resources, investment in systems and equipment, and so on, has to be recognised. All resources and activities that have such an impact have to be integrated regardless of whose responsibility they are. This can only be done in an overall corporate plan that is based on a notion of relationship building and maintenance. As we concluded in an earlier study (Grönroos, 1982), a market orientation needs to be instilled in all plans through a market-oriented corporate plan. This plan would then serve as a governing *relationship plan*. Hence we can formulate the third proposition about how to plan relationship marketing.

Proposition 3

Relationship marketing cannot be planned in traditional marketing plans, because many of the marketing resources and activities are simultaneously planned in other plans. Instead a market orientation has to be instilled in all plans and these have to be integrated through a market-oriented corporate plan as a governing relationship plan.

Market Segmentation

As relationship marketing is based on a notion of relationships with identifiable customers that should not be treated as unknown persons but as individuals representing households or organisations, traditional segmentation is less appropriate. Instead of getting some of the business of a large segment, the firm should strive to get as much as possible of every individual customer's business (cf. Peppers and Rogers, 1993). The basic idea behind market segmentation still holds true, of course. However, the nature of segmentation is changing dramatically. It is no longer enough to distinguish between homogeneous groups of customers based on average measures. Much more detailed and individualised information in the form of, for example, customer information files (cf. Vavra, 1994) or other types of databases have to be compiled. Firms serving mass markets cannot, of course, make such files as individual and informative as firms that have a limited number of customers. However, the basic principle should be the same in both situations. Costs of developing such databases may also restrict the amount of information that can be obtained and retrieved. Hence the fourth proposition about how to distinguish between customers can be formulated.

Proposition 4

In relationship marketing information about potential and existing customers to be used for marketing decisions and activities cannot be based on traditional market segmentation techniques only. Choice of customers to serve and decisions about how to serve them have to be based on individual customer information files and other types of databases.

Market Research and Market Share Statistics

Measuring market share is an important way of monitoring relative sales of a product when the product is marketed to a mass market of unknown customers. Sales statistics are relatively easily compiled. Studies of customer perceived quality and customer satisfaction measurements normally cannot be done on an equally regular basis. As a consequence, high market shares are sometimes regarded as a proxy for customer satisfaction. As we concluded in an earlier section, market share can be maintained at least for some time even when customer satisfaction deteriorates. When a firm has direct contacts with its customers, information about the needs, desires, expectations and future intentions of customers as well as about their quality and value perceptions and about satisfaction can be obtained directly in these contacts. This, however, requires an intelligent system for registering the pieces of information that a large number of employees throughout the organisation is exposed to on a daily basis. This is vastly neglected today. However, only such direct management of the customer base gives management current and accurate information, not only about sales but also about the needs, expectations and intentions and the level of satisfaction among the customers. Hence we can formulate a fifth proposition about the need to manage the firm's customer base directly and not through market share statistics and ad hoc customer studies only.

Proposition 5

In relationship marketing the firm should manage its customer base directly through information obtained on a daily basis in the continuous interfaces between the customers and employees of the firm, and only support this with market share statistics and ad hoc studies of customer needs and expectations, and of perceived quality, value and satisfaction.

THE REBIRTH OF MODERN MARKETING

The marketing mix management paradigm was developed to suit the requirements of marketing during the peak of the industrial society. Today it is only helpful to some types of businesses, such as many consumer goods industries, and even there it is being questioned. By going back to the roots of the marketing phenomenon, relationship marketing offers a new approach to managing the market relationships that is more geared to the nature of an ever-growing number of market-places and marketing situations. However, it is important to understand the paradigmatic nature of this perspective. It is above all a philosophy that guides the planning and management of activities in the relationships between a firm and its customers, distributors and other partners.

The relationship philosophy relies on co-operation and a trusting relationship with customers (and other stakeholders and network partners) instead of an adversarial approach to customers, on collaboration within the company instead of specialisation of functions and the division of labour, and on the notion of marketing as more of a market-oriented management approach with part-time marketers spread throughout the organisation than as a separate function for specialists only (Grönroos, 1996).

Common mistakes when discussing relationship marketing follow from a failure to understand this philosophical shift. We have to realise that it is *a new paradigm, not a just a new model*, that is emerging. Sometimes relationship marketing is used more or less as a synonym for direct marketing or database marketing, or for establishing customer clubs, and it becomes just another instrument in the marketing mix toolbox to be used in accordance with the marketing mix management philosophy. In other situations relationship marketing is used as a synonym for developing partnerships and alliances and networks. However, it is much more than that. It requires a totally new approach to some of the fundamental thoughts in marketing, as is implied by the five propositions suggested in the previous section. The transition from a transaction-oriented marketing mix-based practice of marketing to a relationship-oriented one is not an uncomplicated process. The old paradigm has deep roots in the minds of marketers as well as non-marketers in a company. And it still has a much easier-to-use toolbox of marketing instruments available than the emerging new paradigm can offer at this point.

Hence the transition towards a relational-oriented marketing approach can often be understood as a learning curve, as is illustrated by the transition curve in Figure 2.1 (cf. Strandvik, 1995). In the beginning, firms that wish to implement a relationship marketing approach are normally still very focused on their products. Hence only easily developed relational activities are introduced. Typical examples are customised sales letters and information bulletins, customer clubs and so on. Such activities do easily backfire, especially if the customer is mistreated in other respects, for example when using a service, in a recovery or complaints situation or in just about any interactions with the firm. Firms in this stage do not yet fully understand the philosophical nature of relationship marketing. Singular exchanges are still the basic focus of marketing. Today, most firms that are applying a relationship marketing approach are probably somewhere in this stage of the transition process. A true transition towards a relationship marketing strategy requires a focus on resources and competencies in the relationship.[2] In principle, the product is but one resource among others, although it is, of course, the necessary prerequisite for a successful relationship. The relationship itself becomes the focus of marketing (Grönroos, 1996).

However, as was noticed earlier, the roots of the old paradigm are very deep in the minds of everybody in a firm regardless of whether they are in managerial positions or not, or whether they are full-time marketers or part-time marketers to be. Therefore it may be difficult to instil the idea of a new philosophical approach to marketing in the organisation according to which marketing is the business of practically everybody as part-time marketers and as managers of interactive marketing performed by part-time marketers. Getting the commitment of everybody to the new marketing philosophy and its consequences for marketing in practice may be difficult or even impossible. As we have observed in another context (Grönroos, 1994), 'the use of the marketing mix paradigm and the 4 Ps has made it difficult for the marketing function to earn credibility' (p. 356). This is another example of the negative effects of the marketing mix impact machine. Some

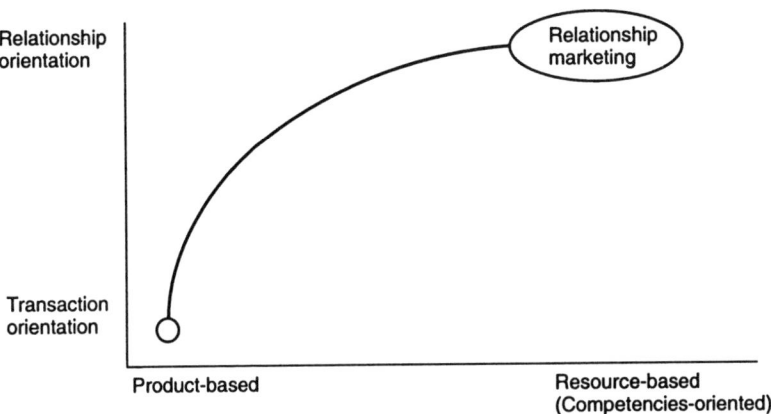

Source: Adapted from Strandvik (1996).

Figure 2.1   Changes in the marketing paradigm: the transition curve

firms have solved this problem not only by scaling down or altogether terminating their marketing departments but also by *banning the use of the term 'marketing'* (compare Grönroos, 1982, 1994). Terms such as 'customer contacts' and 'customer satisfaction' have been used in firms instead of 'marketing' to mean the same thing, the management of the firm's market relationships. Probably we sometimes need this kind of semantics. It is not too far-fetched to assume that in the future this is going to happen in a growing number of cases. Hence we have a sixth and final proposition about relationship marketing as the rebirth of marketing is offered.

Proposition 6

To create an understanding of relationship marketing among managerial and non-managerial staff throughout the organisation and to develop a culture where relationship marketing is implemented, it may be necessary to replace the term 'marketing' with a neutral and psychologically more easily accepted term to describe the task of managing the firm's market relationships.

Notes

1. This section is adapted from an article to be published in the *Asia–Australia Marketing Journal*, vol. 4, 1996.
2. It is interesting that this changing demand from the market has had an impact on the strategy field that parallels the development of the relationship approach in marketing. Resources and core competencies are emphasised in the emerging strategy literature (cf. Hamel and Prahalad 1994).

References

Abbott, L. (1955) *Quality and Competition* (New York: Columbia University Press).
Baggozzi, R. P. (1975) 'Marketing as Exchange', *Journal of Marketing*, 39, October, 32–9.
Berry, L. L. (1983) 'Relationship Marketing', in L. L. Berry, G. L. Shostack and G. D. Upah (eds), *Emerging Perspectives of Services Marketing* (Chicago: American Marketing Association) 25–8.
Berry, L. L. (1986) 'Big Ideas in Services Marketing', *Journal of Consumer Marketing*, 3 (2), 35–43.
Berry, L. L. and A. Parasuraman (1991) *Marketing Services. Competing through Quality* (New York: Free Press).

Berry, L. L. and A. Parasuraman (1993) 'Building a New Academic Field – The Case of Services Marketing', *Journal of Retailing*, 69 (1), 13–60.

Bitner, M. J. (1995) 'Building Service Relationships; It's All About Promises', *Journal of the Academy of Marketing Science*, 23 (4), 246–51.

Blomqvist, R., J. Dahl and T. Haeger (1993) *Relationsmarknadsföring. Strategi och metod för servicekonkurrens* (Relationship marketing. Strategy and methods for service competition) (Gothenburg: IHM Förlag).

Borden, N. H. (1964) 'The Concept of the Marketing Mix', *Journal of Advertising Research*, 4 (2), June, 2–7.

Chamberlain, E. H. (1933) *The Theory of Monopolistic Competition* (Cambridge, Mass.: Harvard University Press).

Christopher, M., A. Payne and D. Ballantyne (1992) *Relationship Marketing. Bringing Quality, Customer Service and Marketing Together* (London: Butterworth).

Craig-Lees, M. and M. Caldwell (1994) 'Relationship Marketing: An Opportunity to Develop a Viable Marketing Framework', *1994 Research Conference Proceedings, Center for Relationship Marketing*, Emory University, Atlanta, GA, June.

Culliton, J. W. (1948) *The Management of Marketing Costs* (Boston, Mass.: Harvard University Press).

Dixon, D. F. and K. J. Blois (1983) 'Some Limitations of the 4P's as a Paradigm for Marketing', *Marketing Education Group Annual Conference*, Cranfield Institute of Technology, UK, July.

Frisch, R. (1933) 'Monopole – Polypole – la notion de force dans l'économie' (Monopoly – polypoly – the driving force concept in the economy), *Nationalokonomisk Tidsskrift*, Denmark, 241–59.

Grönroos, C. (1982) *Strategic Management and Marketing in the Service Sector* (Helsingfors, Finland: Swedish School of Economics and Business Administration) (published in 1983 in the USA by Marketing Science Institute and in the UK by Studentlitteratur/Chartwell-Bratt).

Grönroos, C. (1989) 'Defining Marketing: A Market-Oriented Approach', *European Journal of Marketing*, 23 (1), 52–60.

Grönroos, C. (1990) 'Relationship Approach to the Marketing Function in Service Contexts: The Marketing and Organisational Behavior Interface', *Journal of Business Research*, 20 (1), 3–12.

Grönroos, C. (1994) 'Quo Vadis, Marketing? Toward a Relationship Marketing Paradigm', *Journal of Marketing Management*, 10, 347–60.

Grönroos, C. (1995) 'Relationship Marketing: The Strategy Continuum', *Journal of the Academy of Marketing Science*, 23, (4), 252–4.

Grönroos, C. (1996) 'The Relationship Marketing Logic', *Asia–Australia Marketing Journal*, 4 (forthcoming).

Grönroos, C. and E. Gummesson (1985) 'The Nordic School of Service Marketing' in C. Grönroos and E. Gummesson (eds), *Service Marketing – Nordic School Perspectives*, Stockholm University, 6–11.

Gummesson, E. (1987) 'The New Marketing – Developing Long-Term Interactive Relationships', *Long Range Planning*, 20 (4), 10–20.

Gummesson, E. (1990) *The Part-Time Marketer* (Karlstad, Sweden: Center for Service Research).

Gummesson, E. (1995) *Relationsmarknadsföring. Från 4P till 30R* (Relationship marketing. From 4P to 30R) (Malmö: Sweden, Liber-Hermods).

Håkansson, H. (ed.) (1982) *International Marketing and Purchasing of Industrial Goods* (New York: Wiley).

Hamel G. and C. K. Prahalad(1994) *Competing for the Future. Breakthrough strategies for seizing control of your industry and creating the markets of tomorrow* (Boston, Mass.: Harvard Business School Press).

Hunt, S. D. and R. M. Morgan (1994) 'Relationship Marketing in the Era of Network Competition', *Marketing Management*, 3 (1), 19–30.

Kent, R. A. (1986) 'Faith in Four P's: An Alternative', *Journal of Marketing Management*, 2 (2), 145–54.

Kotler, P. (1992) 'It's Time for Total Marketing', *Business Week ADVANCE Executive Brief*, 2.

McCarthy, E. J. (1960) *Basic Marketing* (Homewood: Irwin).

McGarry, E. D. (1950) 'Some Functions of Marketing Reconsidered', in R. Cox and W. Alderson (eds) *Theory in Marketing* (Chicago: Richard D. Irwin).

McKenna, R. (1991) *Relationship Marketing. Successful Strategies for the Age of the Customer* (Reading, Mass.: Addison-Wesley).

McKitterick, J. B. (1957) 'What is the Marketing Management Concept?' in F. Bass (ed.), *The Frontiers of Marketing Thought in Action* (Chicago: American Marketing Association).

Mickwitz, G. (1959) *Marketing and Competition* (Helsingfors, Finland: Societas Scientarium Fennica) (available from University Microfilms, Ann Arbor, Mich.).

Mickwitz, G. (1966) 'The Copenhagen School and Scandinavian Theory of Competition and Marketing', in M. Kjaer-Hansen (ed.), *Readings in Danish Theory of Marketing* (Copenhagen: Erhvervsokonomisk Forlag) (originally published in *Det Danske Marked*, May 1964).

Normann, R. (1983) *Service Management* (New York: Wiley).

Peppers, D. and M. Rogers (1993) *One-to-One Future: Building Relationships One Customer at a Time* (New York: Currency/Doubleday).

Piercy, N. (1985) *Marketing Organisation, An Analysis of Information Processing, Power and Politics* (London: George Allen & Unwin).

Rapp, S. and T. Collins (1990) *The Great Marketing Turnaround* (Englewood Cliffs, N.J.: Prentice-Hall).

Rasmussen, A. (1955) *Pristeori eller parameterteori – studier omkring virksomhedens afsaetning* (Price theory or parameter theory – studies of the sales of the firm). (Copenhagen: Erhvervsokonomisk Forlag).

Reichheld, F. F. and W. E. Sasser, Jr. (1990) 'Zero Defections: Quality Comes to Service', *Harvard Business Review*, 68, September–October, 105–11.

Romilla (1916) *Reklame-laere* (Advertising) (Trondhjem, Norway: Aktietrykkeriet).

Sheth, J. N. and A. Parvatiyar (eds) (1994) *Relationship Marketing: Theory, Methods and Applications*, 1994 Research Conference Proceedings, Center for Relationship Marketing, Emory University, Atlanta, GA, June.

Sheth, J. N. and A. Parvatiyar (1995) 'Relationship Marketing in Consumer Markets, Antecedents and Consequences', *Journal of the Academy of Marketing Science*, 23 4, 255–71.

Sheth, J. N., D. M. Gardner and D. E. Garrett (1988) *Marketing Theory: Evolution and Evaluation* (New York: Wiley).

Smith, A. (1950) *The Wealth of Nations. An Inquiry into the Nature and Cause of the Wealth of Nations* (London: Methuen) (first published 1776).

Smith, W. R. (1956) 'Product Differentiation and Market Segmentation as Alternative Marketing Strategies', *Journal of Marketing*, 21, July, 3–8.

Stackelberg, H. von (1939) 'Theorie der Vertriebspolitik und der Qualitätsvariation' (Theory of business policy and quality variations), *Schmollers Jahrbuch*, 63/1.

Stauss, B. (1994) *Total Quality Management: Customer Orientation without Marketing?*, Working paper No. 43, Wirtschaftswissenschaftlichen Fakultät Ingolstadt der Katolischen Universität Eichstätt, Germany.

Strandvik, T. (1995) *Visionär kvalitet* (Visionary quality), Research report, Swedish School of Economics and Business Administration, Finland (forthcoming).

Taylor, F. W. (1947) *Scientific Management* (London: Harper & Row) (a volume of two papers originally published in 1903 and 1911 and a written testimony for a Special House Committee in the USA in 1912).

Vavra, T. G. (1994) 'The Database Marketing Imperative', *Marketing Management*, 2 (1), 47–57.

Waterschoot, W. van and C. Van den Bulte (1992) 'The 4P Classification of the Marketing Mix Revisited', *Journal of Marketing*, 56, October, 83–93.

Webster, Jr., F. E. (1992) 'The Changing Role of Marketing in the Corporation', *Journal of Marketing*, 56, October, 1–17.

Webster, Jr., F. E. (1994) 'Executing the New Marketing Concept', *Marketing Management*, 3 (1), 9–18.

3 Another Oxymoron in Marketing: Marketing Strategy

Robin Wensley

The essence of the argument in this chapter is that the link between marketing and strategy, at least as they are commonly understood, is becoming more and more tenuous under the twin pressures of changing fashions and more refined analysis. Changing fashions in management are shifting attention away from strategy formulation and analysis towards strategy process and implementation. More refined analysis in marketing recognises that on both economic and statistical grounds it is very unlikely that one can reduce heterogeneity and diversity to a relative simple decision rule for commercial success.

These developments suggest that the field of marketing itself needs to respond in various ways. In particular marketing needs to recognise, in the current strategy jargon, its own domain of distinctive competence. This has two components: theory and research related to buyer behaviour,[1] and the functional focus on the nature and activities of marketing management. We also need to recognise more clearly the other side of this distinctive competence: that as marketing scholars and indeed practitioners move into areas which are, at best, on their periphery they inevitably begin to interact with the distinctive competencies of other fields of inquiry and it is important to recognise what marketing can contribute to such debates. This chapter attempts to refine the former issues but at the same time demonstrate some of the problems raised by the latter concern.

FROM FORMULATION TO IMPLEMENTATION

From the late 1960s to the mid-1980s at least, management strategy seemed to be inevitably linked to issues of product-market selection. Perhaps ironically this was not primarily or mainly as a result of the contribution of marketing scholars or indeed practitioners. The most

significant initial contributors, such as Bruce Henderson and Michael
Porter, were both to be found at or closely linked to the Harvard
Business School, but were really informed more by particular aspects of
economic analysis: neo-marginal economics[2] and industrial organisational economics, respectively. However, in various institutions the
marketing academics were not slow to recognise what was going on
and also to see that the centrality of product-market choice linked well
with the importance attached to marketing. It has previously been
argued, however, that this expansion of the teaching domain had a
much less significant impact on the research agenda and activity within
marketing itself, where the focus continued to underplay the emerging
importance of the competitive dimension (Day and Wensley 1983).
This relatively atheoretical development continued into the process of
codification of this new area, most obviously in the first key text by
Abell and Hammond (1979), which was based on a, by then, well
established second year MBA option at Harvard.[3]

In retrospect this period was the high point for the uncontested
impact of competitive market related analysis on strategic management.
With the advantage of hindsight, it is clear that a serious alternative
perspective was also developing, most obviously signalled by Peters and
Waterman (1982), which was to have a very substantial impact on what
was taught in strategic management courses and what was marketed by
consultancies. It was also a significant book in the sense that, although
not widely recognised as so doing, it also attempted to integrate at least
to some degree earlier academic work by other relevant academics such
as Mintzberg (1973), Pettigrew (1973) and Weick (1976).

As the decade progressed, it was inevitable that at least to some
degree each side recognised the other as a key protagonist. Perhaps one
of the most noteworthy comments is that in which Robert Waterman
challenges the value of a Michael Porter based analysis of competition.
Waterman (1988) argues that the Porter approach does not work
because 'people get stuck in trying to carry out his ideas' for three
reasons: (1) there is usually no single, easily identified competitor; (2)
business is a positive sum game: at one level firms compete fiercely, at
another level they help each other; and (3) competitors are human: they
are neither dumb nor superhuman. Equally, the economists have not
taken such attacks lying down: more recently Kay (1993) attempted to
wrest back the intellectual dominance in matters of corporate strategy
and Porter (1990) extended his domain to the nation-state itself.

The story, of course, has also become complicated in other ways,
many of which are outside the scope of this chapter. In terms of key

perspectives, Tom Peters (1988) has become more and more polemical about the nature of success, and C.K. Prahalad has, with Gary Hamel, refined his original notion of dominant logic to reflect in general terms the importance of transferable capabilities and technological interdependencies in the development of strategic advantage.[4] Of course, Peter Senge (1990) reiterated the importance of information structures and Michael Hammer (1990) introduced a 'new' approach labelled 'business process analysis'.

In terms of the disciplinary debate, what was originally broadly a debate between economists and sociologists now also involves psychologists, social anthropologists and, if they are a distinct discipline, systems theorists. However, in the context of this chapter, the key change in emphasis has been the one from analysis to process, from formulation to implementation. Perhaps the single most important contributor to this change has been Henry Mintzberg, who has developed over the period an extensive critique of what he calls the 'Design School' in Strategic Management, culminating in his 1994 book. In this he even challenges the notion of planning in strategy and sees another oxymoron:

> Thus we arrive at the planning school's grand fallacy: because analysis is not synthesis, strategic planning is not strategy formation. Analysis may precede and support synthesis, by defining the parts that can be combined into wholes. Analysis may follow and elaborate synthesis, by decomposing and formalising its consequences. But analysis cannot substitute for synthesis. No amount of elaboration will ever enable formal procedures to forecast discontinuities, to inform managers who are detached from their operations, to create novel strategies. Ultimately the term 'strategic planning' has proved to be an oxymoron. (1994, p. 321)

Whilst Mintzberg's approach and indeed critique of strategy analysis is itself rather polemical and overstated,[5] there is little doubt that the general emphasis in strategic management has shifted significantly towards implementation and away from formulation and planning.

RULES FOR SUCCESS AMIDST DIVERSITY

Ever since Chamberlain (1933) and/or Robinson (1933), often depending on one's cultural heritage, it has been recognised that a competitive model based on homogeneous firms is inappropriate. Whilst their approach was broadly based on the heterogeneous nature of demand, more recently one can argue that this maxim, extended to the wider issue of firm heterogeneity itself, has been rediscovered in the development of the so-called 'resource based view of the firm', to which we will return later, with the emphasis on the differential portfolio of assets or resources which are owned by any one firm.

This very observation has itself raised questions for any attempt to derive relatively simple rules for strategic success beyond the self-evidently tautologies such as 'exploit your distinctive capabilities'[6] but the issue is compounded when we consider the heterogeneity of the demand side as well. In some developments of the resource-based view such heterogeneity is included in the asset base of the firm, much as the rationale for the downward-sloping demand curve in the original Robinson analysis was at least partly implicit assumptions about consumer response. It is, however perhaps clearer to try and retain a distinction between advantages as a result of access to or ownership of resources[7] which can be transformed into marketable offerings and advantages which are purely in the form of preferential access to a particular market itself.

A more useful way of looking at demand-side heterogeneity is from the user[8] perspective directly. Arguably from its relatively early origins marketing or at least the more functional focused study of marketing management has been concerned with managerially effective ways of responding to this heterogeneity, particularly in terms of market segmentation. Indeed, it would be reasonable to suggest that, without a substantial level of demand heterogeneity, there would be little need for marketing approaches as they are found in most of our textbooks. While there remains a substantial debate about the degree to which this market-based heterogeneity is indeed 'manageable' from a marketing perspective (cf. Wensley, 1995a, 1996; Saunders, 1995), to which we will partly return later, our concern at the moment is merely to recognise the substantial degree of heterogeneity and consider the degree to which such diversity on both the supply and demand side facilitates or negates the possibility of developing robust 'rules for success'.

To address this question, we need to consider the most useful way of characterising the competitive market process. This is clearly a substantial topic in its own right with, amongst others, proponents of various analogies or metaphors including game theory, sports games and military strategy. As we develop these various approaches one aspect becomes clear: the determining nature of the rule structure decreases as we move along the spectrum or, in more technical language, the operational rules become more endogenously rather than exogenously determined. The most endogenous systems in this sense seem to be found in the evolutionary ecology analogy which since Hannan and Freeman's (1976) original work has been recognised as one of interest in the strategy field.

It is undeniable that in the field of ecology we observe wide diversity in terms of both species and habitat, but we also observe two critical aspects which must inform any attempt to transfer this analogy into the field of strategy. The first is the interactive relationship between any species and its habitat, nicely encapsulated in the title of the book by Levins and Lewontin (1985): 'The Dialectical Biologist'. Particularly in the context of strategy it is important to recognise that the habitat (for which read market domain) evolves and develops at least as fast as the species (for which read the individual firm).[9]

The second aspect addresses directly our question of 'rules for success'. How far can we identify, particularly through the historical record, whether there are any reliable rules for success for particular species characteristics? Of course, it is very difficult to address this question without being strongly influenced by hindsight and most observations are seen as contentious. However, Stephen Jay Gould (1987, 1990) who has perhaps most directly considered this issue in his various writings, particularly the analysis of the Burgess Shale, comes to the uncompromising conclusion that it is difficult if not impossible to recognise any species features or characteristics that provide a reliable ex ante rule for success.

Hence, it would seem that we should at least be very cautious in any search for rules for success amidst a world of interactive diversity.

BUYER BEHAVIOUR

Just as there is diversity amongst firms so, perhaps even more so, there is diversity amongst customers. The existence of such diversity is beyond doubt, its interpretation is another matter. Indeed, it is arguable that the managerial response to customer diversity, market segmentation, is at the very core of the marketing management approach. However, while overall diversity may be beyond doubt, the interpretation of the nature of market segmentation is rather more problematic.

In a recent debate about the empirical evidence for market segmentation, Wensley (1995a) asserts that at best few of the assumptions of market segmentation, particularly as represented in the marketing textbooks, are actually seen in empirical work. Obviously at least at some level this is a matter of degree but Wensley (1995a) argues that, certainly when it comes to actual patterns of buyer behaviour, in general the actual effect of any segmentation approach is merely to reflect the behavioural variability in each 'segment' that was in the original total sample, rather than to reduce it. Saunders (1995), however, argues that this interpretation is flawed on three grounds:[10]

1. That the original studies of what might be termed the 'English' school, including Ehrenberg, Goodhart and Collins, recognised that some degree of segmentation existed and that Wensley fails to recognise this.

2. That this is an area of research where different researchers using different methods actually 'see' different phenomena and, in particular, various American studies have had no problems with 'not only recognising segments but tracking them through time also'.

3. That whatever the 'academic' debates, it has been shown to work over and over again in marketing practice.

Broadly speaking much of the debate around (1) is a fairly simple one around 'onus of proof': what should we regard as a 'significant' reduction in segment variability? It is worth reconsidering the conclusion that Collins drew from his original work:

This is not to deny that segmentation does exist in terms of consumer requirements within a product field, but only to say that if it exists it fails to lead to any similar patterning of behaviour in respect of brand-choice. It seems reasonable to suppose that different consumers, at some point in time, do have different requirements. The problem is to reconcile this with the regular patterning of brand-duplication. (1971, p. 157)

Saunders is right to point out that Wensley's analogy to fractal patterns is misleading in that any segmentation scheme, by its very nature, is likely to reduce overall variability in the process of generating subgroups, the question is more by how much and how consistently through time?

This brings us to consider (2). How do we interpret the claim that because they looked in a different way, various American researchers not only find segments but are able to track them? A closer inspection of the relevant work reveals that many focus in terms of segmentation on buying volume itself. This means that overall their conclusions are hardly different from those already recognised by Wensley himself in his summary that 'in general heavy buyers continue to be heavy buyers'.[11] The more substantive point is to return to the basic logic of any market segmentation procedure.

Wensley and Saunders agree on the centrality of market segmentation to marketing as a whole, at least to marketing management. Indeed, rather ironically Saunders uses the same authority as Wensley to reinforce this point. The central element of the debate seems to be, as we have discussed before, Wensley's assertion that empirical research does not generally support the managerial version of market segmentation, whilst Saunders claims, in the final analysis, that since it works in practice it must be true. This brings us to the central issue of marketing management itself.

MARKETING MANAGEMENT

There seems general agreement that the focus of marketing on marketing management can be traced in particular to two significant individuals: Wroe Alderson (1957) who focused attention on the functional nature of marketing and Philip Kotler (1967), who in both the title and the content of his famous textbook first explicitly emphasised the managerial aspect of marketing, compared with the more descriptive nature of previous texts.

As with all major shifts in emphasis there have been some unintended consequences, three of which are of particular relevance. First is the extent to which such a definition of marketing focuses very directly on the activities of the marketing function within organisations. More recently there has been a very live debate about the extent to which such a focus confuses the differences between 'marketing as a function' and 'marketing as a philosophy'.[12] Second, there is the extent to which this focus on the functional nature of marketing disguises the problematic nature of marketing activity itself. Not surprisingly, therefore, this perspective on marketing has failed to encourage a more critical analysis of the role of marketing in human society as more broadly constituted. This is either in terms of the validity of the underlying assumptions particularly when attempts are made to extend marketing to new domains such as the public services (see Wensley, 1990) or, more broadly, when questions are raised about the interpretation of market and marketing behaviour itself (see, for instance, Buttimer and Kavanagh, 1995; Brownlie and Desmond, 1995).

Third, and most importantly for the particular focus of this chapter, is the degree to which the managerial focus can rest on a logical syllogism: the fact that markets are an important phenomenon does not mean that they can be 'managed' in a particular way. Management in this sense seems to imply control, a word which of course, featured in the title of Kotler's textbook; and yet, in this sense, we have to appreciate that the very people that we are talking about managing are ourselves as consumers. This raises two additional questions: what can we really claim in terms of marketing management and how far can we seriously assert that 'it works'?

In terms of the former question it is evident that it is seen as necessary to undertake various activities, which are generally defined within the marketing domain, such as, in the traditional approach, selling, advertising and market research. The fact that these activities are undertaken within most commercial organisations means that they have to be managed in the sense that choices have to be made and budgets have to be observed. However, the important distinction is that in managing these activities we are not managing the market-place. Indeed, the more current organisational concern with overall operational strategy and the nature of longer-term interorganisational relationships even raises the direct question as to whether this traditional definition of activities is appropriate.

Further, the test of effectiveness, or even efficiency, is unclear. The question inevitably involves the implied 'compared with what?'. It is perhaps easiest to draw an analogy with the equivalent question in terms of financial portfolio investments. Here there is a clear option between so-called 'passive' portfolios and actively managed ones. Particularly when we take into account the additional transaction costs of active management, it is often not clear at all whether the managed funds actually work in the sense of outperforming the passive option. However, it is important to realise that the passive option is not a 'naive' one: it is a carefully constructed portfolio which is then left on its own, subject to some rule-based adjustments related to a notion of overall 'balance'.

The equivalent question therefore in the case of marketing management is not really active management with doing nothing at all. Rather it is the question of the additional value added of analysis and actions which can only genuinely be undertaken with the particular level of sophistication being considered. In marketing terms, therefore, it is the added value of more sophisticated forms of positioning particularly in cases of multiple products, brands or even brand variants. Here, as Ehrenberg and others have previously pointed out, we also face a rather more complex form of empirical evaluation. The mere fact that, when available for sale, a range of different relatively substitutable items sell rather than one single one cannot be regarded as evidence of segmentation. Whilst this might be argued as a test that segmentation works, it is no more a test of this proposition than of others such as that differentiation or, indeed, fragmentation, works.

ECONOMICS AS A PROCESS

The current intellectual tradition of marketing strategy rests on the economic notion of Sustainable Competitive Advantage (SCA). In this it is a subset of the tradition of industrial organisation economics and, particularly, the work of writers such as Bain and Caves. Whilst Bain (1962) focused attention on barriers to market entry, some of which were market-based but others of which were more related to, say, technology, Caves (1980) and then, even more so, Porter, extended this analysis to the concept of mobility barriers within any particular industry. At a theoretical level, their joint paper (Caves and Porter, 1977) remains a critical one in that in theory terms Porter achieved limited advance in his two subsequent texts (Porter, 1980, 1985).[13] One important characteristic of this work is the extent to which the notion of sustainablity is both central and ill-defined.

Competitive advantage, or its mirror in welfare terms, the 'distortion of efficient resource allocation' was seen, following Joe Bain's (1962) earlier work, as the result of barriers to new competition. The developments proposed by Caves and Porter (1977) were that such barriers were (1) 'partly structural but at least partly endogenous' and (2) applicable not only to industry entry issues but also as 'a general theory of the mobility of firms among segments of an industry, thus encompassing exit and inter-group shifts as well as entry'. In their conclusion they state:

> By formulating the entry process as an investment decision made under uncertainty and conjectural interdependence, and by recogniz-

ing that subgroup structures of industries impede intra-industry
mobility, we have sought to generalize the theory of barriers to
entry into a theory of mobility barriers that takes a consistent and
comprehensive view of the decision-making behaviour of both
nascent and going firms. (1977, p. 261)

However, in the context of our analysis, the most evident lacuna in the
paper is the extent to which the longevity of any particular mobility
barrier is seen as relatively unproblematic. There seems little discussion
of the equivalent Schumpeterian view, that one should assume any
such barrier to competition is itself a wasting asset. Indeed, this
limitation is most evident in the fact that their analysis leads them to
a conclusion which is driven by a rather comparative-static perspective
compared with a dynamic one: 'The queue of potential entrants to a
group will, in general, consist of established firms in other markets,
going firms in other groups, and entirely new firms' (p. 261).

In a similar vein, Porter in his later work, for instance only states
that the fundamental basis of above average performance is SCA and
then points out that in the context of his (in)famous three generic
strategies each strategy has risks attached to it, including the potential
competitive impact of the alternative strategies. The summary table he
uses helps to emphasise the extent to which he apparently sees the risks
as residing in the dynamic and changing behaviour of both competitors
and customers (or buyers in his terms). In this, of course, he is right but
misleadingly so in that the definition of sustainability becomes virtually
tautologous: 'The sustainability of a (generic) strategy requires that a
firm possess some barriers that make imitation of the strategy difficult'
(1985, p. 20). As Inkpen and Choudhury (1995) point out, the problem
with such a definition is that we explain the observable phenomenon
(persistence of a specific competitive advantage) by an unobservable
one (the existence of barriers to imitation) to achieve virtually nil
explanatory power:

IO strategists define strategy in such terms as the 'continuing search
for rent', with rent defined as the excess return to the owners of
resources. But from a practical perspective, this statement is mean-
ingless . . . the researcher with . . . [such a] focus would look for
evidence to explain why the firm's idiosyncratic resources failed to
create a competitive advantage . . . by examining mobility barriers,
entry barriers, asset specificity, nonimitable resources and so on.
(1995, p. 314)

Thomas and Carrol (1994) considered how far the broader notion of competitive groupings within an industry can be related to the more specific and interrelated concepts of strategic groups, cognitive communities and networks of interacting firms. Nath and Gruca (1995) in recent work in the health care industry argue that, given that they find significant convergence between multiple measures of the group structure in a mature, geographically delimited competitive environment, the concept of a strategic group is a theoretical construct and not just a methodological artefact.

In so doing, however, in the context of sustainability we are considering the notion of strategic groups and hence barriers to competition in a rather unimportant context. The critical context in terms of longer-run sustainability is the extent to which the notion of groups has validity in the context of a dynamic and turbulent environment. Here, as Wensley (1994) comments, the prospects for any intermediate group based analysis are much less promising.

Such broader considerations, alongside analogous issues in the field of economics recognising the dynamic and process view of the system (cf., for instance, Langlois, 1986), have led a number of marketing authors to suggest a rather different perspective which might be broadly labelled 'Austrian' (Wensley, 1982; Jacobson, 1992; Dickinson, 1992; Hunt and Morgan, 1995). Such a view emphasises the extent to which the competitive market process is both one of discovery of new opportunities through entrepreneurial actions and the subsequent inevitable erosion of advantage through competition.

In a recent paper, Hunt (1995) further develops his approach on a 'new' paradigm and links it with the current focus in strategy, mentioned earlier, on the resource-based view of the firm. The recent genesis of the resource-based view is seen as the 1984 article by Wernerfeld although, as he recognises, many of the basic ideas are to be found in Penrose (1959).[14] Wernerfeld, in reviewing the impact of his article ten years on, comments:

> In the fall of 1981, I found myself, as a young economist, teaching business policy and competitive analysis for the first time. Because of my background in game theory, I was worried about the consistency of many recommendations from Harvard teaching notes. For example if all MBAs learn to identify the 'most attractive' niche, who will get it and why will competition not destroy the attractiveness? Similarly, the manifest heterogeneity of strategies seemed to imply that many (even large) firms have made 'elementary' mistakes. The

resource-based view started as my attempt to satisfy myself that one could build a consistent foundation for the classical theory of business policy. (1995, p. 172)

He goes on to argue that to achieve success firms need to apply a combination of strategic knowledge which is independent of the specific opponent alongside, once the opponent is known, with knowledge which deals with ways to exploit differences. As Wernerfeld (1984) implies, the heyday of marketing strategy was when the strategic problem at the firm level could be defined in terms of undifferentiated rules relating to product-market selection such as 'invest in market share for high growth markets', but we are now in a world in which it is essential to understand the nature and impact of the differences between firms which, in the context of marketing, can be taken to mean their relative market positions.

THE MARKETING CONTRIBUTION

This chapter started by suggesting that marketing needed to return to its roots and be less concerned with the strategy domain and its own fluctuating fads and fashions. What is the nature of these roots? The saga of the definition of marketing is well known: every time one is developed a new alternative is offered in its place. In view of our wish to consider marketing's roots we will eschew current definitions provided either by professional bodies or recent authors, and look to two other sources: the *Oxford English Dictionary* and history.

Our first source certainly suggests that the attempts to differentiate marketing from selling have yet to impinge on the OED. Marketing is variously described as the activity related to the verb 'to market' (as in buying or selling) or, perhaps more specifically: 'the action or business of bringing or sending (a commodity) to market'. An alternative historical source of insight is provided by Paul Converse, who in his 1930 text uses the following definition: 'Marketing, in a broad sense, covers those business activities that have to do with the creation of place, time and possession utilities' (1930, p. 3).

To some degree, therefore the functional or marketing management perspective predates Alderson (1957). However, at this earlier stage of development, definitions of marketing also tended to be very descriptive, and often very institutional, such as in the considerable focus that Converse (1930) gave to a detailed description of the nature of the distribution structure particularly for manufactured products. A rather more recent interpretation of such definitions would be to emphasise the understanding and nature of market behaviour with particular emphasis on the buyer.

Hence the two areas in which we should perhaps apply renewed focus in developing the field of marketing: the behaviour of markets and the nature of marketing management. In terms of the behaviour of markets, marketing faces two challenges: first, to cope with and exploit the burgeoning amount of data with respect to buyer behaviour. In doing this we face challenges not to be misled by statistical sophistication or philosophical minefields but at the same time to be informed about such perspectives. In this context it might be as well to suggest that all researchers should be required to read John O'Shaughnessy's book, *Explaining Buyer Behaviour*, along with one of the various and often referenced texts on multivariate analysis before embarking on any empirical work.

Second, and somewhat related, is the need to uncouple, at least to some degree, the link between managerial interest or, even, naive managerial imperatives and market understanding. This side of the study of market behaviour must take a critical (in the best sense of the word) stance with respect to practice. To at least some extent we must live up to our rhetoric and consider the nature of the market from the buyer's perspective. We need, for instance, to emulate such works as Roland Marchand's *Advertising the American Dream* (1985), in deconstructing and interpreting the often uncomfortable relationship between marketers with their claims of customer-orientation and their deeper prejudices:

> John Benson, the president of the American Association of Advertising Agencies, confessed in 1927, 'To tell the naked truth might make no appeal. It may be necessary to fool people for their own good. . . Average intelligence is surprisingly low. It is so much more effectively guided by its subconscious impulses and instincts than by its reason.' Most of the ad agents who accepted the 'irresponsible public' viewpoint were inclined to interpret Benson's phrase 'for their own good' not as suggesting a hope for intellectual or cultural uplift of the mass audience but rather as recognising the need to stimulate consumption in order to maintain prosperity. (1985, p. 85)

The study of marketing, however, cannot as a whole distance itself from the nature of marketing management. The existence of large numbers of managers within professional associations in the marketing domain represents a critical element in the legitimacy of marketing itself. Any serious study of marketing management must consider the extent to which there is both evidence of transferable good practice as well as an underlying body of, to use current jargon, knowledge and understanding which can inform practice. Beyond this there is also an aspect of the current shift in overall emphasis discussed above which should hearten many in marketing. The move from formulation to implementation is also in some sense a move from analysis to action: this is very consistent with the perspective that has imbued much of our teaching in marketing: at some point issues are resolved by action.[15]

Finally, we return to the original title of the paper: is marketing strategy an oxymoron? Of course as usual the answer is, it all depends on what we mean. We have argued that the central issues in marketing and strategic management, as domains of research and teaching, are indeed moving apart significantly from what was an, admittedly temporary, coincidence. However, there will continue to be an important part of marketing itself which is 'strategic', particularly in the researching and interpretation of the wider impacts of individual marketing activity, be it in terms of the evolution of the firm's market position or the social milieu in which all firms operate.

Notes

1. The term 'buyer' is used here intentionally rather than alternatives such as customer or consumer. This is for a number of reasons: first, I have previously tried to apply some finer distinctions in the use of the other terms (Wensley, 1990) and second, although more commonly in the USA, the notion of buyers has been seen as rather more generic (cf. particularly O'Shaughnessy, 1992).

2. Labelling the intellectual pedigree for Bruce Henderson and the Boston Consulting Group is rather more difficult than for Michael Porter. This is partly because much of the approach developed out of consulting practice (cf. Morrison and Wensley, 1991) in the context of a broad rather than focused notion of economic analysis. Some of the intellectual pedigree for the approach can be found in Henderson, who was at Harvard also, and Quant (1958) but some basic ideas such as dynamic economies of scale have a much longer pedigree (see, for instance, Jones, 1928).

3. The book itself is clearly influenced by the work related to the Profit Impact of Market Strategy (PIMS) project, as well as work in management consultancies such as McKinsey, ADL and, perhaps most importantly, Boston Consulting Group, whose founder, Bruce Henderson, had close links with Derek Abell. The MBA course itself started in 1975 with a

broad notion of 'filling the gap' between what was seen then as the marketing domain and the much broader area of Business Policy, so encompassing issues relating to Research and Development, Distribution and Competitive Costs. The course itself was a second year elective and rapidly expanded to four sections with a major commitment on development and case writing in 1976 and 1977.

4. For instance, see Bettis and Prahalad (1995), Prahalad and Hamel (1990) and Prahalad and Bettis (1986).

5. In fact Mintzberg himself goes on to argue three roles for 'corporate planning': (1) a more refined approach in traditional contexts, (2) a focus on techniques which emphasise the uncertain and emergent nature of strategic phenomena and/or (3) a more creative and intuitive form of strategic planning (see Wensley, 1996).

6. I have intentionally forsworn using the term 'core competencies' because, as discussed above, I believe some of the work in this area represents a genuine attempt to identify transferable advantages residing either in organisational routines or technological synergies. However, it must be said that many actual applications of the 'core competencies approach' do fall well short of a rigorous definition such as provided by Bogner and Thomas (1994):

    Firms with core competencies are more than just highly adept at executing core skill sets. In addition they have built appropriate cognitive traits which include:

    (i)   recipes and organisational routines for approaching ill-structured problems.

    (ii)   shared value systems which direct action in unique situations, and

    (iii) tacit understandings of the interactions of technology, organisational dynamics and product markets.

7. The notion that, in terms of strategic actions, it is not the narrow notion of ownership of resources but the broader one of influence over their disposition that is important owes much more to the 'network' perspective, which is another key influence on the current developments in strategy but rather outside the scope of this chapter, than to the strict resource-based view. For a recent discussion of some of these issues, see Dubois and Torvain (1995).

8. Again I will avoid terms such as 'customer' or' consumer' and focus attention on defining the individual or group concerned purely in terms of product or service usage.

9. Of course, the issues contained here are much more complex than this simple summary. However, even at this level it is worth recognising that the whole notion of 'niche' strategies can often be misrepresented. As ecologists often emphasise, there is no sense in which a species can be defined separately from its niche: they are co-determined in that a niche is a species just as a species is its niche. Much of the representation of niche strategies in the management literature manages to suggest a false notion of niche as some sort of pre-existing pigeon-hole in the environmental space waiting for a firm (species) to come along!

10. We should not, however, overestimate the extent of the disagreement. For instance, Hooley and Saunders (1992) quote apparently with approval Baumwoll (1974) in their introduction to segmentation research: researchers are anxious to find a magic formula that will profitably segment the market in all cases and under all circumstances. As with the medieval alchemist looking for the philosopher's stone, this search is bound to end in vain (p. 154).

11. This is not true of some of the work to which Saunders refers (cf. Chintagunta 1994) as well as some of the recent American work to which he does not refer (cf. Russell and Kamakura, 1994); however, in both of these cases there are significant concerns in interpretation (Wensley, 1995b), which mean that the claim that such work not only identifies segments but also tracks them is certainly misleading.

12. Michael Baker himself has been one of the most active contributors to this debate (see, for instance, Baker, 1994).

13. Indeed, Caves (1980), in what might be seen as a rather sceptical comment about the whole theoretical side of the development, chose to characterise the mobility barriers approach as a 'dynamised add-on' in his subsequent review.

14. McKiernan (1995) in an informative review of the historical development of the various approaches to strategy and policy, emphasises particularly the important legacy of Edith Penrose's work. It is, however, noteworthy that, whilst Wernerfeld clearly recognises the pedigree of the resource-based view of the firm, Hunt, despite extensive referencing of other economic work, seems to miss it.

15. For a rather earlier discussion of such issues in terms of marketing teaching, see Law and Wensley (1979).

References

Abell, D. and J. Hammond (1979) *Strategic Market Planning* (Englewood Cliffs, New Jersey: Prentice-Hall).

Alderson, W. (1957) *Dynamic Marketing Behavior: A Functionalist Approach to Marketing Theory* (Homewood Ill.: Richard D. Irwin).

Bain, J.S. (1962) *Barriers to New Competition* (Cambridge, Mass.: Harvard University Press).

Baker, M.J. (1994) 'One more time – what is marketing?', in M.J.Baker (ed.), *The Marketing Book* (Oxford: Butterworth–Heinemann).

Baumwoll, J.P. (1974) 'Segmentation Research: the baker vs the cookie monster', *Proceedings of the American Marketing Association Conference*, 3–20.

Bettis, R.A. and C.K. Prahalad (1995) 'The Dominant Logic: Retrospective and Extension', *Strategic Management Journal*, 16, 5–14.

Bogner, W. and H. Thomas (1994) 'Core Competence and Competitive Advantage: A model and illustrative evidence from the pharmaceutical industry', in G. Hamel and A. Heene (eds), *Competence Based Competition* (Chichester: Wiley).

Brownlie, D. and J. Desmond (1995) 'Apocalyptus interruptus: a parable', in S. Brown, J. Bell, and D. Carson (eds) *Proceedings of the Marketing Eschatology Retreat,* University of Ulster, Belfast, September.

Buttimer, C. G. and D. Kavanagh (1995) 'Markets and Madness', in S. Brown, J. Bell and D. Carson (eds), *Proceedings of the Marketing Eschatology Retreat,* University of Ulster, Belfast, September.

Caves, R. E. (1980) 'Industrial Organisation Corporate Strategy and Structure', *Journal of Economic Literature,* XVIII, March, 64–92.

Caves, R. E. and M. E. Porter (1977) 'From Entry Barriers to Mobility Barriers: Conjectural Decisions and Contrived Deterrence to New Competition', *Quarterly Journal of Economics,* May, 242–61.

Chamberlain, E. H. (1933) *The Theory of Monopolistic Competition* (Cambridge, Mass.: Harvard University Press).

Chintagunta, P. (1994) 'Heterogeneous Logit Model Implications for Brand Positioning', *Journal of Marketing Research,* XXXi, May, 304–11.

Collins, M. (1971) 'Market Segmentation – the Reality of Buyer Behaviour', *Journal of the Market Research Society,* 13 (3), 146–57.

Converse, P. D. (1930) *The Elements of Marketing,* 1st edn (New York: Prentice-Hall).

Day, G. S. and R. Wensley (1983) 'Marketing Theory with a Strategic Orientation', *Journal of Marketing,* Fall, 79–89.

Dickinson, P. (1992) 'Towards a General Theory of Competitive Rationality', *Journal of Marketing,* 56, 69–83.

Dubois, A. and T. Torvain (1995) 'Overlapping control boundaries in industrial networks', *11th IMP Conference,* September, Manchester, 345–67.

Gould, S. J. (1987) *Time's Arrow, Time's Cycle* (Cambridge, Mass.: Harvard University Press).

Gould, S. J. (1990) *Wonderful Life,* (London: Hutchinson).

Hammer, M. (1990) 'Re-engineering Work: Don't Automate, Obliterate', *Harvard Business Review,* July–August, 104–12.

Hannan, M. T. and J. Freeman (1976) 'The Population Ecology of Organisations', *American Journal of Sociology,* 82 (5), 929–63.

Henderson, J. M. and R. E. Quant (1958) *Microeconomic Theory: a mathematical approach* (New York: McGraw-Hill).

Hooley, G. J. and J. Saunders (1993) *Competitive Positioning: The Key to Market Success* (New York: Prentice-Hall).

Hunt, S. D. (1995) 'The Resource-Advantage Theory of Competition', *Journal of Management Inquiry,* December, 4(4), 317–32.

Hunt, S. D. and R. M. Morgan (1995) 'The comparative advantage theory of competition', *Journal of Marketing,* April, 59(3).

Inkpen, A. and N. Choudhury (1995) 'The Seeking of Strategy Where It Is Not: Towards a Theory of Strategy Absence', *Strategic Management Journal,* 16(4), May, 313–23.

Jacobson, R. (1992) 'The Austrian School of Strategy', *Academy of Management Review,* 17(4), 782–807.

Jones, H. J. (1926) *The Economics of Private Enterprise* (London: Pitman and Sons).

Kay, J. (1993) *Foundations of Corporate Success* (Oxford: Oxford University Press).

Kotler, P. (1967) *Marketing Management: Analysis, Planning, Implementation and Control* (Englewood Cliffs, New Jersey: Prentice-Hall).

Langlois, R. (1986) *Economics as a Process* (Cambridge: Cambridge University Press).

Law, P. J. S. and R. Wensley (1979) 'Marketing Teaching', *European Journal of Marketing*, 13 (1).

Levins, R. and R. Lewontin (1985) *The Dialectical Biologist* (Cambridge, Mass.: Harvard University Press).

Marchand, R. (1985) *Advertising the American Dream* (Berkeley, CA: University of California Press).

McKiernan, P. (1995) *Historical Evolution of Strategic Management* (Aldershot: Dartmouth).

Mintzberg, H. (1973) *The Nature of Managerial Work* (New York: Harper & Row).

Mintzberg, H. (1994) *The Rise and Fall of Strategic Planning* (New York: Prentice-Hall).

Morrison, A. and R. Wensley (1991) 'A Short History of the Growth/Share Matrix: Boxed Up or Boxed in?', *Journal of Marketing Management*, 7(2), April, 105–29.

Nath, D. and T. S. Gruca (1996) 'Convergence across alternative methods for forming strategic groups', *Strategic Management Journal* (forthcoming).

O'Shaughnessy, J. (1992) *Explaining Buyer Behaviour* (Oxford: Oxford University Press).

Penrose, E. (1959) *The Growth of the Firm* (Oxford: Basil Blackwell).

Peters, T. J. (1988) *Thriving on Chaos* (London: Macmillan).

Peters, T. J. and R. H. Waterman (1982) *In Search of Excellence* (New York: Harper and Row).

Pettigrew, A. M. (1973) *The Politics of Organisational Decision Making* (London: Tavistock).

Porter, M. E. (1980) *Competitive Strategy: Techniques for Analyzing Industries and Competitors* (New York: The Free Press).

Porter, M. E. (1985) *Competitive Advantage* (New York: Free Press).

Porter, M. E. (1990) *The Competitive Advantage of Nations* (New York: Macmillan).

Prahalad, C. K. and R. A. Bettis (1987) 'The dominant logic: A new linkage between diversity and performance', *Strategic Management Journal*, 7(6), 485–501.

Prahalad, C. K. and G. Hamel (1990) 'The core competence of the corporation', *Harvard Business Review*, May–June, 79–91.

Robinson, J. (1933) *The Economics of Imperfect Competition* (London: Macmillan).

Russell, G. and W. Kamakura (1994) 'Understanding Brand Competition using Micro and Macro Scanner Data', *Journal of Marketing Research*, XXXI, May, 289–303.

Saunders, J. (1995) 'Market Segmentation: Invited Response to "A Critical Review of Research in Marketing"', *British Journal of Management*, 6 (Special Issue).

Senge, P. (1990) *The Fifth Discipline: The art and practice of the learning organisation* (New York: Doubleday).

Thomas, H. and C. Carrol (1994) 'Theoretical and empirical links between strategic groups, cognitive communities and networks of interacting firms', in H. Daema and H. Thomas (eds), *Strategic Groups, Strategic Moves and Performance* (New York: Pergamon).

Waterman, R. (1988) *The Renewal Factor* (New York: Bantam Press).

Weick, K. E. (1976) 'Educational Organisations as Loosely Coupled Systems', *Administrative Science Quarterly*, 21, 1–19.

Wensley, R. (1982) 'PIMS and BCG: New Horizon or False Dawn', *Strategic Management Journal*, 3, 147–53.

Wensley, R. (1990) 'The Voice of the Consumer? Speculations on the Limits to the Marketing Analogy', *European Journal of Management*, 24(7), 49–60.

Wensley, R. (1994) 'Strategic Marketing: A Review', in M. J. Baker (ed.), *The Marketing Book* (Oxford: Butterworth–Heinemann).

Wensley, R. (1995a) 'A Critical Review of Research in Marketing', *British Journal of Management*, 6 (Special Issue).

Wensley, R. (1995b) 'Market Segmentation: Analytical puzzles and/or managerial problems', *LBS/Warwick Marketing Workshop*, London, December.

Wensley, R. (1996) 'Book Review: Henry Mintzberg and Kevin Kelly', *BAM Newsletter*, Spring, 6–9.

Wernerfeld, B. (1984) 'A resource-based view of the firm', *Strategic Management Journal*, 5(2), 171–80.

Wernerfeld, B. (1995) 'The resource-based view of the firm: ten years after', *Strategic Management Journal*, 16, 171–4.

4 The Evolution of Distribution Channels for Consumer Goods

Susan A. Shaw and John A. Dawson

INTRODUCTION

The choice of channels of distribution is fundamental in establishing the strategic direction for a business. The decision on channel affects the assortment and characteristics of goods made available to the final consumer and the processes by which they are made available (Cespedes, 1988–9). The choice of channels used has a major impact on the totality of the processes performed by the business and its overall performance in the market. The inclusion of a chapter on channel evolution and the theory of channel management therefore complements other chapters in this volume. We hope that it helps to redress partially what Michael Baker (1992) has suggested is an unjustly neglected topic in marketing. The purpose of the contribution is twofold: first, to provide a summary analysis of the ways in which distribution channels for consumer products have been changing; second, to assess the implications of these changes for research into channel theory. The emphasis throughout the chapter is on the European experience, on consumer goods channels and on channels involving large retail businesses. While this area is a small subset of all marketing channels, by focusing on this subset it is possible to explore in detail some important issues which have ramifications for research into all distribution channels.

THE EVOLUTION OF DISTRIBUTION CHANNELS FOR CONSUMER PRODUCTS

The change over the past three decades in European distribution structures and management systems for consumer products has been profound. This section begins with discussion of changing business structures, followed by examination of the implications of change for power and control in the channel and for the ways in which channels function.

Structural Change

Channel structure can be defined as comprising both the horizontal and the vertical economic arrangements in the channel. This contrasts with the narrower definition given by Stern and Reve (1980) and which is frequently used in channel analysis but which covers only vertical arrangements but including horizontal arrangements enables discussion of the interaction between horizontal changes and vertical arrangements. One of the features apparent in European channels has been attempts to manage more tightly, both competitively and co-operatively, the vertical relationships in order to enhance horizontal competitiveness. At the retail level, the major change in horizontal structures has been the growth in market share and power of a decreasing number of large retail businesses, each operating large numbers of retail outlets, and the parallel massive decrease in the network of shops operated by small firms. Recent analyses by Ducroq (1991), Greipl, *et al.*, (1992), Pilotti (1991), Dawson (1995a) and others have reviewed this change and the structural adjustments taking place. The growth in market power of large firms is reflected in increases in five-firm and ten-firm concentration ratios, by the increase in sales volumes of large firms often operating across several retail sectors, and by the decrease in the number of small firms. Comparisons of the data in Jefferys and Knee (1962), Distributive Trades EDC (1973), Dawson (1982) and Eurostat (1993) indicate the very considerable growth in absolute and relative measures of the large firms. There are some notable differences across sectors but the trends have been particularly strong in the food and everyday goods sector. Table 4.1 shows recent trends in the UK in this sector which includes food and grocery, off-licence, chemist and confectionery, tobacco and newspaper retailers but excludes sales of petrol. While there are substantial difficulties in defining and measuring exact market sizes, a general indication of the trends is possible and from Table 4.1 it is clearly seen that the largest firms have increased their market share substantially within a slowly growing market (Dawson, 1995b).

   In contrast to the strengthening of formal horizontal structures there has been weakening of extended and formal vertical structures with some relocation of functions. Vertical disintegration has occurred as

Table 4.1   The retail market for food, grocery and everyday goods in the UK

	1989	*1992*	*1994*
Market size, 1994 prices			
£ billion	76	77	81
Index	100	101	107
Percentage market shares			
Largest 5 superstore firms	32.5	36.9	39.9
Other multi-outlet supermarket retailers *	13.4	13.4	13.3
Discount grocery store retailers	3.5	5.8	7.0
Specialist food based retailers	13.6	11.0	9.6
Independent food non-specialists	6.3	5.3	4.8
Others	30.7	27.6	25.4

* Non-discount stores

Source: Central Statistical Office, *Annual Reports* of the Institute for Grocery
Distribution.

many retailers have divested themselves of manufacturing interests.
For instance, in 1980 all of the major food retailers in the UK had food
manufacturing interests, while today only one (Sainsbury) has such
interests, but even here these are managed in a completely separate
operation. The same trend has occurred in non-food sectors with, for
example in the UK, the divestment of clothing manufacture by clothing
retailers (Burton, Next and so on), of shoe manufacture by shoe
retailers (Sears) and of drug manufacture by Boots. Elsewhere in
Europe similar changes can be seen: the Goasam group in Spain has
separated its clothing manufacture activity from its constituent retail
companies; ICA in Sweden divested food manufacturing interests in
1993; and FDB in Denmark is steadily reducing its food processing
interests. There is also a greater tendency to contract out activities such
as the management of logistics systems (Smith and Sparks, 1993), store
cleaning, security, building maintenance, advertising and so on, in line
with the widely observed tendency of business in the 1990s to concentrate on 'core' activities, passing responsibilities for non-core activities to specialists. The divestment of manufacturing by retailers has
been offset only partially by increased retail activity by manufacturers
with the emergence of retail chains such as Kodak, Disney, Sony, retail
activity by financial service suppliers and more direct sales from
manufacturers to consumers through activities such as mail order sales.
There have also been changes in channel length. The large size of

orders enables the retailer to deal directly with manufacturers and internalise the merchant wholesaling function. As a consequence, the market share of merchant wholesalers has shrunk in line with the growth of retail corporate chains.

There has been an overall increase in retail capacity, with increases in retail space, increased space productivity and extended trading hours, which has outstripped the increase in retail sales. This together with the growth of large organisations results in a fall in the number of horizontal units (firms and establishments) supporting vertical channel structures. Furthermore, each retailer is tending to use a smaller number of suppliers. The reason for this is threefold: central purchasing by the retailer, closer relationships with suppliers (discussed below) raise the cost of dealing with large numbers of suppliers, and changes in suppliers which enable them to provide more of a retailer's needs. These factors, coupled with the drive by manufacturers to achieve scale economies has led to decreasing numbers of suppliers, although through more international trade the range of international sources used by retailers has probably increased.

Rising Retailer Power

While vertical disintegration, in a formal sense, has occurred, this has been combined with an increase in retail control over the vertical and horizontal aspects of channel structure. Centralisation of decision making by retailers, particularly sourcing decisions, has reduced the autonomy of the individual retail outlet within the business. This reflects the central exploitation of economies of scale in buying, marketing and other aspects of management, exploitation of economies of replication and, in some cases, economies of scope at both store and business level (Shaw *et al.*, 1989). The ending of retail price maintenance initiated the process in several countries by increasing the freedom of the retailer to vary final selling prices. The process has continued as retailers have developed their own brand products which require central management and have installed logistics systems centrally driven by point of sale information. In consequence the importance of negotiated discounts and large-scale buying as a source of competitive advantage has increased and so retailers have sought ways to exert more control over their vertical channel relationships with other firms and their horizontal relationships within their firm.

The increase in market shares of large retailers, coupled with centralised systems of decision taking, has been a cause of changes in the internal polity, that is the allocation, possession and use of power within channels. There are differences in the way in which different writers have defined the power construct, but a generally used definition in the academic literature is of the 'ability of one channel member to influence the decision variables of another channel member or one firm's potential for influence on another's beliefs and behaviour' (Frazier, 1990). Using this definition, the high levels of concentration of retail buying in a few decision points in many, if not all, sectors imply that the relative power of these decision points must have increased, given the lack of comparable changes on the supply side. Certainly the phenomenon of increased retailer power has been commented on in British literature (Knox and White, 1991; Moir, 1990; Hogarth Scott and Parkinson, 1993; Crewe and Davenport, 1992) and can be found more generally elsewhere (Marfels, 1992; Pelligrini, 1990; Messinger and Narasimhan, 1995; McLaughlin, 1995). Few of these commentators, however, define the term. There is also a tendency to assume that possession of power automatically results in its use; only infrequently are the ambiguities explored of the retailer's possession of power coupled with its non-use. This power can be defined, using the measures of Frazier (1983) as reward power (the benefit of the large accounts on offer), coercive power (the threat of loss of the account) and expert power (the knowledge and expertise of retailers in marketing, logistics, new product development and so on). In cases where contracts are involved there is legitimate power. Retailers also have information power (French and Raven, 1959; Raven and Kruglanski, 1970) resulting from the retailers' access to market information via scanning systems at point of sale and customer card programmes. Manufacturers have power to withhold supplies and some manufacturers have strong national brands which retailers wish to stock. In many cases, however, retailers have alternative sources of supply which limit the ability of manufacturers to impose sanctions on retailer behaviour other than when a manufacturer brand is very important, for example newspapers, or the manufacturer has an exclusive product, for example in the popular recorded music sector.

Interest in the implications of power is not new, with power and conflict dominant themes in research on channels (Frazier, 1990) but studies are often from a manufacturer perspective and do not reflect the realities of European distribution channels. There are, however, new issues. Aspects which formerly denoted manufacturer power, such as national brands and extensive communication with the final consumer, have declined as sources of power while the magnitude and range of areas of influence of retailers have increased. First is the changed impact of power over information, already cited. In markets in which each of a small number of major retailers has a significant market share, sales data of the individual firm are revealing of the consumer behaviour of a major marketing segment. Data from the scanning of items at point of sale is the property of the retailer, not the manufacturer, and is rapidly surpassing the traditional sources of market data used by manufacturers derived from consumer panel data. The latter, because they are based on the records of a sample of the population, can never reach the accuracy achieved by universal scanning systems. Negotiations are under way, in several European countries, to sell to manufacturers access to aspects of scanning data via links between market research agencies and the retailers but the information publicly available will only be partial. Scanning data are now being linked to consumer profile data through the use of data from customer loyalty schemes. This gives the retailer a unique ability to identify particular types of consumers with considerable precision and to employ consumer-oriented product development initiatives.

A second example is of the balance of communication with the consumer which has changed in many product sectors, from one where manufacturers communicated directly with the consumer in order to stimulate sales and encourage brand loyalty to one where the retailer plays a greater role in communications. The role of in-store display of the product assortment has been enhanced and expenditure on above-the-line promotional activities by retailers has increased. The increases in expenditure by major retailers in the UK on advertising 1982–95 can be seen in Table 4.2. Manufacturers communicate less with final consumers because the filtering of the retailer is now stronger.

Channel Characteristics

Changes in channel structures and power relationships have been accompanied by several changes in the processes of channel management with the development of retailer led vertically administered channels (McCammon, 1970; Dawson and Shaw, 1989, 1990).

Responsibility for the management of supply, for example, manufacture, assembly or component procurement still rests with the supplier but the retailer exercises higher levels of authority over operations, for example in specification and control of quality. Retailers own and control product assortments but, because of increasing product variety, shorter product life cycles and better ability to control

Table 4.2   Advertising expenditures[1] for selected sectors and major retailers

Total advertising expenditure (£m)		1982	1988	1994
Food manufacture		406	563	484
Drink		133	227	256
Retail food and general merchandise[2]		294	482	777
Household stores		118	204	251
Total advertising expenditure (£m)	1986	1989	1992	1995[3]
Sainsbury (supermarkets)	6.4	9.2	19.5	40.4
Tesco (supermarkets)	9.2	13.3	26.7	36.5
Texas (DIY)	9.7	14.0	22.5	25.3[4]
B and Q (DIY)	8.6	16.1	18.2	23.2
MFI (furniture)	21.4	17.0	21.1	22.1
Currys (electricals)	14.9	14.4	16.5	
Dixons (electricals)	15.4	12.4	13.9	63.7[5]
Woolworth (general merchandise)	7.8	21.7	17.7	20.4
Comet (electricals)	9.9	12.0	19.6	19.4
Boots (chemists)	8.9	10.3	14.9	18.2
ASDA (supermarkets)	9.3	9.8	11.0	15.5

Notes:
[1] Press, TV and radio at card rates.
[2] Includes mail order.
[3] Year October 1994–September 1995.
[4] Homebase in 1995.
[5] 1995 figure is for Dixons Group which includes Currys and Dixons.

Source: Register-MEAL.

the timing of range launches, retailers now have a more flexible assortment in terms of qualitative, quantitative and timing factors. Retailers have more choices available to them. In making these choices retailers have sought greater control over product assortments by becoming involved in specification of products and processes and by taking control at an earlier stage in the channel, rather than just selecting from predetermined products over which they had no influence. Retailers also have sought to develop distinctive identities because identity is considered a core activity which is central to competitiveness (Kapferer, 1986; Corstjens and Corstjens, 1995). An important manifestation of this is in the development of retailer branded products which now represent a significant proportion of sales in many different product areas. In British food retailing, for example, retail brands have shown a rapid increase in market share and now have a market of over 36 per cent for grocery products (Taylor Nelson AGB, 1994; IGD, 1995a). In clothing, DIY products, household furnishing and many other areas retail brands are widespread. This is a feature present not only in the UK. Major international retailers, for example IKEA, Promodès, Ahold, Toys Я Us and Disney Store have notable retail brand presence, while retail brands are of growing importance in the marketing activity of domestic retailers in European markets from Finland to Portugal. As retailers seek to develop the range of retail brands, more and more suppliers, even with strong manufacturer brands, are involved in the supply of retailer brand products. Some retailers have developed sophisticated brand strategies. For example, in the UK the large food retailers have now followed the lead of non-food retailers in creating a variety of brand positioning for themselves with budget, standard and premium retail brand items within the same product category (Laaksonen, 1994).

A second trend is towards much greater integration of processes in channels. This involves process integration across several firms. An example is in operational management, with the establishment of joint delivery and ordering cycles to meet needs for in-store availability and least cost operation (Crewe and Davenport, 1992; Mentzer, 1993; Ottimo and Pilotti, 1994). The aim is to achieve 'synchronisation of all channel activities in a manner that will create the greatest net comparative advantage for the consumer' (Langley and Holcomb, 1992). The benefits of just-in-time delivery systems, cross docking in distribution centres and consistency of quality and service for the retailer can only be achieved by organisations who work closely together at both strategic and operational level (GEA, 1994; P-E International, 1994). GEA define this process as one where 'both retailers and suppliers share proprietary internal or external data and/or share policies and processes used in decision-making with the clear objective of sharing the benefits'. It is easy to emphasise the benefits of such integration and also easy to ignore the real operational problems of implementation. GEA describe supplier–retailer collaboration as containing five components: operating standards, product replenishment, store assortment, promotion and product development. In their study of practice in European countries they point to variations in levels of achievement across a variety of measures. The UK is described as very advanced in most of these aspects while Greece and Spain are little developed, with Germany, France and Italy occupying intermediate positions. A prediction of the GEA study is that all countries are moving towards the UK model. The result of this integration is a longer term orientation because of the benefits of joint strategic planning, the costs of setting up systems and the search costs which would be incurred for alternative suppliers. The conclusions of GEA and their predictions of European convergence are seductive but based on untested assumptions about the convergence of currently different cultures across Europe.

These two trends have implications for the location of functions both in the channel and within the business of individual channel members. Since the emphasis is on the overall performance of the channel, there is a willingness to seek improved performance, even if it changes the traditional perceptions of roles. For example, Hawkes (1995) suggests that in the food sector the supplier may be required to take responsibility for store audits, store stocking and quality control while the retailer takes greater responsibility for product concepts, product positioning and advertising. There are, however, considerable differences in practice in the allocation of roles in the channel with firm- and sector-specific differences to be observed. Suppliers may now be given access to retail sales data by store so that the supplier can assume responsibility for replenishing stocks without prior orders from the retailer (Houlder, 1995). Retailers and suppliers have always influenced each other but now it is possible to have integration where before integration could not be handled. Within the business, the growth of quick response systems with high levels of interaction within the channel has led to a growth in the importance of logistics as a component of customer satisfaction (Mentzer *et al.*, 1989), in order to manage ordering, distribution, storage and forecasting. For companies supplying both retail and manufacturer brand products the size of the marketing department has probably decreased and activities have been focused to service the accounts of key trade customers, analogous to the industrial marketer, rather than primarily being concerned with marketing at consumer level. The retailer now has a stronger responsibility for marketing to the consumer.

Finally, the retailer's role in influencing the structure of the channel itself has grown as the retailer's role as a catalyst of change has increased. The development of third party distribution systems and regional distribution centres for store delivery are a manifestation of this. While systems are often managed by external specialists, it is the retailer's drive for efficiency in distribution which has led to the drive to reduce physical distribution and stock holding costs through the development of just-in-time systems (GDI, 1988; Smith and Sparks,

1993). The role of the retailer as stimulator of new product development is another example (Senker, 1988). In their search for unique differentiated products, retailers have developed capabilities for the generation of new product ideas, product testing and quality management and thus have played a part in stimulating the development of manufacturers. Retailers have acted as a catalyst for the development of new information technology systems, usually working in partnership with system suppliers (Simmet, 1990). While fundamental technological developments in information handling and communications have their origin in developments outside the channel, retailers have provided a major stimulus to the development of new applications and of dedicated retail channel systems (IGD, 1995b; Herman, 1994).

The combination, over the last 20 years, of external impetus and internal dynamics has had a profound effect on the structure of channels for consumer products in Europe and on the economic and social processes which take place within those channels. We now turn to the role played by academic work on channels in providing explanations of the logic of operation and prescriptions for managers in these channels.

DISTRIBUTION CHANNEL THEORY: THE GAPS

Although there have been suggestions that knowledge of channels is limited, the volume of research on channels is considerable (Frazier, 1990). The focus of interest has changed in line with changes in the themes addressed by marketing academics in the core marketing literature. Prior to 1970 most interest was in the identification and explanation of the economic functions performed in marketing channels. Subsequently interest grew in the behavioural aspects of channel management with theoretical and empirical research grounded in the concepts of power, influence strategies, control and conflict. This literature used constructs drawn from the enhanced interest of marketing academics in exchange relationships, although the interest in power and influence strategies was probably greatest in the marketing channel literature. Considerable research was carried out on the sources of power and the management of power within channel relationships (see, for example, Gaski, 1984; Frazier, 1983, 1990). Reviews of this literature can be found in Frazier (1990). More recently, with the evidence of the increasing role played by vertical marketing systems in channel management, discussed earlier, interest has grown in the broader issues associated with the management of relationships. Particular interest has been shown in the constructs which generate satisfaction in channel members with relationships which, as a consequence, are likely to endure. Knowledge about the factors creating trust and reciprocity in relationships has been added to constructs of power and influence factors (see, for example, Ruekert and Churchill, 1984; Anderson and Weitz, 1989; Anderson and Narus, 1990; Frazier and Rody, 1991; Skinner *et al.*, 1992).

Existing theory, however, still fails to explain certain aspects of channel management systematically and thus there are considerable gaps in our understanding of the processes which operate within channels. First, there are gaps in existing analysis, the first of which is in the treatment of channel functions. After research in the 1970s, channel functions have been a largely neglected issue. There are several aspects of this neglect, led by the limited range of functions considered in much of the literature. Much research assumes that the relevant channel functions are primarily the sales and marketing of a predetermined product mix from the supplier (usually a manufacturer). A widely researched scenario is one which deals with decisions to be made by manufacturers in their relationships with large numbers of distributors, where the latter perform only marketing functions (see, for example, Anderson and Weitz, 1989; Anderson and Narus, 1990). There is little consideration of new product development processes or the processes for creating new systems because these are regarded as being internal to the manufacturer and thus outside the range of interest in a study of channel management. Production management and scheduling have received similar treatment. Similar comments can be made about the way in which other channel functions such as financing and management of physical flows are treated. After the identification of these functions in the 1970s and consideration as to how the performance of these functions influenced channel configuration, these topics have been largely disregarded in the marketing literature despite the changes described earlier in this chapter. Without an understanding of the totality of functions performed in the channel, other aspects of channel management such as communication and flows of control cannot be understood properly.

Given the lack of interest in channel functions, the lack of interest in the location of these functions in the channel is inevitable. In the main, the rationale for the allocation of functions is not discussed. This is particularly evident in the writings on power and dependence in the 1980s and even later (Brown *et al.*, 1995). Thus, for example, the literature largely ignores the interactions between power, control, authority and location of functions in the channel, although these identities interact considerably: for example, power can affect the location of functions and the location of functions can influence power. Some of the recent literature on relationship management has recognised that the location of some functions is changing (Webster, 1992), is interested in a wider range of variables affecting channel management and has emphasised the importance of overall optimisation of channel performance. So far, however, there is no theory to explain location of functions within integrated relationships or discussion of the implications of more integration of functions for the management of relationships. It is unclear what are the causes of the migration of functions to different locations; clearly there are processes at work other than power. Writers suggest the elements of inter-business relationships which are likely to lead to more efficient management of activities but show little interest in the actual organisation and management of those activities. From over 70 articles on channel management in major journals between 1980 and 1994, only four consider the location of functions in any detail and one of these is only concerned with the location of sales functions. Yet understanding the reasons for the location of different functions in different places in the channel is a necessary part of understanding channel management. For example, if quality control and in-store availability are organised by the supplier rather than by the retailer, this defines the necessity of a relationship based on high levels of continuing information exchange and on considerable trust so that the retailer is willing to delegate activities. Another example is in the different balance of marketing activities for the supplier in a channel for retailer brand products compared to a situation where the retailer purchases manufacturer brand products. In the former situation the emphasis is likely to be on establishing systems where the retailer and supplier work together on product specifications, design and supplying products and services to meet those specifications. In the latter, the marketing activities of the supplier are likely to include downstream product promotion and a less interactive role in the design of product specifications.

The spatial aspect of the location of functions has been almost totally ignored in the literature. The changes in the location of functions in the channel influence the comparative advantage of alternative spatial locations of the providers of channel functions. In this context the location of regional distribution centres (RDCs), wherein the logistics function is physically co-ordinated, is important to the cost efficiencies of the change in the location of this function within the channel and the transaction costs involved in intra-channel relationships. As the range of activities at RDCs has expanded, so their optimal spatial location and their optimal spatial network have changed. The spatial provision of these facilities is important for understanding the responsibility for and location of functions within the channel. There are other spatial aspects of channel structure and performance which have not been explored in the marketing literature, for example the ways that the changed channel management procedures allow access to national distribution by regionally focused producers, and the potential for conflict between the spatial concentration of decision making by retailers and the operation of a spatially highly disaggregated network of facilities. The spatial location of suppliers may be an important factor in sustaining long-term relationships in the new channel structures. Discussion of these issues, and other similar ones, are notably absent from the academic literature on channels.

Most existing channel research is primarily concerned with the interface between businesses and does not address the relationship between the channel and the internal functioning of the business. It is increasingly difficult to separate relationships which are inter-firm, channel–firm, inter-channel and intra-firm because changes in the internal management strategies and systems of one channel member influence the internal management of channel partners. The relationships influence channel structures and performance and hence influence inter-channel competition. An example can be drawn from retail category management which integrates buying and merchandising systems within the retailer, working also with the supplier in a joint team (Nielsen, 1992; McLaughlin and Hawkes, 1995). Category management by the retailer requires the parallel adoption of category management systems by the supplier so that multiple functions within the supplier are co-ordinated to meet the needs of the retail category manager. This also changes the relationship between functions within the business in order to change the operation of the channel. Because a product category, for example haircare products, is distributed through several different channels, category management in one channel, for example supermarkets, can influence changes in other channels, for example independent drug stores served by a wholesaler.

Value-oriented channel management means that logistics managers require a greater understanding of marketing-led concepts such as customer satisfaction but, equally, marketing managers require a greater understanding of logistics in order to identify the potential for meeting customer needs and creating new needs. A similar analogy can be drawn with production. Total quality management, required by the retailer, places greater emphasis on operations and production, undertaken by the manufacturer. This requires that some functions, which have been traditionally manufacturer-oriented, are more customer-led and reflect the importance of customer service. Equally, marketing must be able to understand production management in order to define with customers what should be offered. This is a topic which has only been addressed to a limited extent in the literature on channels in marketing journals (Mentzer *et al.,* 1989; Christopher, 1992), although the interface of other functions with marketing has been examined in the logistics literature (Coyle and Andraski, 1990; Langley and Holcomb, 1992; Novack *et al.*, 1992; Mentzer, 1993). The concentration in the marketing channels literature on behavioural factors such as trust and satisfaction is valuable in indicating the antecedents for the development of optimal channel performance. Trust and commitment in themselves, however, are unlikely to be enough to sustain the relationship. What is now required is the specific understanding of the systems which can be set up to deliver both competitive and co-operative advantage, that is logistics, production management, new product development, retail branding, format development and so on, and the way in which different functions interconnect to achieve these advantages. The conclusion that the need is to obtain better understanding of the technical aspects of channels and relationships runs counter to current popular paradigms of post modernism and eschatology in marketing which emphasise a seemingly limitless variety of formless and unstructured activity. Channels are neither formless nor unstructured. The need for a structured understanding of processes is a logical direction for research, given the high degree of channel and functional integration which are now observable.

The lack of interest in functional issues is probably one cause of a similar lack of research interest in the channel in its entirety rather than in sets of dyadic relationships. An additional cause may simply be the difficulty of envisioning the entirety of the channel. Recently, Crewe and Davenport (1992) and Shaw (1994) have noted the need to consider the entire chain to understand its functioning. Shaw shows how retailers influence directly and indirectly the activities of the suppliers of suppliers. Crewe and Davenport note the way that risk is transferred to subcontractors in the clothing industry, while relationships of retailers with suppliers remain close and stable. This suggests that to understand channel relationships we need to go beyond an emphasis on channels relationships involving one supplier and an intermediary to a view that looks at channels as a retailer driven value chain, ignoring traditional views of roles and concentrating instead on the way that value is delivered by the chain as a whole and in effect who makes what profit where. This constitutes a modern day extension of the 1930s, 1950s and 1960s studies on 'why does distribution cost so much?' (Braithwaite and Dobbs, 1932; Stewart *et al.*, 1939; Barger, 1955; Cox, 1965).

The second aspect of the channel as a totality is the treatment of networks of channel relationships other than those associated directly with product aspects of the value chain. The general marketing literature considers the role of networks (see, for example, Anderson *et al.*, 1994) of various types but the network approach has received little treatment in the marketing literature on channels for consumer goods, although most channels have substantial networks of other relationships which influence management and development. Such networks can influence the power balance in channels since they can be an important source of competitive and co-operative advantage. In conceptual terms a channel is a particular type of network but there has been relatively little cross-fertilisation of the work of the network school with work on channel dynamics. An example, cited earlier, is the role of third party distribution in facilitating channel flows which illustrates how approaches of the network school and the channel schools might be synthesised. The development of internal logistics systems managed by third party specialists (which could be studied in a network context and including financial, technological and business service networks) can be said, for instance, to have played an important role in developing the competitive position of firms in food retailing and in clothing retailing through the achievement of associated economies of scale, releasing economies in information use and affecting the power, control, trust and reciprocity relationships between retailers and suppliers (studied by the channel school). Other examples could be cited of the roles played by financiers of channel operations, the role of packaging design agencies in new product development for retail brands, property companies in real estate provision, and software system development houses in new approaches to merchandising and building customer loyalty for products and stores. In all these cases there is a need to combine a network approach and a channel approach in order to understand the complexity which constitutes the totality of the channel.

Networks involve complex relationships with customers or suppliers who are in competition with each other. For example, suppliers who have multiple accounts with a number of dominant retailers have to make these relationships compatible with each other. For the retailer, for example, if high levels of information transmission are necessary for the integrated relationship with the supplier to work properly, what are the rules about the security of that information or its use by the supplier in other relationships with competing retailers? This issue has been considered briefly in a food context by some authors (Knox and White, 1991) but no theory or conceptual framework of behaviour has been developed to address these and other comparable situations. While there are few studies which consider the channel in its totality, whether or not as a network, there are even fewer studies, even of an episodic nature, which consider the mechanisms and processes of integration within the network. For example, there is anecdotal material of a journalistic nature which considers the role of the individual chief executive officer in providing the integrative view, and there is some material which considers the role of specific technologies in integrating the channel (Houlder, 1995) but explicit analysis of the process is usually absent. Furthermore, there is an implicit view that networks comprise competing firms when there is some evidence to suppose in the existing literature, and in the real world, that co-operative firms may constitute core aspects of networks.

DISTRIBUTION CHANNEL THEORY: THE NEED FOR INTEGRATION

Implicit in the foregoing critique is a general concern that partial approaches to channel research do not allow understanding of the way in which channels evolve over time. Therefore the second general claim is that most writing has been partial and not integrative, so that understanding of both the functioning and management of distribution channels is impaired. While, as Hunt (1991) points out, no one would propose that to explain anything we must study everything, explanation must go deep enough to provide marketing academicians with an understanding of the phenomenon being studied (Popper, 1960). This has not always been the case with channel research. While there have been review articles and attempts to take a holistic approach, most research has concentrated on relatively narrow aspects of channel management. The result is that most research has examined episodes and events rather than the dynamic forces present. For example, of the 33 articles published in the *Journal of Marketing* and the *Journal of Marketing Research* over the period 1980–95, only two deal with channel management issues in a dynamic context. Even the most recent literature on relationship management does not consider the management of change. Of the above 33 articles, only five consider interactions with the external environment relevant to an understanding of channel structure and management. Yet external factors such as developments in information technologies have had a profound influence on the way in which channels operate. While retailers may have adapted systems to suit their specific needs, the availability of the core technologies and external facilitators were prerequisites to this development (Burt and Dawson, 1991). Developments in temperature control systems for food transport and storage radically affected channel management and relationships, not least in new product development and in-store merchandising. Developments in international communications, by increasing supply opportunities for retailers, have affected power balances, particularly in European clothing retailing. This is not to deny the role of the internal dynamism of retailers and some manufacturers in stimulating change in channels but to suggest that a suitable enabling environment is a precondition for change. The stance is of environmental possibilism rather than environmental, or organisational, determinism. Because we lack a theory of the relationship between internal and external change forces we also lack a theory of retail and channel evolution and with it a full understanding of the dynamics of a channel at any particular moment.

THE NEXT STAGE

Two things are needed if we are to develop channel research in the directions suggested above. The first is a conceptual framework which can be used as a basis not only for understanding channels in a static context but also for understanding the processes in their evolution. The second is a consequent agenda of issues for research. A possible conceptual framework is presented in Figure 4.1. It seeks to emphasise the components that comprise the channel:

the actors and participant institutions;
the structure of the channel in terms of vertical, horizontal and spatial organisation;

channel processes in terms of flows and behavioural relationships;
external factors affecting channel structures and processes;
the extent and form of interactions amongst these four components.

Figure 4.1 indicates the main directional flows, distinguishing at the same time institutions, influences and processes. The full range and nature of interactions are not shown. Channel structures are seen as resulting from the underlying economics of operations and external forces such as public policy which influence those economics. Product flows and behavioural processes are in turn influenced by institutions in the channel through the effect of power, trust, reciprocity and dependence relationships among channel members. There is also a role for managerial vision and dynamism as a force explaining channel evolution, as there is also for the role played by external facilitators in defining the processes which take place in the channel. Location of functions and behavioural relationships in the channel influence each other and influence the pattern of activities which will be undertaken within members of the channel. A channel is not, however, a simple linear system for change. The internal dynamics of the channel expressed through channel flows and behavioural relationships have a further influence on structures and institutions through feedback which affects the economics of operations. This new framework builds on the Stern and Reve political economy framework (1980) mentioned earlier but covers the forces affecting channel evolution more explicitly and by indicating the main directions of change attempts to provide greater explanatory power.

This framework can then be used to address some key issues in building an understanding of channel processes and performance. Particular issues suggested by earlier discussion of existing theory include the following.

What processes of change are linear and continuous and which are externally triggered, non-linear and discontinuous?
Are particular forms of channel structure and particular types of processes and behavioural relationships more likely to create channel environments where change and development, in effect, are encouraged? Are these encouraging of innovation in products, in business processes, in relationships and/or in channel integration?
Are particular configurations of networks involving external facilitators more likely to create channel environments where change, development and innovation are encouraged?

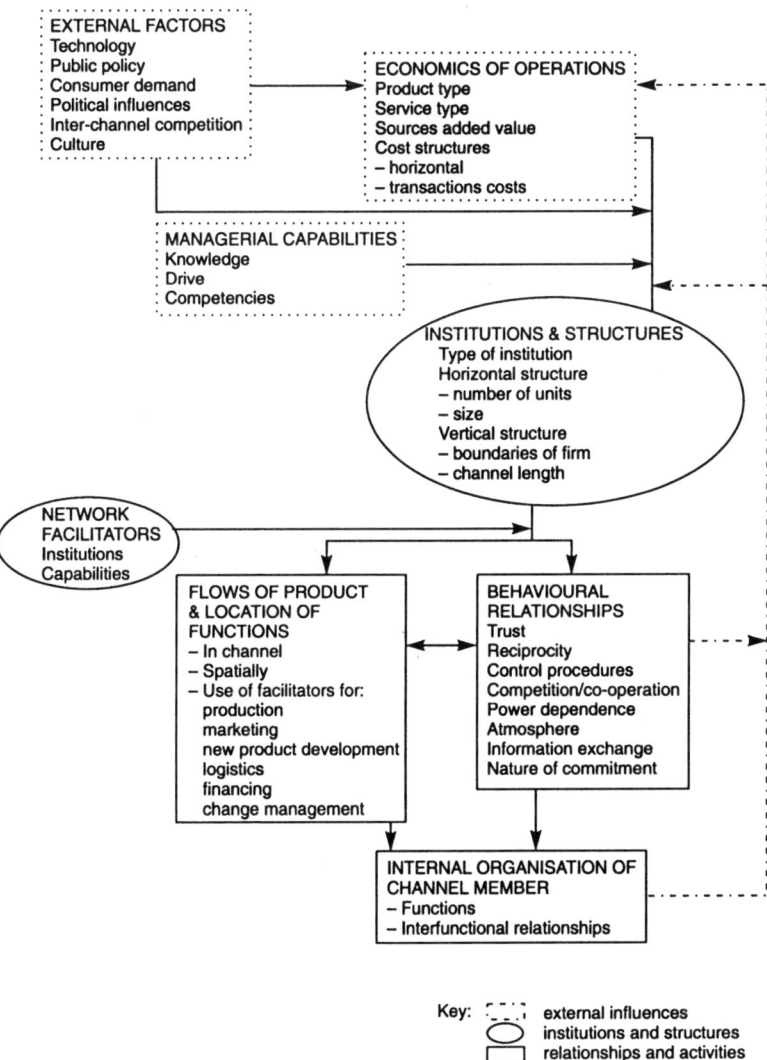

Figure 4.1   Revised conceptual framework for channel research

How do channel members both build close relationships with each other and remain responsive to external forces, particularly new forms of competition?

How does membership of a channel influence the responsiveness of internal management structures and processes within the business with respect to product and process innovation?

What is likely to be the impact of the greater need for integration of functions and central control in the channel on longer term channel structures and levels of competition and co-operation between channels?

Are particular channel structures and relationships likely to be more responsive to the impact of external factors such as changes in technology and public policy than other channels?

How do the spatial and structural aspects of the organisation of the channel interact?

Distribution channels for consumer goods in Europe have undergone profound change in the 25 years since the publication of Michael Baker's introductory text, *Marketing* (Baker, 1971). Contrasting the current situation with that described in Baker, the channels have changed, the key agents have changed and the relationships have been transforned. Baker points out that, although the 1960s were a decade of considerable output of academic publication on distribution, 'it is significant that little of the research represented in this literature has been concerned with the strategic implications of channel choice' (p. 174). It is still highly debatable whether over the last 25 years the academic study of channels has kept pace with the changes in the real world despite the widespread acceptance that the choice of channels is a decision 'of acute importance to the marketer'.

References

Anderson, J.C. and J.A. Narus (1990) 'A Model of Distributor Firm and Manufacturer Firm Working Partnerships', *Journal of Marketing*, 54(1), 42–58.

Anderson J.C., H. Hakansson and J. Johanson (1994) 'Dyadic Business Relationships within a Business Network Context', *Journal of Marketing*, 58(4), 1–15.

Anderson, E. and B. Weitz (1989) 'Determinants of Continuity in Conventional Industrial Channel Dyads', *Marketing Science,* 8(Fall), 310–23.

Baker, M. J. (1971) *Marketing: An Introductory Text* (London: Macmillan).

Baker, M. J. (1992) *Marketing Strategy and Management*, 2nd edn (London: Macmillan).

Barger, H. (1955) *Distribution's Place in the American Economy since 1869* (Princeton: Princeton University Press).

Braithwaite, D. and S. P. Dobbs (1932) *The Distribution of Consumable Goods* (London: Routledge).

Brown, J. R., J. L. Johnson and H. F. Koenig (1995) 'Measuring the Sources of Marketing Channel Power: A Comparison of Alternative Approaches', *International Journal of Research in Marketing*, 12, 333–54.

Burt, S. L. and J. A. Dawson (1991) 'The Impact of New Technology and New Payment Systems on Commercial Distribution in the European Community', *Commission of the European Communities, DGxxiii, Series Studies, Commerce and Distribution*, 17.

Cespedes, F. V. (1988–9) 'Channel Management is General Management', *California Management Review*, 33, 99–118.

Christopher, M. (1992) *Logistics and Supply Chain Management: Structures for Reducing Costs and Improving Services* (London: Pitman).

Corstjens, J. and M. Corstjens (1995) *Store Wars: The Battle for Mindspace and Shelfspace* (Chichester: Wiley).

Cox, R. (1965) *Distribution in a High Level Economy* (Englewood Cliffs: Prentice-Hall).

Coyle, J. J. and J. C. Andraski (1990) 'Managing Channel Relationships', *Annual Conference Proceedings, Council of Logistics Management* Chicago, 245–58.

Crewe, L. and E. Davenport (1992) 'The Puppet Show: Changing Relationships within Clothing Retailing', *Transactions of the Institute of British Geographers*, 17, 183–97.

Dawson, J. A. (1982) *Commercial Distribution in Europe* (London: Croom Helm).

Dawson, J. A. (1995a) 'Retail Change in the European Community' , in R. Davies, (ed.), *Retail Planning Policies in Western Europe* (London: Routledge) 1–30.

Dawson, J. A. (1995b) 'Food Retailing and the Food Consumer', in D. W. Marshall (ed.) *Food Choice* (London: Blackie) 77–104.

Dawson, J. A. and S. A. Shaw (1989) 'The Move to Administered Vertical Marketing Systems by British Retailers', *European Journal of Marketing*, 23(7), 42–52.

Dawson, J. A. and S. A. Shaw (1990) 'The Changing Character of Retailer–Supplier Relationships', in J. Fernie (ed.) *Retail Distribution Management* (London: Kogan Page) 19–39.

Distributive Trades EDC (1973) *The Distributive Trades in the Common Market* (London: HMSO).

Ducroq, C. (1991) *Concurrences et Stratégies dans la Distribution* (Paris: Vuibert).

Eurostat (1993) *Retailing in the European Single Market* (Luxembourg: Eurostat).

Frazier, G. L. (1983) 'On the Measurement of Interfirm Power in Channels of Distribution', *Journal of Marketing*, 55 (1), 52–69.

Frazier, G. L. (1990) 'The Design and Management of Channels of Distribution', in G. Day, B. Weitz, and R. Wensley, (eds.) *The Interface of Marketing and Strategy* Strategic Management Policy and Planning 6 (Boston: JAI Press) 255–304.

Frazier, G. L. and Rody, R. C. (1991) 'The Use of Influence Strategies in Interfirm Relationships in Industrial Product Channels', *Journal of Marketing 55*, (January), 52–69.

French, J. and B. Raven (1959) 'The Bases of Social Power', in D. Cartwright (ed.), *Studies in Social Power* (Ann Arbor: University of Michigan Press) 150–67.

GDI (1988) *Logistics 2001 in* Europe (Zurich: GDI).

Gaski, J. F. (1984), 'The Theory of Power and Conflict in Channels of Distribution', *Journal of Marketing*, 48, Summer, 9–29.

GEA Consulenti Associati di Gestione Aziendale (1994) Supplier–Retailer Collaboration in Supply Chain Management (London: Coca-Cola Retailing Research Group – Europe).

Greipl, E. von, H. Laumer and U. Chr. Täger (1992) *Entwicklung der Empirishen Handelsforschung in der Bundesrepublik Deutschland* (Munich: IFO).

Hawkes, G. (1995), 'Chips with Everything: Client Management and IT', in G. Brace and L. Patten (eds), *Food and Beverage Europe* 1995, (London: Sterling Publications), 55–72 .

Herman, G. (1994) *The Impact of Information Technology in Retail* (London: Pearson Professional).

Hogarth Scott, S. and S. T. Parkinson (1993) 'Retailer–Supplier Relationships in the Food Channel: A Supplier Perspective', *International Journal of Retail and Distribution Management*, 21 (8), 11–18.

Houlder, V. (1995) 'Tighter links in the Chain', *Financial Times*, 22 June, 21.

Hunt, S. D. (1991) *Modern Marketing Theory: Critical Issues in the Philosophy of Marketing Science* (Cincinnati: South Western Publishing Company).

Institute for Grocery Distribution (1995a) *Grocery Retailing 1995: The Market Review* (Watford: IGD Business Publications).

Institute for Grocery Distribution (1995b) *IT Trends in the Grocery Industry* (Watford: IGD Business Publications).

Jefferys, J. B. and Knee, D. (1962) *Retailing in Europe*, (London: Macmillan).

Kapferer, J-N. (1986) 'Beyond Positioning: Retailer's Identity', *Retail Strategies For Profit and Growth* (Amsterdam: ESOMAR) 167–75.

Knox, S. D. and H. F. M. White (1991) 'Retail Buyers and their Fresh Produce Suppliers: A Power or Dependency Scenario in the UK?', *European Journal of Marketing*, 25 (1), 40–52.

Laaksonen, H. (1994), 'Own Brands in Food Retailing Across Europe', *Oxford Report on Retailing* (Oxford : Oxford Institute of Retail Management).

Langley, C. J. and Holcomb, M. C. (1992) 'Creating Logistics Customer Value', *Journal of Business Logistics*, 13 (2), 1–28.

Marfels, C. (1992) 'Concentration and Buying Power: The Case of German Food Distribution', *International Review of Retail, Distribution and Consumer Research*, 2(3), 233–44.

McCammon, B. C. Jr. (1970) 'Perspectives for Distribution Programming', in L. P. Bucklin (ed.), *Vertical Marketing Systems* (Glenview, Ill. Scott Foresman) 32–51.

McLaughlin, E. W. (1995) 'Buying Practices in the Fresh Fruit and Vegetable Industry in the USA', *International Review of Retail, Distribution and Consumer Research*, 5 (1), 37–62.

McLaughlin, E. W. and G. F. Hawkes (1995) 'Category Management in the US Grocery Distribution Channel: A New Mechanism for Grocery Co-ordination', *Eighth International Conference on Research in the Distributive Trades*, CESCOM, Milan, September, A14, 15–24.

Mentzer, J. T. (1993) 'Managing Channel Relations in the 21st Century', *Journal of Business Logistics*, 14 (1), 27–41.

Mentzer, J. T., R. Gomes, and R. E. Krapfel Jr. (1989) 'Physical Distribution Service: A Fundamental Marketing Concept?', *Journal of the Academy of Marketing Science*, 17 (1), 53–62.

Messinger, P. R. and C. Narasimhan (1995), 'Has Power Shifted in the Grocery Channel?', *Marketing Science*, 14(2), 189–223.

Moir, C. (1990), 'Competition in the UK Grocery Trades', in C. Moir and J. A. Dawson (eds), *Competition and Markets* (London: Macmillan), 91–118.

Nielsen, (1992) *Category Management* (Chicago: American Marketing Association).

Novack, R. A., L. M. Rinehart, and M. V. Wells (1992) 'Rethinking Concept Foundations in Logistics Management', *Journal of Business Logistics*, 13 (2), 233–67.

Ottimo, E. and L. Pilotti (1994) 'Electronic Data Interchanges and Producer–Retailer Relationships', *Università Bocconi, Note di Ricerca*, 32.

P-E International (1994) *Supply Chain Partnerships: Who Wins?* (Egham: P-E International).

Pelligrini, L. (1990) *Economia della Distribuzione Commerciale*, (Milan: EGEA).

Pilotti, L. (1991) *La Distribuzione Commerciale*, (Turin: Utet).

Popper, K. R. (1960) *The Poverty of Historicism* (London: Routledge & Kegan Paul).

Raven, B. and A. Kruglanski (1970) 'Conflict and Power', in P. Swingle (ed.), *The Structure of Conflict* (New York: Academic Press) 69–109.

Ruekert, R. W. and G. A. Churchill (1984) 'Reliability and Validity of Alternative Measures of Channel Member Satisfaction', *Journal of Marketing Research*, 21 (May), 226–33.

Senker, J. (1988) 'Technological Co-operation Between Manufacturers and Retailers to Meet Market Demand', *Food Marketing*, 2(3), 88–99.

Shaw, S. A. (1994) 'Competitiveness, Relationships and the Strathclyde University Food Project', *Journal of Marketing Management*, 10, 391–407.

Shaw, S. A., D. Nisbett and J. A. Dawson (1989) 'Economies of Scale in UK Supermarkets: Some Preliminary Findings', *International Journal of Retailing*, 4 (5), 12–26.

Simmet, H. (1990), *Neue Informations und Kommunikations-technologien im Marketing des Lebenmitteleinzelhandels* (Stuttgart: Poeschel).

Skinner, S. J., J. B. Gassenheimer and S. W. Kelly (1992) 'Co-operation in Supplier Dealer Relations', *Journal of Retailing*, 68 (2), 174–93.

Smith, D. L. G. and L. Sparks (1993) 'The Transformation of Physical Distribution in Retailing: The Example of Tesco plc', *International Review of Retail, Distribution and Consumer Research*, 3 (1), 35–64.

Stern, L. W. and T. Reve (1980) 'Distribution Channels as Political Economies: A Framework for Comparative Analysis', *Journal of Marketing*, 44(3), 52–64.

Stewart, P. W., J. F. Dewhurst and L. Field (1939) Does Distribution Cost Too Much? (New York: Twentieth Century Fund).

Taylor Nelson AGB (1994) *Packaged Grocery Private Label 1983–92* (London: Taylor Nelson AGB).

Webster, F. E. (1992) 'The Changing Role of Marketing in the Corporation', *Journal of Marketing*, 56 (4), 1–17.

5 Using Relationship Marketing and Organisational Learning for Competitive Advantage during Innovation

Patricia W. Meyers and
Gerard A. Athaide

Without his knowledge, Professor Michael Baker and his work on new product development and innovation provided the fundamental impetus for this chapter. Indeed, Professor Baker played a very important role in forming the research career of the first author. Several years ago (not even the rigours of academic citation will force the exact date from me – some things are best left hazy) this author was pursuing an interest in innovation in search of a dissertation topic. The area was then being 'rediscovered' in the USA and certainly worthy of more study. The difficulty then was finding an appropriate conceptual framework with which to winnow ideas. Some of Professor Baker's work came to light during a daily foray to the library in search of previous thinking on innovation. His careful discussion of a two-by-two grid with innovation in the fourth, high-growth and high-risk, cell offered a parsimonious foundation upon which to build. The dissertation proposal was written, accepted, completed and ultimately led to several more pieces such as the one included here. Much later, I met Professor Baker at an American Marketing Association Conference where I had the pleasure of being the track chair for his paper with Susan Hart (Hart and Baker, 1993) that offered a framework with which to view new product development. His careful pursuit and continuous improvement of thinking about innovation still inspires.

One of the hallmarks of his work has been an emphasis upon the relationships between sellers and buyers and how important these are to marketing in general and to innovation and new product development in particular. The study reported here continues this stream of inquiry by including organisational learning as an important continuing process within marketing relationships during successful new product development when it involves new technology.

New product development is an important contributor to a firm's growth and prosperity. This is particularly true in high-technology industries where rapid changes in buyer needs or 'dominant' technological designs necessitate frequent new product introductions (Weiss and Heide, 1993; Madique and Zirger, 1985). At least three driving forces, intense global competition, highly fragmented and demanding markets, and rapidly advancing technologies, now place the interest upon new product development processes at the forefront of business concerns (Clark and Wheelwright, 1993). For success, firms must learn rapid and effective new ways to address changing market needs, technological advances and competitor moves as they develop and launch new products.

Unfortunately, the failure rates for new products remain very high (Lucas and Bush 1984). Some of this failure has been attributed to the faulty organisation of the new product development process (NPD) itself. These problems are related to the way the technology in question is developed relatively early in the NPD cycle and to the way the market for new products is detected and formed during early commercialisation of innovations (Leonard-Barton, 1990).

For firms that market new, industrial products to business organisations this NPD failure has been attributed partly to ineffective management of relationships with customers during new product development and early launch (More, 1986). In fact, existing research strongly implies that relationships between sellers and buyers[1] are particularly crucial for the successful commercialisation[2] of new, high-technology innovations (Ettlie, 1986; Meyers and Athaide, 1989, 1991; Parkinson, 1985). Since a major component of these relationships is the exchange of information especially about buyers' perceptions and use of new products (More, 1986; Moriarty and Kosnik, 1989), it appears that sellers use the information generated during such relationships to learn and to build competitive advantages. Recent work does point out that when markets and technologies are new to a selling firm a major focus of relationship activities directed by the seller toward buyers is the generation of new knowledge (Leonard-Barton, 1995). This learning adds to an unfolding understanding of user needs and technical capabilities (Attewell, 1993). Learning during relationships also often takes the form of making tacit or local knowledge explicit, codified and communicable (Nonaka and Takeuchi, 1995). The mechanisms by which sellers generate and manage this learning as an 'asset' (Glazer, 1991) are not clear, however. Thus, while existing research indicates that the relationships which selling organisations have with their buying organisations (or organisational customers) are extremely important to the new product development process, scholars have little empirical work upon which to base understanding and theory development about this important process. In addition, practitioners have little but their own past experience upon which to base the management of these relationships. For these reasons, this paper reports exploratory research efforts to investigate more fully the organisational seller–buyer relationship during new product development, specifically how the management of such relationships by the selling organisation can involve effective organisational learning and competitive advantage in the market-place. In particular, the following research questions appear worthy of investigation:

- What kinds of information and knowledge are generated by sellers during the course of their relationship with buyers?
- How do sellers use this information to learn, that is generate new knowledge that can lead to competitive advantage?

To explore answers to these research questions and to formulate propositions for future research we conducted an extensive field study of one high-technology firm in the north-east United States, a supplier of health care-related applications software.

This chapter contains three major sections reporting the process and findings of the study. First, we describe our research approach and method. Next, we provide an overview of the company and its relationship marketing strategies. We conclude with our findings and propose propositions and directions for future research.

METHOD

Previous work indicates that high-technology firms generate competitive advantage by maintaining intensive relationships with customers in niche markets (Leonard-Barton, 1988; Meyers and Athaide, 1989, 1991; von Hippel, 1978). This is particularly true for sellers of new applications software where technological advantages as well as buyers' needs and usage patterns are initially unclear (Voss, 1985). Consequently, a successful applications software firm was a desirable site for our study. One that develops and markets computer software to the health care industry was identified, using an expert panel.[3]

Since very little theory existed to guide our research, a clinical, grounded theory approach was adopted (Glaser and Strauss, 1967). Participant observation, archival research, and an extensive series of taped, semi-structured interviews were conducted over a period of 13 months. While more than 25 employees were included in this research, the primary interviewees included six: the project manager (from the development applications department), the customer support manager, the technical support engineer, the marketing manager, the regional sales manager and the marketing vice president. In addition, relevant archival data such as company documents and memoranda and industry reports served as useful contextual information. The interview transcripts and researcher notes were coded following established case methodology techniques (Miles and Huberman, 1984, 1994; Yin, 1984). To increase validity, the two researchers acted as coders and worked through discrepancies through discussion and re-examination of the field notes and transcripts. Codes used in this paper focused on information generated by the field site company about customers during the development and launch of a new product. Codes also included the processes by which this information was interpreted to form new knowledge that generated competitive advantage.

Because theory is sparse in this area the authors also compared their findings to existing literature in related fields. This was done in an effort to increase exploratory construct validity and to explore the possibility of generalisation as theory develops (Eisenhardt, 1989). These comparisons to related work are included throughout this chapter to show the development of the researchers' ideas as an integral part of the qualitative research process. This approach, while encouraged during theory development, is a departure from established practice in confirmatory research and is highlighted now to help the reader interpret and evaluate the process and contribution of this study.

THE COMPANY

Medco (not its real name) was founded in 1982 to market and support a wide variety of computer software products addressing the needs of health care delivery organisations (for example, health maintenance organisations, hospitals, multi-physician practices). This field study centres around the development and launch of a new software package called TIMESHARE (the actual name has been disguised), designed to automate the daily business functions of physicians' group practices such as general practitioners, radiologists and anaesthesiologists. Medco began by buying a medical practice management software package and hooking physicians to it. The company then modified the program repeatedly until the in-house development of TIME-SHARE. TIMESHARE links physicians' offices to a mainframe computer at Medco via telephone lines. Some of the features of TIMESHARE include streamlining appointment scheduling, expediting insurance payments by transferring bills electronically to major insurance carriers, and enhancing cash flow from patients by quickly generating accurate bills and by reminding patients regularly and automatically when they do not pay. The software utilises a fourth generation language transportable across all hardware platforms from PCs to mainframes. By 1992, Medco had approximately $150 million in annual sales, 120 employees and an annual sales growth rate of 20 per cent or more over each of the previous three years.

Development applications, customer support and marketing represent the three major functional groups at Medco. The *applications area* develops programs for the physicians' environment. This area houses the programming staff which writes the computer programs, designs the screen layouts and debugs new programs. *Customer support* is responsible for solving customer problems. It is divided into in-house customer support representatives and external field representatives. The in-house reps answer customer queries over the telephone as well as via electronic mail. Customer problems that can only be addressed by an on-site visit are handled by the field reps. The *marketing department* includes two primary responsibilities: first, it is responsible for generating sales leads by developing brochures, advertising the product, and doing mass mailings to physicians; second, the sales staff is solely responsible for actual selling, that is, visiting prospective customers, conducting product demonstrations and closing the sale.

All three major functional groups at Medco play an active role in building and maintaining relationships with customers. The company slogan, 'Part of your business that's our business' was developed through a company-wide contest and reflects the organisation's strong commitment to partnership with customers. The marketing vice-president asserted: 'We build a relationship with people over time. That's true with marketing, customer support, technical support, really with everybody. It's like a family.' This philosophy was confirmed by the regional sales manager who observed: 'We don't want to be a vendor, we want to be a partner. That's really what we want to do. We want to be a part of their business and we want to work that way, cooperatively.' This seller–buyer cooperation started early during the development of TIMESHARE. As the marketing manager reflected, 'We had a physicians' advisory committee . . . we used to meet with them and said, "If we were developing a system, what would you want?" We had all their input.'

Since TIMESHARE represents a discontinuous innovation (Robertson and Gatignon, 1986) for most prospective buyers (strong change required in buyer behaviour and perceptions), Medco spends a considerable amount of time conducting needs analyses for buyers and demonstrating the product in order to clarify the potential benefits of product adoption. Following a decision to adopt, customers are provided with intensive training at Medco. In addition, the product is installed on weekends so that it does not interfere with the delivery of health care.

Recognising that buyers require considerable 'hand-holding' during the initial implementation phase, the company maintains an extensive Customer Support Center. Buyers can call the Help Desk from 8 am to 5 pm, Mondays to Fridays, to report any hardware or software problems. Communication can take place via telephone, fax or electronic mail and a field rep will visit buyers on-site to resolve any problems that cannot be solved by the Help Desk. In fact Medco exhibits an active commitment to solving customer problems in real time that is well captured by the following remarks of the marketing vice president: 'We have a system that we log problems on [the computer]. Whenever anybody calls with a problem we log it, whatever it is, and we assign it to someone. And it is followed up until it is resolved.'

Medco also keeps in touch with its customers after implementation. For example, the company organises quarterly user group meetings and publishes a monthly newsletter. As the technical support engineer noted: 'We send [customers] bulletins concerning regulatory changes. . . Any information we feel they would need to help them.' It is clear that Medco follows a relationship marketing approach that has been successful in the market-place. We now discuss our findings concerning our initial research questions about the types of information generated during relationships and how this information is used to form new knowledge that helps gain competitive advantage for the seller.

FINDINGS

Overview

Our findings indicate that two mechanisms help Medco achieve competitive benefits from its relationships with buyers. First, Medco uses information obtained from its relationships to respond to buyers' needs in real time, that is to remain 'market-oriented' (Kohli and Jaworski, 1990). Second, the cumulative information generated from its relationships helps the organisation to learn to manage both its product and its relationships more effectively. Each mechanism is now discussed.

Related literature is noted during the discussion of the general constructs of our findings. Observations or events reported during our interviews provide more detailed understanding of how the general constructs may apply in the specific context being considered here. In essence, we show how new information and knowledge generated by Medco while working closely with its customers led to responsive actions that improved competitiveness. In turn, Medco was also able to reflect on their actions and then improve their customer relationships through organisational learning.

Market Orientation and Marketing Relationships

According to Kohli and Jaworski (1990), two key elements of a market orientation include generating intelligence on customers and designing appropriate responses to this information. These two elements were prominent during Medco's relationships with its buyers. Medco gathered and responded to information in four general areas: buyer needs, competitive offerings, buyers' regulatory environment and buyers' internal environment. Figure 5.1 illustrates how this market orientation, as evidenced by marketing relationships, leads to competitive advantages through purposefully generating information and then responding actively to it. The constructs and process are now described.

Buyer Needs

Buyers of new high-technology products often cannot articulate their needs (Bentley, 1990; Moriarty and Kosnik, 1989). In Medco's case,

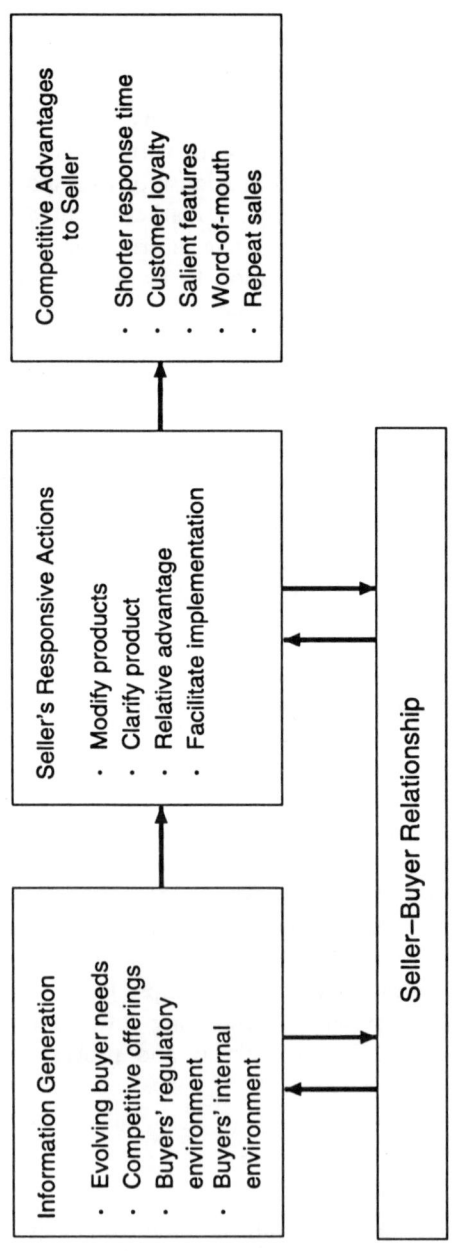

Figure 5.1   Deriving competitive advantages through marketing relationships

although buyers were able to articulate their needs (for example, buyers were aware that they needed software which would increase their cash collection), they could not detail the process involved to get there. The regional sales manager observed that customers 'know what they need down here [that is, as an outcome], but they don't know what they need in the middle to get them down there. They know they want their receipts to turn over faster. They know they need to do appointment scheduling. They know they need a monthly report.' Anderson, *et al.*, (1987) have also noted that buyers in high-technology industries are often uncertain about the appropriate solution to their problems. Consequently, Medco spends a lot of time to begin with (prior to adoption) assessing buyer needs and gauging the technical competence of the buyer.

After implementation, however, as buyers become familiar with the technology, they gain self-confidence (DeBruicker and Summe, 1985) and reach the point of demanding product modifications to suit the local environment. Rice and Rogers (1980) refer to this process as reinvention. As if aware of this research, Medco also assesses buyers' needs *after implementation*. This input provides direction for saleable product modifications and follow-on offerings. As the project manager observed:

> What's important to a programmer might not necessarily be important to a user. . . . . you realise how big little changes are. A lot of times we'll ignore little changes and put in some big, full-blown system when maybe we should cut two keystrokes down to one, or turn that field from green to red instead of trying to turn the whole system red. That's what's good about meeting with customers.

Medco uses the information gained upfront during the needs analysis to assess the technical competence of the buyer. Every effort is then made to clarify the relative advantages of adopting TIMESHARE by demonstrating the product and communicating its benefits using simple language that the buyer can understand. This process moves the customer down the 'ladder of abstraction' so that buyers can make purchase decisions based on product attributes like reliability or speed of processing instead of higher level abstractions like 'quality' and 'value' (Zeithaml, 1988). In addition, interactions with buyers after implementation are used to generate ideas for future product enhancements.

Competitive Offerings

Medco does not buy competitors' products and reverse engineer them to establish benchmarks for comparison. Instead it relies on its customers to provide information about the current features of competitive offerings as well as forthcoming product upgrades. The project manager revealed: 'They [the customers] may say, "Competitors' product X and product Y have these features. What do you have? Where do you see your product going?" or "they [the competition] have all these things. How can we do that with your system?" ' Medco takes advantage of this information on potential competitors in two ways. First, it uses this knowledge to demonstrate the relative advantages of adopting TIMESHARE in relation to competitive products. Second, product attributes offered by competition serve as a useful source of future product modifications/enhancements for TIME-SHARE.

Buyers' Regulatory Environment

The health care industry in the USA is highly turbulent and characterised by frequent changes in the regulatory environment (Carter, 1990). These legislative changes mandate product modifications. Medco's managers rely on customers to keep them posted about important changes in the regulatory environment. As the technical support engineer observed: 'They [the customers] tell us stuff. Sometimes we find out a regulatory change from a customer who first wants to tell us so that we'll make sure to get it out to everybody else.'

In fact Medco initiated quarterly meetings with physicians and their staffs at which Medco applications and support personnel solicit information relating to the external environment. The customer support manager noted that this information generation deals with:

> What's going on in your medical equipment world and what regulation changes . . . What are Congressmen doing. It's almost like a user group and not so much oriented on the system as it is on 'Let's keep each other informed on what's taking place within our specialty.'

Since regulatory changes demand immediate modifications in the software, Medco uses customer input about new regulations to make necessary product modifications. In addition, details regarding the new regulations are communicated to other physicians' groups in their customer base who are unaware of the change. This positions Medco as a knowledge provider for customers about their own regulatory environment.

Buyers' Internal Environment

Medco gathers information on two key aspects of the buyer's internal environment: identifying the decision maker and understanding the politics of the customer organisation. Lucas and Bush (1984) noted that identifying the decision maker in organisational buying situations is extremely difficult. Medco's marketing manager agreed:

> One of the obstacles for a marketing rep is to find out who is really in charge here . . . . you can spend all the time in the world with Sally and she thinks it's great and wants it. But as soon as you go to the doctor's office: 'What's this? IBM? I hate IBM! I ain't buying this, I'm buying this other one.'

In addition, Medco tries to understand the politics of the adoption decision at the buyer organisation. The customer support manager stated: 'If the administrator makes a decision to go with the system, the staff are sometimes not receptive to that decision or didn't feel like they had a part brought into that decision.'

Ettlie (1986) observed that for discontinuous innovations effective implementation requires a two-member team: one each from the seller and buyer organisations who work hard at integrating the technology in the buyer environment. Since these innovations produce disruptions in existing business practices (Robertson and Gatignon, 1986), user acceptance of the innovation can be slow. Medco therefore sees the decision maker as an internal change agent, responsible for generating support for the innovation; then Medco provides support for this advocacy.

In spite of the seller's efforts, however, lack of enthusiasm for the innovation by users might inhibit realisation of full benefits. In such cases knowledge of the political situation at the buyer's organisation can prove beneficial in identifying the source of the problem. As the customer support manager remarked, 'We will go to the doctor or we will go to the administrators and say, "We have a problem here. This is the situation, this is what is going on, we need the people's support. If they give it to us this will work. If it works in 120 offices, it will work for your office." ' Consequently, Medco avoids a scenario that is all too common in high-technology environments: failure to achieve desired benefits is blamed on the technology instead of human and behavioural factors (Meldrum and Millman, 1991).

The foregoing discussion of relationship marketing activities as a form of market orientation indicates that information generated during relationships is acted upon by the seller to clarify the product's relative advantages, modify products and facilitate implementation. In addition, these responsive actions by the seller can result in competitive advantages such as faster detection of and response to evolving customer needs, greater customer loyalty and high switching costs, discovery and incorporation of salient product features as the customer needs them, positive word-of-mouth and repeat sales. Thus the following propositions are proposed for future research:

P1:   When marketing new, high-technology innovations, sellers' success depends on their ability to generate information on evolving buyers' needs, competitive offerings and the buyers' external and internal environment.

P2:   Successful sellers of more radical innovations use the information generated to learn how to (1) clarify the product's relative advantage, (2) modify the product to buyers' specifications, and (3) facilitate the buyers' implementation process.

P3:   As a consequence of information generation during relationship marketing, sellers will derive competitive advantages such as faster response time, customer loyalty, early incorporation of salient features, positive word-of-mouth and repeat sales.

Organisational Learning

In addition to the observations and responsive actions that Medco made regarding its product and customers, the company also used the information generated through its relationships with buyers to reflect upon and change its own core beliefs and actions. The learning organisation does more than process existing information. It creates new information and different points of view, even when these new insights contradict existing organisational norms (Nonaka and Yamanouchi, 1989). This new learning is similar to what Argyris and Schon (1978) have called 'double-loop' learning in which a company adopts different ways of viewing and understanding the world. Thus learning organisations go beyond the lessons of past successes to explore and understand their markets (Hamel and Prahalad, 1991). We found that Medco learned new ways to understand and organise its relationships with customers. Sometimes these new insights refined their existing frames of reference; sometimes the learning created very different norms for relating to the customer. In the following description of findings we provide evidence of Medco's organisational learning in four areas: the choice of relationship partner; knowledge of the customer implementation cycle; management of customer expectations; and the use of information as a product. As Figure 5.2 illustrates, this learning leads to competitive advantages through effective relationship management.

Choice of Relationship Partner

Moriarty and Kosnik (1989) observed that high-technology firms often mistakenly believe that success depends upon coming up with great products and selling them to anyone who has the money to buy them. This situation was definitely true for Medco during the early days of its existence. The company went after any and all customers and built intensive relationships with them. The considerable investments required to maintain these relationships, however, have convinced Medco that relationships are more efficient and effective with certain customers. Some segmentation characteristics for intensity of relationship are beginning to emerge. The following statement of the regional sales manager reflects this realisation:

> Not only is it a return on the investment. . . in the training and supporting versus what we're getting on the processing and software sale. But also in terms of . . . is it going to be a good referral? These are the types of accounts we're not going to go after. They cost us too much to support. . . Maybe it's not the account you really want, but if it gets you in that building, you take it. . . . specialties, too, are a big deal. There are certain doctors who will make a lot more than other doctors. It just makes sense to go where people have money to spend.

The following proposition can be derived:

P4:   As a result of their cumulative relationship experiences, successful sellers learn how to be selective when choosing relationship

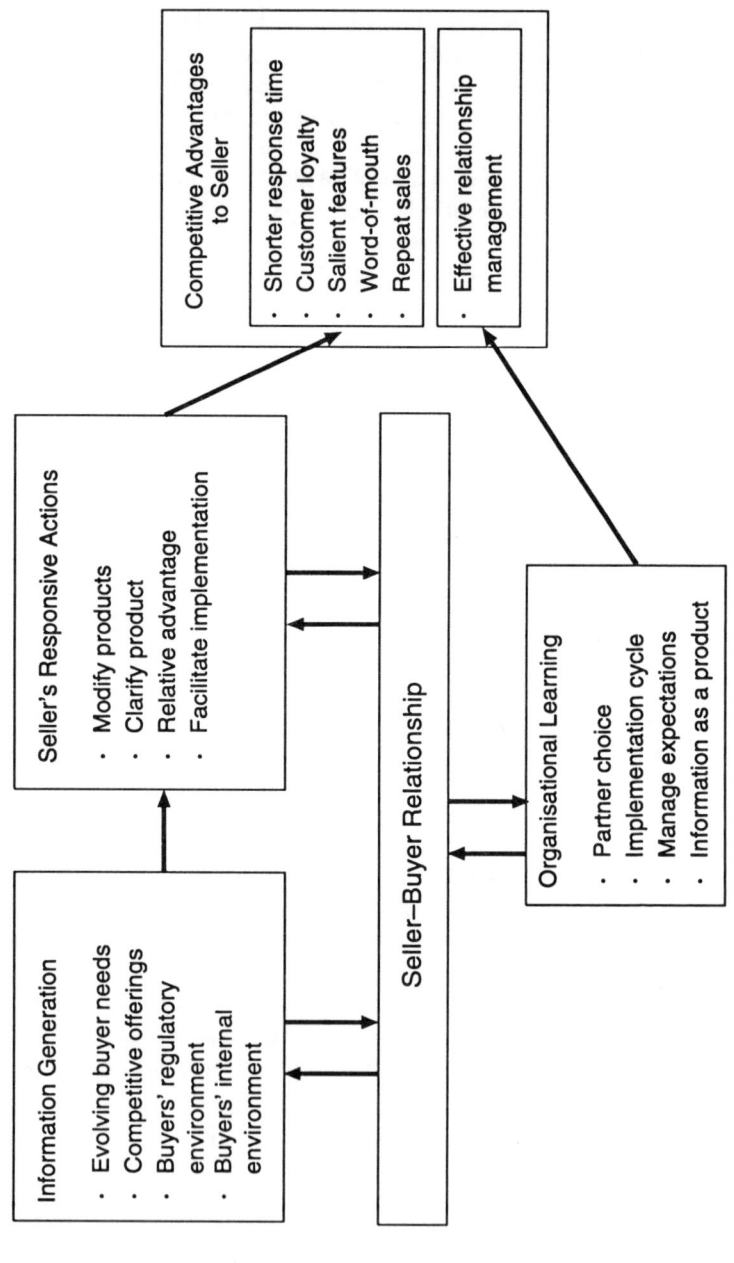

Figure 5.2   Using marketing relationships and organisational learning to generate competitive advantages

partners. They develop a set of relationship segmentation characteristics that identify candidates with higher payoffs to their relationship investments.

Customer Implementation Cycle

Reflecting on its relationships with customers, Medco learned that customers go through a cycle when implementing a discontinuous innovation such as TIMESHARE. For customers, initial euphoria (caused by high expectations) gives way to implementation difficulties and consequent frustration with the system. Medco's customer support manager captured this succinctly when he noted:

> When they sign, they love the idea of being computerised. A month into it they hate it and we know it . . . they are unsure of what they are doing, they have no confidence. It is really an insecure time. . . we recognise this . . . and we try to do a lot more hand holding at that time . . . . six months [later] they love us. Because all of a sudden they realise what this time and effort in the first one to three months has yielded . . . it is almost predictable. It's good to have that knowledge that we are going to go through that . . . and that cycle is almost a natural cycle that any customer goes through to various degrees.

Medco uses this knowledge of the implementation cycle for their product to manage its relationships more effectively by providing personalised support when buyers enter the frustration phase of the cycle. Therefore:

P5: Successful sellers of high-technology products learn how to match resource expenditures with buyers' variable demand for the resource.

Managed Expectations

When the company began, marketing reps tended to promise more than the product could deliver. The company has learned, however, that it is far better to explore and manage the expectations of potential buyers. The customer support manager noted: 'We can't do everything. And we've gotten a lot better at telling people we aren't going to do that. No sense in fooling you, this is it. . . . But we can offer you this. . . we almost never give them a roadblock. We always offer some solution.' A good illustration of Medco's new approach to managing expectations is its handling of new product releases. The project manager reflected:

> In the dark old ages, two years [ago], we didn't really have a software development plan . . . If somebody wanted something done tonight, no matter what we did, we did it tonight. . . . Then we moved into what we call a 'release mode'. We are moving in the direction of planned enhancements where we save a whole bunch of changes and put them on every three or four months.

This bundling of modifications enables Medco to save on programming and publication costs. In addition, this clear, direct setting of expectations – which they almost always meet – lays the foundation for building trust, an important requirement for successful relationships.

P6:   Over time, sellers' success depends on their ability to discover, manage and meet buyer expectations and build trust.

Information as Product

Glazer (1991) noted that products can be placed along an information–intensiveness continuum. For more information-intensive products, the information itself can be marketed as an asset since this information can provide potential buyers with relative advantages (Webster, 1969). Medco has moved modifications to the TIMESHARE product closer to the information-intensive end of the continuum. For example, initially all consultative services were provided as part of the product offering. Today many of these services are sold separately on an annual contract basis. Thus the information-intensive feature of the initial product – in any case current needs assessment – has become a complementary product in its own right. This development required that the organisation go through an 'unlearning' process because the prevailing company philosophy required that no stone be left unturned to please the customer. The regional sales manager summed up this unlearning process well: 'In a way we're doing an office consultation while we're installing the system . . . I started doing a lot of that and I said that we ought to be charging for that service. We were giving a lot away free.'

P7: Successful sellers of more radical innovations learn to market the ability to generate customer information as an asset in itself distinct from the initial product offering.

DIRECTIONS FOR FUTURE RESEARCH

In addition to providing propositions, our findings suggest at least two important questions for future research.

What is Marketing's Role in Relationship Marketing?

Our case study of one successful innovator company revealed that all major functional groups at Medco play an important role in the relationship marketing process. For example, software designers interact with buyers to determine product enhancements while customer support staff help resolve emerging problems in real time. The crucial question then becomes, 'what is marketing's role in the process?' Perhaps, as Webster (1992) argues, marketing should be responsible for managing information dissemination within the organisation to ensure prompt responsive actions. Marketers may also contribute new techniques to systematise and manage relationship investments over the course of new product development and commercialisation.

How can Marketing Encourage Organisational Learning and Unlearning?

At Medco, information is shared via daily meetings attended by managers from marketing, customer support, design and applications. In addition, frequent cross-functional reassignment stimulates alternate perspectives. Medco uses this information to learn how to manage its relationships more efficiently and effectively. Development and commercialisation stages for more radical technologies often overlap. Managerial guidelines and shared understandings of product benefits are provisional – changing quickly as familiarity and knowledge accumulate. Perhaps marketers will be the coaches who facilitate joint creation of meaning within both the buyer and the seller. There is evidence, in addition, that Medco also uses new information to 'unlearn' that is to *actively forget* existing ways of doing business. For example, the existing organisational philosophy required that customer support be provided at no charge throughout commercialisation. Realising that 'information' was a marketable asset, the organisation initiated user fees for the provision of customer support. This transition was difficult at Medco because it required giving up a deeply entrenched philosophy of marketing the product. Thus marketers and new product managers may have particular responsibility as change agents during organisational learning.

The marketing functions of sales, customer support, forecasting, new product planning and development at Medco offered ample opportunities for organisational learning and unlearning, especially in dynamic, technology-intensive and competitive markets. It appears worthwhile to investigate how other organisations use these opportunities to learn and unlearn so that these activities can be understood and managed over the development and commercialisation cycles. We hope others will join us in these exciting efforts.

Notes

1. For purposes of this chapter, 'buyer' refers to an industrial firm that is adopting the new product. It is used here to be roughly synonymous with 'customer'. We do acknowledge that several individuals and roles will make up the buying center. We chose to represent the buyer firm as a single entity, however, as this is more parsimonious and in keeping with the level of analysis.
2. Following Nevens *et al.* (1990), commercialisation is defined as a process which begins when an organisation identifies an unmet need, continues with product development and marketing and includes subsequent efforts to enhance the product. According to Voss (1988), commercialisation therefore includes the three stages of new product development, implementation and post-implementation.
3. Following studies (Maidique and Zirger, 1984; Meyers and Athaide, 1991), the firm was classified as 'successful' because it had survived beyond the start-up stage (in fact it had been in existence for nine years) and had shown profits and growth for the preceding three years. The expert panel that identified this company as a knowledgeable software provider consisted of four members: one business consultant, one business school dean and two local business leaders.

References

Anderson, E., Chu Wujin, and B. Weitz (1987) 'Industrial Purchasing: An Empirical Exploration of the Buyclass Framework', *Journal of Marketing*, 51, July, 71–86.

Argyris, C. and D. A. Schon (1978) *Organisational Learning* (Reading, Mass.: Addison-Wesley).

Attewell, P. (1992) 'Technology Diffusion and Organisational Learning: The Case of Business Computing', *Organisation Science*, 3(1), February, 1–19.

Bentley, K. (1990) 'A Discussion of the Link between One Organisation's Style and its Connection with its Market', *Journal of Product Innovation Management*, 7, 19–34.

Carter, N. M. (1990) 'Small Firm Adaptation: Responses of Physicians' Organisations to Regulatory and Competitive Uncertainty', *Academy of Management Journal*, 33 (2), 307–33.

Clark, K. B. and S. C. Wheelwright (1993) *Managing New Product and Process Development* (New York: The Free Press).

DeBruicker, F. S. and G. L. Summe (1985) 'Make sure your customers keep coming back', *Harvard Business Review*, 63 (1), 92–8.

Eisenhardt, K. (1989) 'Building Theories from Case Study Research', *Academy of Management Review*, 14, October, 532–50.

Ettlie, J. E. (1986), 'Implementing Manufacturing Technologies: Lessons from Experience', in Donald Davis and Associates (eds), *Managing Technological Innovation* (San Francisco: Jossey-Bass) 72–104.

Glaser, B. J. and A. L. Strauss (1967) *The Discovery of Grounded Theory* (Chicago: Aldine).

Glazer, R. (1991) 'Marketing in an Information-Intensive Environment: Strategic Implications of Knowledge as an Asset', *Journal of Marketing*, 55, October, 1–19.

Hamel, G. and C. K. Prahalad (1991) 'Corporate Imagination and Expeditionary Marketing' *Harvard Business Review*, 69, July-August, 81–92.

Hart, S. and Baker, M. J. (1993) 'Learning from Success: Multiple Convergent Processing for Effective New Product Development', in P. Rajan Varadarajan and Bernard Jaworski (eds), *Classical and Contemporary Perspectives on Marketing Thought*, Proceedings of the American Marketing Association Winter Marketing Educators' Conference, 137–42.

Kohli, A. K. and B. J. Jaworski (1990) 'Market Orientation: The Construct, Research Propositions and Managerial Implications', *Journal of Marketing*, 54, April, 1–19.

Leonard-Barton, D. (1988) 'Implementation as Mutual Adaptaion of Technology and Organisation', *Research Policy*, 17 (5), 251–67.

Leonard-Barton, D. (1990) 'Implementing New Production Technologies: Exercises in Corporate Learning', in M. A. von Glinow and S. A. Mohrman (eds.), *Managing Complexity in High Technology Organisations* (New York: Oxford University Press) 160–87.

Leonard-Barton, D. (1995) *Wellsprings of Knowledge* (Boston, Mass.: Harvard Business School Press).

Lucas, G. H., Jr. and A. J. Bush (1984) 'Guidelines for Marketing a New Industrial Product', *Industrial Marketing Management*, 13, 157–61.

Maidique, M. A. and B. J. Zirger (1984) 'The new product learning cycle', *Research Policy*, 14 (6), 299–313.

Meldrum, M. J. and A. F. Millman (1991) 'Ten Risks in Marketing High-Technology Products', *Industrial Marketing Management*, 20 (3), 43–50.

Meyers, P.W. and G.A. Athaide (1989) 'Implementing technological innovations: Developing strategic knowledge through relational marketing', paper presented at the 1989 AMA Summer Educators' Conference, San Antonio, Texas.

Meyers, P.W. and G.A. Athaide (1991) 'Strategic Mutual Learning Between Producing and Buying Firms During Product Innovation', *Journal of Product Innovation Management*, 8, 155–69.

Miles, M.B. and A.M. Huberman (1984) *Qualitative Data Analysis: A Source Book of New Methods* (Beverly Hills, CA: Sage).

Miles, M.B. and A.M. Huberman (1994) *Qualitative Data Analysis*, 2nd edn (Thousand Oaks, CA.: Sage).

More, R.A. (1986) 'Developer/Adopter Relationships in New Industrial Product Situations', *Journal of Business Research*, 14, December, 501–17.

Moriarty, R.T. and T.J. Kosnik (1989) 'High-Tech Marketing: Concepts, Continuity and Change', *Sloan Management Review*, 30 (4), 7–17.

Nevens, M.T., G.L. Summe and B. Uttal (1990) 'Commercializing technology: What the best companies do', *The McKinsey Quarterly*, (4), 3–22.

Nonaka, I. and H. Takeuchi (1995) *The Knowledge Creating Company* (New York: Oxford University Press).

Nonaka, I. and T. Yamanouchi (1989) 'Managing Innovation as a Self-Renewing Process', *Journal of Business Venturing*, 299–315.

Parkinson, S.T. (1985) 'Factors Influencing Buyer–Seller Relationships in the Market for High-Technology Prodcts', *Journal of Business Research*, 13, February, 49–60.

Rice, R.E. and E.M. Rogers (1980) 'Reinvention in the Innovation Process', *Knowledge: Creation, Diffusion, Utilization*, 1, June, 499–514.

Robertson, T.S. and H. Gatignon (1986), 'Competitive Effects on Technology Diffusion', *Journal of Marketing*, 50 (3), 1–13.

von Hippel, E.A. (1978) 'Users as Innovators', *Technology Review*, 80 (3), 3–11.

Voss, C.A. (1985) 'The Role of Users in the Development of Applicaions Software', *Journal of Product Innovation Management*, 2, June, 113–21.

Voss, C.A. (1988) 'Implementation: A key issue in manufacturing technology: The need for a field of study', *Research Policy*, 17, 55–63.

Webster, F.E., Jr. (1969) 'New Product Adoption in Industrial Markets: A Framework for Analysis', *Journal of Marketing*, 33, July, 35–9.

Webster, F.E. Jr. (1992) 'The Changing Role of Marketing in the Corporation', *Journal of Marketing*, 56, October, 1–17.

Weiss, A.M. and J.B. Heide (1993) 'The Nature of Organisational Search in High Technology Markets', *Journal of Marketing Research*, 30, May, 220–23.

Yin, R.K. (1984) *Case Study Research: Design and Methods* (Beverly Hills, CA: Sage).

Zeithaml, V.A. (1988) 'Consumer Perceptions of Price, Quality and Value: A Means-End Model and Synthesis of Evidence', *Journal of Marketing*, 52 July, 2–22.

Zirger, B.J. and M.A. Madique (1990) 'A Model of New Product Development: An Empirical Test', *Management Science*, 36, July, 867–83.

6 The Measurement, Methodologies and Models of New Product Success Studies

Susan J. Hart

INTRODUCTION

> The problem is that, depending on how one defines success, one is likely to find different success determinants. (Cooper and Kleinschmidt, *Journal of Marketing Management*, 11 (4), May 1995, p. 315)

The 'problem' mentioned above, appositely cited from Michael's journal, is the point of departure for this contribution. Not that the problem is new: Carter and Williams' (1957) study (also lamented for its peer-neglect by Michael in a recent comment on 'The Commodification of Marketing Knowledge') found that technical progressiveness had varying relationships with the measures of success that they used. Furthermore, speculating on the direction of the relationship between technical progressiveness and profitability, they suggest 'it may be that profits are the stimulus or the necessary means for progressiveness' (p. 185), a point skilfully avoided by many involved in researching new product success. The aim of this chapter is to offer a conceptually based model for measuring new product success. An earlier review of new product success measurement provides the background to the following discussion, while the recent contribution by the Product Development and Management Association Task Force and findings of studies of new product success and failure (S/F) measures are integrated into the model. Intrinsic to the S/F studies are three issues, which are rarely developed explicitly: the level of analysis, the relationships among dimensions and the influence of time. In analysing the reluctance to deal directly with these issues, we encounter two themes present in the recurrent soul-searching of the marketing academy:

diversification at the expense of advancement and empiricism at the expense of theory building. The remainder of this chapter is organised into four sections. The first reviews the S/F literature to highlight the principal dimensions embedded within the measures of new product success and failure. The second critically evaluates the major methodologies employed by researchers to measure new product S/F. The third discusses the interrelationships among the dimensions of S/F, concentrating on the implicit associations among linking concepts of the level of analysis, cause and effect and time. The fourth combines these linking concepts into an overall framework into which past and future investigation of new product S/F might be placed.

THE NATURE OF NEW PRODUCT SUCCESS

Why is it Important?

Underpinning the literature in new product development (NPD) and innovation is the belief in the relationship between the extent of innovation (a term used to cover various instances of 'new', 'product' and 'development') and an organisation's fate. Marketing literature makes frequent mention of shortening product life cycles, faster rates of technological change, increasing sophistication of buyers, all contriving to reinforce companies' need for successful new products for continued commercial health and survival. Several authors have shown that new products account for increasing shares of total current companies' sales and profits suggesting that, on the whole, the new product business is being carried out effectively (Cooper, 1983; Hopkins, 1980; Hultink and Robben, 1995; Abede and Christiaans, 1986). Such a suggestion, however, is dependent upon the assumption that an increasing proportion of sales and profits from new products is an appropriate measure of output, when it might well be viewed as a measure of input or activity, especially considering that over the past 20 years, the absolute number of new products has also increased (Edgett *et al.*, 1992). This trend has been consistent over a number of studies in the past 25 years. The National Industrial Conference Board in 1967 reported that 70 per cent of the industrial goods companies they studied expected to be increasingly dependent upon new products for growth, while McDonald and Eastlack (1971) found that among their study of over 200 Fortune 500 companies, growth was expected to come mostly from new products. Inexorably, therefore, the trend in numbers of new products being developed has been upwards, leading to, not only an increased incidence of 'success', but also an increased number of opportunities for 'failure'.

New product failure rates reported in the literature over a thirty-year period vary widely. In his book, *Marketing New Industrial Products,* Michael Baker cites failure rates of 20 per cent and 30 per cent from the studies of Ross Federal Research and Booz Allen Hamilton, respectively. Crawford's (1977, 1987) review of failure rates concluded that the failure rate for new products is in the area of 30–40 per cent, although consumer products fail more often than industrial products (35 versus 25 per cent). Page (1993) found that the average success rate for new commercialised products was 58 per cent, at a time when the average number of introductions has increased by 140 per cent since the period covered by Booz Allen Hamilton's (1982) study (1976–81). And yet it is still difficult to generalise across the various studies mentioned above, 'owing to the absence of any agreed definitions of 'new product' and 'failure' (Baker, 1975, p. 15).

Despite this problem of definition, a glance through the introductions to research articles on 'what distinguishes success and failure in new product development' reveals authors' fondness for evoking failure rates as justification for their need to provide the business and academic communities with 'empirically based normative advice'. I include several of my own articles in this indictment. Faced with the task of identifying the factors which separate successful from unsuccessful new products, two tasks confront the researcher: identifying those issues which might affect the outcomes and identifying the outcomes themselves. The second of these tasks has been done perfunctorily, with little regard for existing theory, let alone any justification of any underlying assumptions. Below some of the major themes emerging from the new product success literature are examined.

Measurement of New Product Performance: Financial and Non-Financial

Several recent reviews of new product success measures draw attention to the many different measures of new product performance that have been used to identify critical success factors. Measures fall into two broad categories: financial and non-financial.

Financial Measures

Studies using financial measures to assess the performance of new products do so in parallel mode to studies of overall firm performance or at the level of the specific product development programme (Hart and Craig, 1993; Griffin and Page, 1993). Performance indicators which reflect corporate-level financial indicators are used, such as sales (revenue or unit), sales growth, export sales and sales growth, the percentage of sales accounted for by products introduced in the last five years, return on assets, asset growth, return on capital and a wide range of profitability measures, summarised in Table 6.1.

Although rarely stated, the use of such firm-level measures as indicators of new product performance is predicated upon the relationship between new product development (innovation) activity and survival and growth of companies, which is evidenced in studies from DeSimone (1967) to countless anecdotes quoted by management gurus and industrial observers: 'To be successful in international markets industry needs to innovate constantly' (Harvey-Jones, 1986, The Dimbleby Lecture).

While the relationship between NPD and overall corporate financial performance is central to the impetus for NPD within the firm, the use of indicators of corporate financial performance is only appropriate for measuring new product success given an adequate time lapse from the launch of the new product. Indeed, most of the new product S/F studies attempt to identify correlates of success for 'products launched within the last five years' (Cooper and Kleinschmidt, 1987a, 1987b; Cannon, 1986), a period of time during which corporate financial performance is subject to many influences, not least the required level of investment in the development. Furthermore, much of the evidence to suggest the strength of the relationship between innovation and financial performance is related to that particular instance of 'new to the world' products, whereas many studies in the NPD literature fail to address the level of innovativeness in their search for correlates of success and failure. This raises the questions as to whether the performance of all kinds of NPD activity might be assumed visible at the most aggregate levels of company performance and, if so, when such visibility might be achieved. These questions suggest that the assumed relationship between innovation and financial performance, used implicitly to underpin the use of corporate-level financial measures as new product success indicators, is often taken out of its theoretical context. The implication of this is a lack of construct validity.

Many studies, however, do measure the financial performance of the new product by focusing specifically on the outcome of a particular programme of new product development. Profit is variously assessed for a specific new product using different nuances of break-even time, return on investment or internal rate of return, the contribution of the new product to company profits, profit growth and a host of phraseologies designed to rate the achievement of profitability goals for the new product. The new product's sales are also used as barometers of its success, again gauged by varying comparative measurement devices: sales compared to the industry average, to the developers' major competitors, to other recently introduced products or simply, to sales objectives. Market share and market share growth are also used by studies. In the review by Griffin and Page (1993), sales-related measures are viewed as measures of 'customer acceptance', rather than financial success indicators, along with purchase trial rate, repeat purchase rate, customer retention rate, customer satisfaction and customer acceptance. I continue to associate sales with financial measures of success, for although customer acceptance is subsumed in the act of purchase, it does not always lead to purchase, thence sales. Simply put, achievement of customer acceptance is perhaps a prerequisite input to purchase, but the achievement of the former does not automatically lead to the latter.

Many of these product-specific measures of financial success may be criticised for their short-term time horizon. In their now classic treatise on the role of formal management techniques in America's ailing competitive performance, Hayes and Abernathy (1980) refer to the detrimental effect that short-term measures of performance have had on US businesses. They argue that such an emphasis contrasts unfavourably with the Japanese focus on long-term growth. Indeed, Biggadike's (1979) study showed that the successfully launched product is unlikely to be profitable for at least the first four years.

So those researching new product development performance financially are caught in something of a conundrum. On the one hand, corporate-level measures of financial performance at the company level rely implicitly on the assumed relationship between new product and corporate performance, often without due control over important elements of context such as the 'newness' of the new product. On the other hand, more immediate measures of financial success of a new

Table 6.1 Summary of financial measures of new product performance

Level	Conceptual base	Profit		Sales	
		Measure	*Study*	*Measure*	*Study*
Company		Profit growth	Walsh *et al.* (1988)	Turnover growth	Walsh *et al.* (1988)
		Profit margin	Walsh *et al.* (1988) Carter & Williams (1957)	Export sales	Walsh *et al.* (1988)
				Sales generated by products introduced in last 5 years (%)	Cooper (1984); Hart & Service (1988)
New product		Product's profit in relation to acceptability level for this type of investment	Cooper (1979) Calantone & Cooper (1981)	First year market share	Yoon & Lilien (1985)
		Rated profitability (0–10 scale)	Cooper & Kleinschmidt (1995)	Development of new product into a 'product group'	Yoon & Lilien (1985)
		Profit relative to other products launched in the last five years	Cooper & Kleinschmidt (1987a, 1987b)	Initial penetration rate	Choffray & Lilien (1984)
				Diffusion rate	Choffray & Lilien (1984)
		Meeting profit objectives	Cooper & Kleinschmidt (1987a, 1987b)	Meeting sales objective	Cooper & Kleinschmidt (1987a, 1987b)

Measure	Reference	Measure	Reference
Profit for new product minus costs	Cooper (1984); Biggadike (1979)	Sales relative to other new products introduced in last 5 years	Cooper & Kleinschmidt (1987a, 1987b)
Profitability of product over the life cycle	Nystrom (1985)	Importance of new product in generating sales for the company	Cooper (1984)
Payback period	Cooper & Kleinschmidt (1987a, 1987b)	Diffusion coefficient	Voss (1985)
Importance of programme in generating profits for the company	Cooper (1984)	Domestic market share, 3 years after launch	Cooper & Kleinschmidt (1987a, 1987b, 1995)
Ratio of cumulative sales to investment (3 years)	Ayal & Raban (1990)	Foreign market share, 3 years after launch	Cooper & Kleinschmidt (1987a, 1987b)
		'Worthwhile' market share	Rothwell et al. (1974)
		Product survived for more than 4 years	Cannon (1986)
		Product survived for 1 year	Voss (1985)

product programme are criticised for contributing to short-term thinking that does not allow for substantial redevelopment of a company's competitive resource base. This conundrum does not openly present itself in the literature, largely because little attention is given to the concepts and dimensions that ought to underpin the choice of success measures. It follows then that the dimension of time is one which, although rarely examined, has an important influence on the appropriateness of the S/F measures used. Moreover, not only are the S/F measures appropriate to different time perspectives, they are also appropriate to different levels of analysis. The focus by researchers on firm-level measures necessitates a strategic view of new product performance, while a focus on specific products is more likely to assess performance of an operational nature. These points are developed later in the chapter.

Many studies using financial measures of new product performance have surprisingly little to say about the conceptual alignment and overlap among the measures. All too often, 'sales and profits' are packaged together in such a way as to ignore the fact that investment in new products may encourage sales growth without a concurrent growth in profits. Yet the theoretical distinctions among different aspects of financial success have long been borne out by empirical investigation. Carter and Williams (1957) used three dimensions to examine financial success: trading profits as a percentage of fixed assets and stock for the average of two (then) recent years; trading profits for the four years ending in 1952–5 as a percentage of those for 1948–51, and the increase in net tangible assets from 1948 to 1954 as a percentage of the 1951 net tangible assets. They found no evidence of a relationship between technical progressiveness and profits as a percentage of assets, a weak relationship between technical progressiveness and the increase in net tangible assets and a 'stronger relationship' between technical progressiveness and profit increase. The authors note the variances among accounting practices that obscure the financial performance of firms and, with that, the possibility of finding associations between performance and other characteristics. They also highlight the fact that the stronger relationship between profit increase and technical progressiveness cannot be assigned cause and effect direction with any certainty, which relates to the question of whether S/F indicators capture inputs to success and failure or the intrinsic nature of the success or failure.

This results in an aggregate view of financial success which hinges on a seemingly random selection of measures which neither builds a cohesive picture of how the various measures of 'financial success' for new products impinge upon one another, nor takes cognisance of other intervening factors upon which the dimensions measured are contingent. In short, the conceptual development of the construct of financial success, even at the level of the specific programme of NPD, is weak and its measurement lacks validity. In addition, the appropriateness of viewing new product success entirely in financial terms is not automatic. As Michael Baker reminds us in *Marketing New Industrial Products*, we have been unable to 'define a common denominator with which we may judge "success" and "failure" and we must accept that a new product has failed when its originator comes to this conclusion on the basis of his own criteria' (p. 16). In the light of this and similar observations, it has become common to criticise the use of financial measures of success on the basis that other objectives (or criteria) may be more important, especially in the judgement conferred upon any one new product. New product 'failures', according to Madique and Zirger (1985), may result in important organisational, technical and market developments. To illustrate their point, they cite the company whose new product failed commercially, but whose experience with the new technology and market allowed the accumulation of experience necessary to introduce other, successful, new products of a similar type. The firm considered the first new product 'a success' of sorts. Booz Allen Hamilton's list of objectives suggests a wide range of criteria for measuring new product success, based on companies' intentions: the establishment of a foothold in a new market, capitalising on a new technology, erecting barriers for competition, offsetting a seasonal cycle, expanding the product range and using excess capacity, to name a few. In any of these new product situations, it is inappropriate to measure performance of the new product in profit terms alone. Further, it is important to recognise that these objectives operate with respect to different levels of analysis; some are strategic, some are operational. S/F indicators based on objectives must reflect these differing levels, as those used to identify operational success and failure are necessary precursors of strategic success and failure, which again implicates the dimension of time. Yet few studies are built upon a conceptual framework which incorporates these elements.

In response to the criticisms of unidimensional financial measures, researchers have introduced a battery of non-financial indicators of success, which would allow them to cope with the possibility that there may be different types of success. These measures, summarised in Table 6.2, are discussed below.

Table 6.2 Summary of non-financial measures of new product performance

Objectives		Process	
		Regularity of updated and new products	Johne & Snelson (1988)
Degree to which product met objectives over 5 years	Cooper (1984)	Success of programme (global rating)	Cooper (1984)
Degree to which product met original expectations	Hise *et al.* (1989)	Success, failure and 'kill' rates over 5 years	Cooper (1984)
Success rating (1 = failure to 6 = success) of managers	Ayal & Raban (1990)	Number of launches over 5 years	Hart & Service (1988)
Success/failure rate (%)	Cooper & Kleinschmidt (1995)	% of successful launches over 5 years	Hart & Service (1988)
Commercial performance relative to expectation	Sauder (1978)	Time efficiency (0–10 scale)	Cooper & Kleinschmidt (1995)
		ON-time project (0–10 scale)	Cooper & Kleinschmidt (1995)
Success/failure assessment	Shipley *et al.* (1991)	Estimate of over/under-run of project	Might & Fisher (1985)

Table 6.2 (*cont.*)

Market		Technology		Design	
		Degree of novelty of technical solutions	Nystrom (1985)	Design awards	Walsh *et al.* (1988)
		Degree of patent protection	Nystrom (1985) Cordero (1990)	Citations by the Design Council Queen's Award Winner	Ughanwa & Baker (1989)
Extent to which new market was opened by new product	Cooper & Kleinschmidt (1987a, 1987b)	Development time	Nystrom (1985)		
Market potential, uniqueness or interchangeability from buyers' view	Nystrom (1985)	Technical success rating	Cooper & Kleinschmidt (1995)		

Non-financial Measures

Non-financial measures are related to one of the following bases: new product objectives, new product process, markets, technologies and design. In each of these categories, the absence of a rigorous conceptual framework frustrates the generation of theory. Measures of objectives are vague. Ayal and Raban (1990) asked respondents to evaluate whether the new product under study was a success or a failure, without further investigations of the dimensions of either; Hise *et al.* (1989) relate product performance to the 'original expectations' for the new product, again without further enquiry as to the nature of these expectations, while Shipley, *et al.* (1991) use management assessment of success or failure, also without elucidation on the criteria used for such an assessment. While each of these approaches is in keeping with the sentiments expressed by Baker, quoted above, that the criteria for designation of 'success' or 'failure' must rest with those charged with the responsibility for carrying out the development, the lack of specification of the assessment criteria does not allow for meaningful aggregate comparisons across studies and thus inhibits theory building. A number of measures of success relate to the process of development, describing the extent and proficiency of product development activity within the firm. Johne and Snelson (1988) assess 'the regularity of updated products in relation to the competitive nature of the market'. This measure is a surrogate for experience, which is then extrapolated to imbue experienced product developers with the status of leading product innovators. Hart and Service (1988) use 'the number of successful launches over a five-year period' (defined by the respondents themselves) and Cooper (1984) uses 'rate of successes, failures and kills over a five-year period'. Measures such as these *may* be acceptable for assessing NPD performance, but very little work has been carried out to establish the nature and extent of the link between the measures and the dimensions they seek to capture. What does the number of successful launches in a five-year period actually indicate about a company? The number of launches may measure the amount of NPD activity as much as it measures the success of that activity. If refined to incorporate the attrition rate of new product ideas (as in the number of 'kills' in a five-year period), this may measure the innova-tiveness of the process of generation of ideas as much as it measures the proficiency of converting ideas into successful new products. All of these process-related measures may indeed relate to the performance of the new product development programme; what is rarely addressed, though, is *how*. Measurements which focus on process outcomes could be said to assess an operational 'stage' in the performance profile of a new product, which is appropriate for a short term evaluation. If this is true, the level of analysis and time are related elements in the conceptual foundations of new product success measurement which have been sorely neglected.

Other non-financial measures are related to market, technological and design-based success. Cooper and Kleinschmidt (1987a, 1987b) assess market success via 'the extent to which a new market for the firm was opened up by the new product', Nystrom (1985) evaluates technological success via the 'degree of novelty/uniqueness of the technological solutions', while Walsh *et al.* (1988) measure design success via 'number of design awards' and 'number of citations by The Design Council'. Ughanwa and Baker (1989) selected companies winning The Queen's Award for Design as their success sample. While these measures undoubtedly add dimensions to the conceptualisation of new product success and failure which are not captured by financial measures on their own, they can be criticised on two counts. First, few, if any, have been grounded in research which focuses on capturing the experience of managers in their own quest to measure the performance of their new product development programmes. Across the NPD literature as a whole, there is a surprising dearth of information regarding how managers themselves would define research in terms other than financial, adding weight to the accusation that measures across several of these non-financial categories suffer from a general lack of content, face and construct validity. Second, there is little cross-referencing among the studies of new product success and failure, other than in the most superficial manner. The study by Griffin and Page in 1993 reviewed the success measures used in over 70 articles, finding a total of 46 different measures. Separate research studies tend not to build upon previous attempts to conceptualise non-financial success measures, with the result that the very nature of non-financial success, and indeed its links with financial success, have not yet been discussed in detail in the literature.

To summarise the foregoing arguments, there are limitations in the measurement of new product performance arising from both financial and non-financial indicators of success and failure. In both camps there is a severe lack of theoretical development of the dimensions; the conceptual boundaries, alignments and relative importance of financial success and non-financial success are not set out and dubiety persists regarding the validity of measures used to capture both financial and non-financial success. Several of these issues seem to be related to the ill-considered roles of the level of analysis of new product S/F, the way in which the various dimensions may be related and the influence of time on the nature of new product S/F. Before going on to propose ways in which to capture these issues conceptually, as a step in the process of building theory, it is useful to examine the influential role of the dominant methods in S/F research to date. The methodological issues are reviewed below.

THE METHODOLOGICAL ISSUES IN THE THEORETICAL DEVELOPMENT AND VALIDITY OF S/F MEASUREMENT

The shortcomings of the new product S/F literature outlined above are partly related to three sets of related issues of methodology: the provenance of the measures chosen, the data collection method and the analytical techniques used in research.

Provenance of Measures

One of the greatest omissions in the new product success/failure literature is the neglect of managerial input into the items which make up the measurement scales. It is not altogether clear from where many the better known studies of NPD success and failure have derived their conceptualisation of non-financial success. Items representing the various nuances of the concepts, such as the extent to which managers agree that 'the new product helped to open up new markets for the company', are rated by managers, but there has been little attempt to validate the appropriateness of the items as performance measures, let alone any effort to *generate* the items from the business community. Even research using a case study approach, such as that by Rubenstein *et al.* (1976) or Sauder (1978) appears not to have investigated (or has failed to report) the managers' views of what defines new product success beyond the adjectives of 'commercial' or 'technological'. A recent exception, however, is the research by Griffin and Page (1993), which investigated which measures are actually used by practitioners in order to measure the performance of their new product programmes. The findings make interesting reading:

- both researchers and practitioners use the achievement of revenue and profit goals as performance indicators;
- both researchers and practitioners view on-time launch as a performance indicator;
- practitioners use profit margins, market share sales volumes, customer satisfaction and customer acceptance more than researchers do;
- researchers use success/failure rate, per cent sales from new products, product performance, speed to market, completed to budget, subjective assessment and technical success more than practitioners do.

Practitioners appear to demonstrate greater sensitivity to the role of the customer in determining success than do marketing academics! Thus the tenets of Michael Baker's 'research myopia' can be extended: the failure to integrate the most basic of a discipline's principles into the framework for research. It could be argued, of course, that 'customer satisfaction' or 'customer acceptance' are intrinsic to measures of market share or sales volumes, or that there is a time relationship at play which needs to be placed within the conceptual framework. This kind of discussion, however, has been eschewed by the majority of researchers of new product S/F in what may be described as a surprising lack of curiosity, itself resulting in a failure to advance insights into or understanding of the construct of 'new product performance'.

In addition, the study by Griffin and Page (1993) showed that, while firm-level measures of performance, such as 'the percentage of sales accounted for by new products', are frequently used by researchers as outcome measures, they are used only by a quarter of companies in measuring the performance of new product programmes. Furthermore, programme-level measures of performance, such as 'impact of the new product programme on corporate performance', used by researchers are not used at all by practitioners. Thus the level of measurement differs between researchers and managers.

Discussion of the pros and cons of the level of performance measurement, from the researchers' point of view, have been aired above and elsewhere (see Hart and Craig, 1993; Griffin and Page, 1993). Researchers and practitioners have access to different kinds of data, which may partly explain their differing preferences regarding the level of performance measurement. Their objectives in measuring performance outcomes are not necessarily aligned. Griffin and Page (1993) suggest that firms are predominantly interested in how any particular project has proceeded, to determine how a team has performed, which suggests an operational level of interest. On the other hand, researchers are interested in discovering what firms routinely do to propel a series of profitable projects through the new product development process, which suggests a more strategic approach. However, it may also be true that different levels of new product S/F measurement exist within firms, depending, once again, on the level of analysis undertaken: strategic or operational. This difference in focus makes it essential that researchers pursue data collection through the appropriate sources in the firm and recognise that the importance of project-level measures are likely to be greater if new product managers are the respondents. Conversely, firm- and programme-level measures require respondents with a broader view of the strategic elements of new product development.

Issues such as these are infrequently addressed by research: Cooper and Kleinschmidt's (1995) use a number of programme-level performance measures, but their respondents were taken from firms' project teams; Cooper's earlier work on *The Performance Impact of Product Innovation Strategies* (1984) focuses on programme and firm-level measures with respondents representing 'those responsible for their firms' new product efforts from a commercial perspective'; others neglect to mention their organisational sources (Yoon and Lilien, 1985; Choffray and Lilien, 1984). On the other hand, the work of Rothwell *et al.* (1974) identifies four distinct roles – independent of job title – whose views are systematically represented in the data collection strategy they used: the technical innovator, the business innovator, the chief executive and the product champion.

Data Collection Method

Where the measurement of success is carried out at the project level, the practice of having respondents identify the successes and failures before going on to answer questions about their development activities for each is highly likely to affect the responses given for each category of new product. This kind of error is fairly basic, relating as much to first principles of questionnaire design (do not lead respondents) as it does to 'attribution bias' (Weiner, 1986; Curren *et al.*, 1988). It would be surprising indeed if the ratings on the success measures were not, for the most part, 'significantly different' for the successes and the failures, as the respondents themselves have identified those successes and failures!

Analytical Technique

In recognising that new product success can be defined in a number of ways, it has become a fairly common practice to apply multi-item scales to the performance outcomes of development projects or programmes in order to capture the various dimensions. This is then followed by the application of data reduction techniques to identify the 'underlying structure of the data'. The most commonly used techniques are principal components analysis and/or cluster analysis. There are at least two problems with such an approach. First, many batteries of scale items include an 'overall success' rating, which is often included in the data reduction procedures, irrespective of either the 'halo effect' that it is likely to produce or the implications it may have for the interpretation of factors. Second, since there is a long history of research suggesting that there are differences in success dimensions, a more appropriate form of factor analysis would be confirmatory, which can be used when the researcher has specific hypotheses about the factorial structure thought to be responsible for the observed covariance structure of the correlation matrix (Kim and Mueller, 1978). In other words, since researchers have long alluded to the existence of 'different kinds of success', it is surprising that none have attempted to specify what these might be and how the variables used to capture the dimensions might be expected to co-vary. Indeed, the interpretation of factors resulting from principal components analysis does depend upon *some* idea of the relationships between variables and, since several previous studies have identified success dimensions using PCA, using these to prespecify dimensions and test them via confirmatory factor analysis would begin to build a theory of success dimensions. At present, the 'success factors' once constructed on the basis of PCA are not used as a basis for replication and validation; each further research study starts anew, using PCA to identify further statistical artefacts which become the independent dimensions of success in new product development. Once more, these indictments apply to previous research by this author. Scrutiny of expert writing on factor analysis suggests that the tendency to use what is an exploratory technique in lieu of developing the results of previous factor analytic studies is not new (Ehrenberg, 1968; Stewart, 1981).

The consequence of these methodological difficulties across the S/F literature as a whole is an incomplete understanding of the way various dimensions of success and failure in new product development are interrelated. The next section reviews the current position on the relationships among different types of new product success and proposes a conceptual framework to take account of these relationships.

THE INTERRELATIONSHIPS AMONG SUCCESS DIMENSIONS

At this juncture it is helpful to review studies examining the nature of success dimensions, all of which have used PCA as described above. Cooper's (1984) research included eight performance measures, which were reduced to three independent dimensions. The first is the *impact* of the NPD programme on company sales and profits and the percentage of current sales by new products. The second is the *success rate* of new products in terms of the percentage of kills and the percentage of commercial successes and the third is the *relative performance*, which captures the overall success of the new product development programme in relation to objectives, competitors and whether the profits exceeded costs. Three years later, Cooper and Kleinschmidt (1987a) used a similar methodology, this time at the level of individual new product projects. They found another (!) three independent dimensions characterising new product performance: *financial* performance (relative profits and sales, profitability levels and payback period); *opportunity window* (the extent to which a new product opened up new opportunities to the firm in terms of a new category of products and/or new market area) and *market impact*, (domestic and foreign market share). My own permutation of new product success indicators produced *technological, cost* and *profit-based* dimensions of success (Hart, 1993).

Each of these studies' findings make sense in a rudimentary way. All are predicated upon the existence of more than one type of success; none attempts to specify what the dimensions of that success might be; all produce seemingly plausible dimensions, on the surface. But although they identify different dimensions of success, based on a technique which emphasises orthogonality, they fail to address the possibility that the dimensions are related and thus do not consider the nature of the relationships. Thus it is not unreasonable to ask whether the 'success rate' identified by Cooper (that is, the percentage of kills and the percentage of commercial successes) does not represent an input to 'relative performance', which is the overall success of the new product development programme. Similarly, is not the 'extent to which a new product opens up a new market' likely to have an impact on 'market impact'? Might not 'cost-based success' identified in my own work feed into the 'independent' dimension of 'profit-based success'? Thus the observed independence of the success dimensions may be explained, paradoxically, by a relationship whereby some dimensions are in fact inputs to others, distanced, either by the level of analysis or the time perspective, issues examined below.

Griffin and Page (1993) investigated the structure of success dimensions based on a review of over 77 different articles, together with measures actually used by practitioners. Using expert assessment, they generated five categories of success and failure measures from a total of 75 different measures: measures of firm benefits, programme-level measures, product-level measures, measures of financial performance and measures of customer acceptance. This categorisation was validated in two ways. First, responses from a sample of companies describing how they wished to measure new product success, were sorted into the categories which were then correlated. The coefficient was low (0.29) but significant ($p < 0.05$). The low correlation leads the authors to suggest that the five groups constitute almost completely independent groups of measures. However, the five groups do *not* all describe different *dimensions* of success; three groups describe the *level* at which success is measured (firm, programme or product) and contain within them items relating to several *dimensions*; two groups are defined in terms of the dimensions of success: financial performance measures and customer acceptance measures. The grouping named 'financial measures' contains measures of profit and time to break-even, while the customer acceptance grouping contains measures of sales volume, market share, revenue growth, customer acceptance, customer satisfaction level, the number of customers, trial rate, repeat purchase rate and a host of items designed to capture the appeal of the product to the market. As mentioned above, appeal of the product to the customer may or may not lead to sales, depending, among other things, on customer awareness of the new product and the time perspective taken on the measurement of success. There is also an issue of how customer acceptance, satisfaction and appeal are, in fact, inputs to sales performance, rather than surrogates for sales performance. Equally, it is apposite, in terms of building theory, to ask how customer acceptance and sales measures develop (or are prevented from developing) into financial success, given an appropriate time lapse. This is examined in a different context by Buckley *et al.* (1988), who contend that a host of measures of international competitiveness, do, in fact, mix up competitive *potential* and competitive *performance* (that is, the *output* of potential).

Similarly, Hultink and Robben (1995) focused on the managerial importance of performance measures, in both the short and the long term. In their sample of 80 firms measuring success, they found that four of the measures they used were equally important, irrespective of the time perspective: meeting quality guidelines, customer acceptance, customer satisfaction and product performance level. The only measure that was uniquely more important in the short, rather than the long, term was whether or not the product was launched in time, while all the measures which were uniquely important in the long term were financial: meeting revenue, market share, unit sales, profitability and margin goals as well as attaining the internal rate of return or rate of return on interest objectives. This research is of great importance for, as the authors suggest, 'in future studies on the determinants and correlates of new product success timeframe has to be specified' (Hultink and Robben, 1995, p. 13). In addition, their results clearly suggest that, in any conceptual framework developed to underpin S/F research, the financial indicators measure longer-term performance, which may result from the performance indicated by the more intermediate measures. Further, the appropriateness of the time perspective taken will be determined by the defined view of the level of analysis, whether that is strategic or operational.

At this point it may be useful to summarise the complex patterns of conceptual and methodological issues presented thus far. While the early criticisms of S/F measurement pointed out that different dimensions of success may exist, research has failed to consider the interrelationships among the dimensions it has since identified, owing partly to a tendency to submit data gathered on success indicators to frequent, *ab initio* factor analyses and partly to a collective disinclination on the part of researchers to consider earlier research within their own discipline (Baker, 1994, p. 23) and build on earlier conclusions. Some may argue that these two tendencies go hand in hand: that the preponderance of quantitative analyses of extensive datasets actually replaces conceptual development. That said, linkages among the dimensions of success appear to be related to the level of analysis, since performance at the operational level can be seen as input to performance at the strategic level. Further, these levels of analysis are subject also to the timeframe employed. The final section of the chapter presents two frameworks for measuring new product success, based on the dimensions of level of analysis and time.

THE ROLES OF TIME AND LEVEL OF ANALYSIS IN NPD SUCCESS MEASUREMENT

Integrating the findings of more recent research, which has shown that the dimension of time influences managerial thinking on how to measure success, suggests that the relationships among success dimensions may depend on the time horizon viewed by researchers. In short, measures of performance in the shorter term may be seen as inputs to performance in the longer term. For example, although 'time efficiency' (of the process) has been used as a success indicator, it also has an impact on another success indicator, namely, the aspect of being 'launched on time'. Similarly, 'customer acceptance' of a new product may be a measure of performance which can be assessed soon after the new product is launched, but equally it affects the new product's diffusion rates, which in turn, over time will affect sales volumes and revenues. Taking a longer-term perspective again, sales volumes are a necessary input to profitability of the new product itself. Similarly, a success indicator such as 'the extent to which the new product opened up a new market for the firm' requires some time to have elapsed before any judgement can be made. The conceptual framework shown in Figure 6.1 outlines these relationships using the measures used for new product success at the product level.

The point of departure for this framework is different objectives that managers may have for the introduction of the new product, taken from previous research. These include technology-based objectives, such as 'gaining experience of a new technology; market-based objectives, such as gaining a foothold in a new market or blocking competition in a market; and financial objectives, such as 'offsetting a seasonal cycle'. These provide the context for the subsequent measurement of success and, in time, precede the actual measurement of performance. The framework then allows for a number of process-based measures of success, such as time efficiency and process completion. These precede the measure of 'launched on time', which subsumes several of the process measures. Taken together, these measures give, in temporal terms, an intermediate assessment of performance that might be useful for controlling new product process activities. They therefore represent an operational assessment of NPD success within the firm. Moving along the time continuum, the first post-launch measures include those which relate to both the technological and market aspirations for the new product, such as 'gaining experience of a new technology' and gaining a foothold in a new market. The emphasis

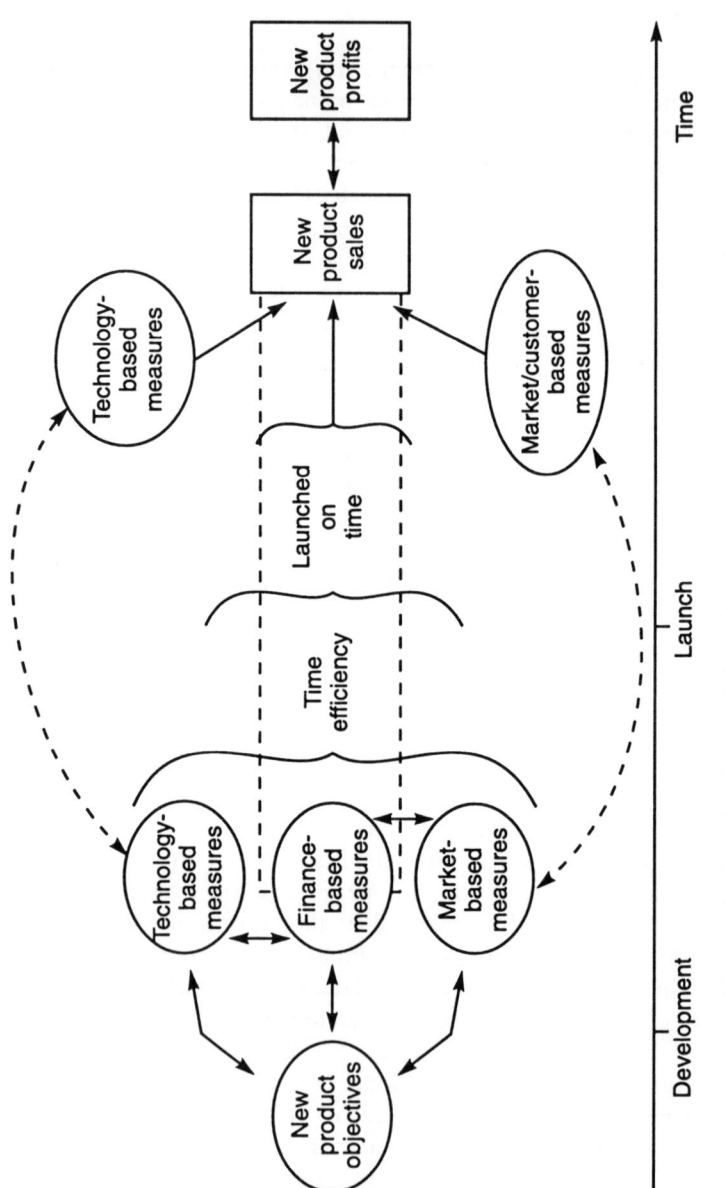

Figure 6.1 New product level interrelationships among success dimensions

given to both or either of these would, of course be linked to the original objectives set for the particular new product under examination. Financial indicators appear towards the end of the continuum, with sales indicators preceding profit indicators. Both are viewed in this figure at the level of the new product.

However, as discussed elsewhere (Hart and Craig, 1993), measures of new product success are routinely taken at the level of the new product programme or, at a higher level of aggregation still, overall company performance. These two levels of measurement can also be placed on a time dimension, in that the extent to which any new product contributes to the overall success rate of the new product programme can only be assessed after a period of time has elapsed to allow comparison of one new product's sales with that of another in the programme. Similarly, whether or not a new product has grown into a category will require, not only a longer time horizon, but also the extension of the original new product into a number of variants which allow it to assume the mantle of a category. The proposed conceptual structure of performance indicators of the programme and firm level are shown in Figure 6.2.

At the new product programme and firm level, the objectives are placed, once again, at the beginning of the time period for the performance assessment, covering technology-, finance- and market-based aspirations. The intermediate phase of evaluation for the programme, or the entire company, necessitates the inclusion of a number of process performance indicators which are viewed as precursors to the next stage of outcomes. These indicators may be used to assess the company's potential for achieving its stated overall new product objectives and as such are inputs to the later measures of outcomes in the framework. That said, because here it is the programme or firm level which is of interest, they are also outcomes in their own right. For example, the regularity of new product launches represents the overall level of new product activity which is, of itself, an indication of the proficiency of processes used to develop individual new products, since the ability to sustain a number of new product launches over time depends, to some extent, on a proportion of these new products being financially successful. This suggests that there is also a time linkage between measures at the individual and programme or firm levels of success measurement. Later indicators of programme and firm-level success can be divided again into the categories of technology and market. Technology-based success indicators include the number of awards made and market-based indicators at this level can now relate

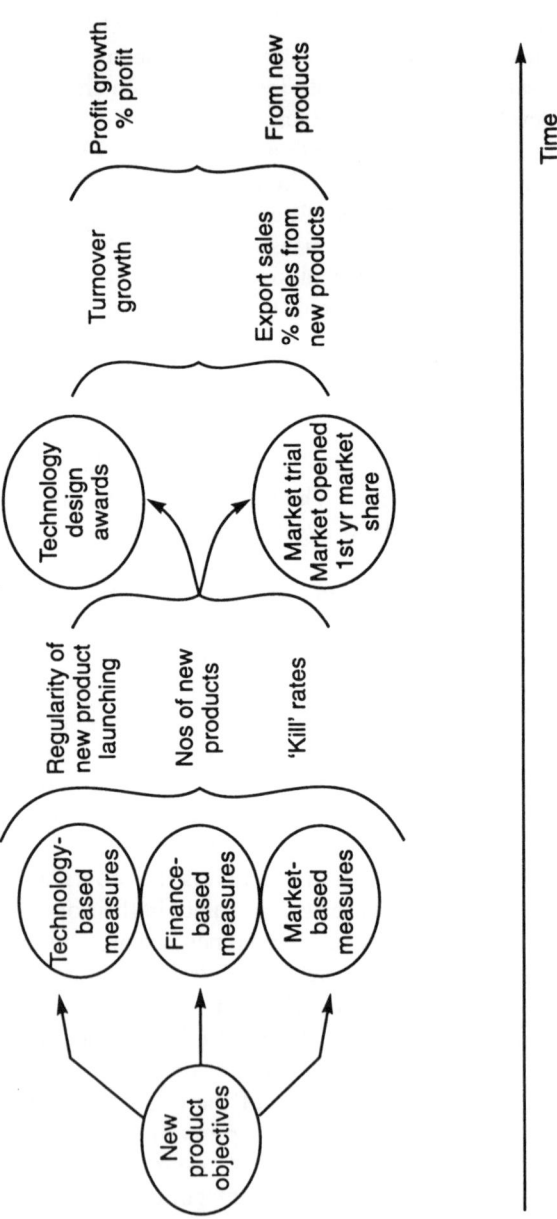

Figure 6.2 New product programme level interrelationships among success dimensions

to whether or not a new category has been opened. The final stages of performance indicators at the programme and firm levels include sales-based measures, such as the achievement of overall targets, growth in turnover and the percentage of sales generated by new products, which provide the necessary new product perspective on profit measures such as profit growth, ROI and the percentage of company profits generated by new products.

Two important caveats accompany these representations of success measures. First, some of the actual measures can operate at both levels, the strategic and the operational. The extent to which sales targets are achieved, the ROI achieved and the levels of customer satisfaction can and do apply to the individual product as well as to the new product programme. It is the interpretation of what the measures mean for the organisation at each level which is important for researchers to distinguish. Second, the measures across the two levels are also related but moderated through the filter of time. For example, a new product which does not achieve its specific sales targets is unlikely *if no action is taken* to contribute very much to overall sales growth, or indeed profit growth. However, the importance of this type of relationship is that the implications for measurement are clear: both levels are necessary to monitor effectiveness and thereby improve a company's ability to develop successful new products continuously.

CONCLUSION

This chapter has attempted to review the measurement of new product success and failure in academic literature as a precursor to developing a more holistic view of the complex interrelationships at play. In so doing, it has highlighted the lack of theoretical development in the S/F literature to date. This shortcoming is due in part to factors identified by Michael Baker in his recent article on 'The 4R's of Marketing' and in part to inattention to the implications of methodological issues, such as data collection, measurement and analytical technique. As a first step in building on previous research, the chapter traces linkages across the measures which are related to the dimension of time and the level of analysis considered within research studies to date. Finally, the role of time is also implicit in the relationship between the two levels of analysis of new product success and failure.

References

Abede, P. V. and R. Christiaans (1986) 'Strategies of Belgian Hi-tec Firms,' *Industrial Marketing Management*, 15, 299–308.

Ayal, I. and J. Raban (1990) 'Developing hi-tech industrial products for world markets', *IEEE Transactions on Engineering Management*, 37(3), August.

Baker, M. J. (1975) *Marketing New Industrial Products* (London: Macmillan).

Baker, M. J. (1994), 'Research myopia: Recent relevance, reinvention and renaissance (The 4 R's of Marketing?)', University of Strathclyde, *Department of Marketing Working Paper*, No. 94/2, February.

Biggadike, E. R. (1979) *Corporate diversification: Entry, strategy and performance* (Cambridge, Mass.: Harvard University Press).

Booz Allen Hamilton (1982) *New Products Management for the 1980s* (New York:).

Buckley, P. J., C. L. Pass & K. Prescott (1988) 'Measures of international competitiveness: a critical survey', *Journal of Marketing Management*, 4 (2), 175–200.

Calantone, R. J. and R. G. Cooper (1981) 'New product scenarios: prospects for success'. *Journal of Product Innovation Management*, 45, Spring, 48–60.

Cannon, T. M. (1986) *Basic Marketing*, 2nd edn (London: Cassell).

Carter, C. F. and Williams, B. R. (1957) *Industry and Technical Progress* (Oxford: Oxford University Press).

Choffray, J. M. and G. L. Lilien (1984) 'Strategies behind the successful industrial product launch', *Business Marketing*, 82–95.

Cooper, R. G. (1979) 'The dimensions of industrial new product success and failure', *Journal of Marketing*, 43, 93–103.

Cooper, R. G. (1983) 'A process model for industrial new product development', *IEE Transactions on Engineering Management*, 30 (1) 2–11.

Cooper, R.G. (1984) 'The strategy–performance link in product innovation', *R&D Management*, 14(4), 247–59.

Cooper, R. G. (1984), 'The Performance Impact of Product Innovation Strategies', *European Journal of Marketing*, 17(5), 5–53.

Cooper, R. G. and E. J. Kleinschmidt (1987a) 'What makes a new product a winner: success factors at the product level', *R&D Management*, 17(3).

Cooper, R. G. and E. J. Kleinschmidt (1987b) 'New products: what separates winners from losers?', *Journal of Product Innovation Management*, 4.

Cooper, R. G. and E. J. Kleinschmidt (1995) 'New product performance: keys to success, profitability and cycle time reduction', *Journal of Marketing Management*, 11 (4), 315–38.

Cordero, R. (1990) 'The measurement of innovation performance in the firm: an overview', *Research Policy*, 19, 185–92.

Crawford, C. M. (1977) 'Marketing research and the new product failure rate', *Journal of Marketing*, 52 (April), 55–61.

Crawford, C. M. (1984) 'Protocol: New tool for product innovation', *Journal of Product Innovation Management*, 2, 85–91.

Crawford, C. M. (1987) *New Products Management* (Homewood, Ill.: Irwin).

Curren, M.T., V.S. Folkes and J.H. Steckel (1988) 'Explanations for successful and unsuccessful marketing decisions: The decision-makers' perspective', *Journal of Marketing*, 56, 18–31.

DeSimone, D.V. (1967) *Technological Innovation: Its Environment and Management* (Washington DC: US Department of Commerce).

Edgett, S., D. Shipley and G. Forbes (1992) 'Japanese and British companies compared; Contributing factors to success and failure in NPD', *Journal of Product Innovation Management*, 9, 3–10.

Ehrenberg, A.S.C. (1968) 'On methods; the factor analytic search for programme types', *Journal of Advertising Research*, 18, March, 55–63.

Griffin, A. and A.L. Page (1993) 'An interim report on measuring product development success and failure', *Journal of Product Innovation Management*, 10(4), 291–308.

Hart, S.J. (1993) 'Dimensions of success in new product development: an exploratory investigation', *Journal of Marketing Management*, 9, 23–41.

Hart, S.J. and A. Craig (1993) 'Dimensions of success in new product development', *Perspectives in Marketing Management*, 3, 207–43.

Hart, S.J. and L.M. Service (1988) 'The effects of managerial attitudes to design on company performance', *Journal of Marketing Management*, 4(2), 217–29.

Harvey-Jones, J. (1986), *The Dimbleby Lecture* (London: British Broadcasting Corporation).

Hayes, R.H. and W.J. Abernathy (1980) 'Managing our way to economic decline', *Harvard Business Review*, July–August, 67–77.

Hise, R.T., L. O'Neal, J.U. McNeal and A. Parasuramen (1989) 'The effect of product design activities on commercial success levels of new industrial products', *Journal of Product Innovation Management*, 6, 43–50.

Hopkins, D.S. (1980) *New Product Winners and Losers*, Conference Board Report No. 604.

Hultink, E.J. and H.S.J. Robben (1995) 'Meaning new product success: The difference that time makes', *Journal of Product Innovation Management*, 12 (5), 392–405.

Johne, A.F. and P. Snelson (1988) 'Marketing's role in successful product development', *Journal of Marketing Management*, 3(3), 256–68.

Kim, J. and C.W. Mueller (1978) *An Introduction to Factor Analysis* (London: Sage).

Madique, M.A. and B.J. Zirger (1985) *The New Product Learning Cycle*, Research Report Series, Innovation and Entrepreneurship Institute, School of Business Administration, University of Miami, Coral Gables, FL, February.

McDonald, B. and Eastlack, E. (1971) 'Growth and New Products', *Business Horizons*, December.

Might, R.J. and W.A. Fisher (1985) 'The role of structural factors in determining project management success', *IEEE*, 32(2), 71–83.

National Industrial Conference Board (1967) 'The marketing executive lacks sweat', *Experiences in Marketing Management*, 13 NICB.

Nystrom, H. (1985) 'Product development strategy: an integration of technology and marketing', *Journal of Product Innovation Management*, 2.

Page, A. L. (1993) 'Assessing new product development practices and performance: Establishing crucial norms', *Journal of Product Innovation Management*, 10(4), 273–91.

Rothwell, R., C. Freeman, A. Horsley, V. T. P. Jervis, A. B. Robertson and J. Townsend (1974) 'SAPPHO updated–project SAPPHO phase II', *Research Policy*, 3, 258–91.

Rubenstein, A. H., A. K. Chakraborti, R. D. O'Keele, W. E. Sauder and H. C. Young (1976) 'Factors influencing innovation success at the project level', *Research Management*, Part 3, May, 15–20.

Sauder, W. E. (1978) 'Effectiveness of product development methods', *Industrial Marketing Management*, 7, 299–307.

Shipley, D., S. Edgett and G. Forbes (1991) 'New product success rates among British and Japanese companies', *EMAC 1991 Proceedings*, 1160–75.

Stewart, D. W. (1981) 'The application and misapplication of factor analysis in market research', *Journal of Marketing Research*, 10, February, 51–62.

Ughanwa, D. O. and M. J. Baker (1989) *The Role of Design in International Competitiveness* (London: Routledge).

Voss, C. A. (1985) 'Determinants of success in the development of applications software', *Journal of Product Innovation Management*, 2, 122–9.

Walsh, V., R. Roy and M. Bruce (1988) 'Competitive by design', *Journal of Marketing Management*, 4 (2), 201–16.

Weiner, B. (1986) *An Attributional Theory of Motivation and Emotion* (New York: Springer-Verlag).

Yoon, E. and G. L. Lilien (1985) 'New industrial product performance: the effect of market characteristics and strategy', *Journal of Product Innovation Management*, 3, 134–44.

7 Rejecting Superior New Technologies

Arch G. Woodside

We have so little information on the outside, on markets, on customers. Nothing – as many people have learned the hard way – is changing faster than distribution channels. (Drucker, 1994)

Baker and Hart (1989) have emphasised that single-factor explanations have been singularly unsuccessful in explaining competitive performance, as well as management decision making and behaviour. As an alternative, research on the patterns, or scenarios, of decision event streams may be useful for both understanding and predicting outcomes, including the success and failure to adopt proven superior technologies. Such research should include mapping of the multiple factor scenarios of both success and failure when implementing combined marketing–buying strategies. Such mapping of failure in marketing–purchasing superior new technologies is the focus of this contribution.

Bringing a superior technical innovation to market is no guarantee of industrial customer acceptance of the innovation and its replacement of a currently used (inferior) product service technology (Sheth, 1981; Ram, 1987; Gatignon and Robertson, 1989). Based on a survey of the research literature described in this report, this proposition holds even when the evidence is overwhelming that the adoption of the innovation will enable the customer to decrease dramatically their product service manufacturing costs and improve both performance and quality of the customer's product service to downstream customers.

Adoptions of new, electronic-based, manufacturing technologies occurred in some US firms in many industries in the 1980s and early 1990s, resulting in the counterintuitive combination of dramatic increases in product quality with dramatic decreases in manufactured costs (see Narasimhan et al., 1993; Woodside, 1994; Gross et al., 1995). This new reality has been named 'The Technology Paradox: as high technology becomes dirt cheap, producers must find new ways to prosper. They have' (Gross et al., 1995, cover page).

However, successfully introducing superior technologies (compared to inferior performing, currently installed technologies) in the marketplace often does not translate into commercial success for these new technologies. For industrial products services, 'typically a long time is required from the introduction of a superior industrial product [and/or technology] until it has replaced half of the uses of the inferior product [or installed base technology]. In one extensive study, the modal time was twelve to fifteen years, with 23 percent of the superior products requiring twenty four to forty seven years. See Martino et al., (1978) and Linestone and Sahal (1976)' (quoted in Moore and Pessemier, 1993, p.76). The causes of delaying and rejecting technological innovations that combine superior performance and lower total costs have received little attention by product innovation researchers.

Ram (1987) introduced the concept of 'innovation resistance' as a summary construct for customers not adopting a superior new technology. While Gatignon and Robertson (1989) explicitly examined both adoption and rejection outcomes of laptop computers for use by salesforces, their 'hypotheses only explain adoption because the lack of previous findings precludes concrete hypotheses about rejection' (p. 36).

Two studies have been reported on delays and rejections of superior new technologies. In these studies, networks of independent industrial firms, and local and national governmental agencies participated informally to block the adoption of superior electronic based, technological innovations to clean up nuclear waste sites (Associated Press, 1994, Dl). The US Government Accounting Office and the Western Governors' Association agreed that 'rapid [and lower cost] cleanup is hampered by a system [distribution network] that relies on traditional technologies selected by "risk averse" cleanup managers who have no incentive to innovate'.

Peter M. Senge (1990, p.348) quotes the general observations of Ed Simon (President and COO, Herman Miller Company) on this widespread enterprise malaise that affects many firms in many industries:

I believe that human beings truly seek to live in a more creative orientation. But people don't realize the incredible extent to which traditional organisations are designed to keep people comfortable and to inhibit taking risks. The learning cycle is a continuous process of experimentation. You cannot experiment without taking risks. Despite rhetoric to the contrary, I believe most American businesses are engaged in building 'no-risk' environments.

The purpose of this chapter is to describe, and examine empirically, several propositions on the causes and realised strategies (Mintzberg and Waters, 1985) that are likely to be found in different industrial marketing–purchasing situations involving rejecting or accepting superior technological innovations. Those are defined as innovations which are independently verified as providing superior operating characteristics and lower total costs compared to currently used products and manufacturing processes. An initial theory of customer rejection of superior manufacturing technologies and product service innovations is developed as a vehicle for summarising a set of related propositions explaining such behaviour.

Empirically, this chapter describes acceptance and rejection by different customers of one industrial technological innovation – fibreglass light poles. This is a high-performing and low lifetime cost product that continues to be rejected by most US light pole buyers. The results of the empirical study serve to emphasise the need for market research on two categories of customer characteristics relevant for new product market strategies: (1) the demographic/psychographic profiles of potential and actual customers of the new product form (such as company and person demographics, and information on buying processes used) and (2) willingness and ability to buy the new product form (see Guiltinan and Paul, 1991, p.59; di Benedetto, 1994).

The following issues are raised with tentative answers based on a literature review and a field study. In what ways are both marketers and customers responsible for rejecting superior technological innovations? In natural field settings, how do a few marketers and customers overcome such rejection and end up successfully adopting superior technological innovations and replacing existing out-of-date technologies? What general observations conclusions appear to follow from case study field research on rejecting and accepting technological innovations?

First, a brief review is presented of relevant literature on successful and unsuccessful marketing–purchasing of industrial innovations. In this review several core and micro propositions are developed; these propositions are relevant for improving environmental scanning and learning in organisations involved in both marketing and adopting superior innovations. Second, the theory of customer rejection of superior industrial technologies is described. Next, a field study to examine these propositions is described. Finally, additional micro propositions are suggested for further research; these are based on results from the field study and the more general, central propositions.

PROPOSITIONS AND FINDINGS FROM THE LITERATURE

Many important core propositions related to marketing and adopting superior technological innovations can be found in the relevant academic and business literatures. First, Drucker (1994, p.108) proposes that technology is no longer a series of parallel streams coming out of major research labs and universities: 'It is chaotic and therefore has to come from outside [for example, from customers, customers' customers, and others in seemingly unrelated industries]. And about this outside we know nothing.' He goes on to observe, 'We must begin to organise information from the outside, where the true profit centers exist. We will have to build a system that gives this information to those who make decisions' (p. 109).

The chaos in designing, marketing and adopting technological innovations is described by Peters and Waterman (1982) in a series of anecdotal reports from many industries. Biemans (1989, 1990) provides details on the chaos of innovation from in depth analyses of 17 cases on marketing and adopting superior technological innovations in the Dutch medical equipment industry. Biemans (1990) relates the central conclusion of his research to earlier observations by Quinn (1985): 'Innovation tends to be individually motivated, opportunistic, customer responsive, tumultuous, nonlinear, and interactive in its development. Managers can plan overall directions and goals, but surprises are likely to abound.' Biemans (1990, p. 539) emphasises that the revealing title of Quinn's article ('Managing innovation: controlled chaos') 'captures the essence of our argument: even though innovation [including marketing and adopting innovation] processes are very much characterized by chaos, in the sense of surprises and unexpected changes, they can still be controlled [by both marketers and adopters] to a certain extent. The three C's of cooperation, coordination, and communication are key elements in successfully developing [commercially viable] innovations because they reduce the level of chaos.'

P1: Managing Technological Innovation Marketing/Adoption is Controlled Chaos

Drucker's and Quinn's central point can be stated as a general, and very insightful, proposition: managing an adoption effectively is to have some success in controlling chaos. Related to P1 is Senge's (1990) detailed observation that most managers develop or use oversimplified and inaccurate mental models of the way the world works, including how marketing and adopting technological innovations occur:

> More specifically, new insights fail to get put into practice because they conflict with deeply held internal images of how the world works, images that limit us to familiar ways of thinking and acting. That is why the discipline of managing mental models – surfacing, testing, and improving our internal pictures of how the world works – promises to be a major breakthrough for building learning organisations. (Senge, 1990)

Quinn's global conclusion (stated formally as P1) can be broken down into a series of micro propositions (MPs). The following are based on Quinn's conclusions and the literature cited.

MP1: Innovations Tend to be Individually Motivated

Learning about superior technological innovations and attempting to transform an organisation from an established older technology to the superior technology is hard work financially and socially. Most people become comfortable with the status quo – working with the established technology – and do not want to make the commitments in time and effort, or to assume the risks involved, in either marketing or adopting the superior new technology. Socially, comfortable co workers may be expected to object to the efforts of champions who are attempting to promote the adoption of new technologies. Nevertheless, a few individuals surface who champion the new technology. From the manufacturing–marketing side, Schon (1967) refers to such unique people as product champions; from the adoption side, von Hippel (1988) identifies such individually motivated persons as lead users; also see Burgleman (1983) and Hutt *et al.* (1988).

A general human tendency toward favouring defensive routines (mental maps of the way activities are done now and should continue to be done) prevents most people from learning new routines or technologies. Defensive routines are habitual ways of acting that protect us and others from threat or embarrassment, but which also prevent us from learning (Argyris, 1985).

Some marketing and adopting implications of MP1 include the following observations. Product champions and lead users must be found or grown for superior technological innovations to flourish. Finding organisations with such people may not be good enough because too few of them (both organisations and individuals) may exist; the power of the installed base of the inferior technology may preclude such people from raising their heads (see Herbig and Kramer, 1993; Herbig *et al.*, 1995). Thus Herbig and his colleagues describe the massive inertia produced by an existing technology's installed base that impedes the adoption of a new technology or new product.

To help overcome the installed base effect, unique marketing programmes may be necessary to help nurture product champions and lead users (for example, see Wilson and Woodside, 1992). Being opportunistic in searching and finding product champions and lead users is a good strategy, but not good enough. To overcome the installed base effect and to achieve commercial success for a new technology, unique marketing programmes need to include the creation or nurturing of new multiple-layer and diagonal inter-firm relationships. The emergence of a network champion (see Woodside and Wilson, 1994; Woodside, 1994) to foster such new relationships is an example of such unique marketing programmes.

MP2: Marketing or Adopting a Technological Innovation is Opportunistic and Requires Interactive Learning

Adoptions of new industrial products and technologies are concentrated in a small number of user firms; this concentration may continue over several years. For example, Cardozo *et al.* (1988, p.106) found a 20/70 concentration. 'For all [new] products combined, the top 21% of customers (28 customers in total) accounted for 70% of total sales during the five year period. Nineteen per cent of customers accounted for 68% of sales. Concentration of sales among the top 5 customers for each [new] product ranged from 55 to 80% of the total purchases of that product.' In their study, repeat purchasers of the new industrial products constituted 61 per cent of all customers and accounted for 93 per cent of all units purchased during a five year period after product introduction.

The strategy implications following the Cardozo *et al.* (1988) findings are that adoption of technological innovations is expected to be concentrated among a few customer firms within any one industry; adoption will not to be widespread across many customers for a long time; for many products, repeat purchases among these few adopters are critical for success of the new technology. Thus, marketers of technological innovations need to recognise and respond to unique customer opportunities by concentrating marketing resources to nurture adoptions and repeat purchases among these few adopters.

Consequently, successful marketing of technical innovations requires interactive learning among: (1) the manufacturer of the new technology; (2) lead user customers; (3) channel members, for example, the manufacturing agent representing the manufacturer; and (4) third party specialists who help overcome roadblocks (for example, technical and financial) in getting the innovation up and running at specific customer sites. In addition, in his study of 17 industrial case studies, Biemans (1989) concludes that one of the major causes of rejection of superior new technologies is that manufacturers of the new technologies often interact insufficiently with third parties during the critical development and testing stages of the innovation. Wilson and Woodside (1992) and Woodside (1994) concluded that additional third parties may be necessary to create and strengthen the weak ties among the multiple participants in the marketing and buying of new technologies.

MP3: Successful Marketing or Adopting of Technological Innovations is Customer Responsive

This micro proposition leads to the often overlooked insight that a request from a customer's customer (the CC) to evaluate (and test on site) the operating and downstream benefits provided by a technology innovation is likely to receive more attention than a request made only by the marketer of the new technology. Given that superior technological innovations usually result in (1) superior performance quality, (2) higher conformance product quality, and (3) lower unit cost to the customer's customer, the CC has a strong vested interest in motivating the supplier firm to adopt the innovation. A related marketing problem as well as opportunity is that the CC may be unaware of the innovation because of the high comfort level his or her supplier has operating with the out-of-date installed technology and the lack of awareness or benefit-building contact by marketers of the new technology with these CCs.

Given the substantial powers of inertia and the installed base of the out-of-date technology, recognising and activating longer routes (designing a 'pull' versus a 'push' strategy) may be more than beneficial for the technological innovation, it may be a necessity. The marketer of the technological innovation may need to recruit the CC to champion the new product or manufacturing process with the CC's suppliers of component parts and finished products.

These observations lead to the strategic and theoretical importance of examining network relationships among firms in the marketing or adopting of technological innovations (see Nicosia and Wind, 1977; Taylor and Kaufmann, 1990; Wisnieski, 1991; Arabie and Wind, 1994; Woodside, 1994). Research on the development of weak ties (Granovetter, 1973) between manufacturers of technological innovations and CCs, and weak ties among each of the three parties with other, 'third-party', participants in successful adoption processes, provides empirical support for these observations (see Biemans, 1989; 1990; Woodside, 1994).

Imparato and Harari (1994) describe the critical impact of customers' customers on new technology adoption by both manufacturers and their channel intermediaries; they label 'looking a customer ahead' their first organising principle for 'jumping the [technological 'S'] curve' by embracing new superior technologies and discarding obsolete installed technologies. Willingness to look a customer ahead is the exception rather than the rule among managers in established organisations. Cooper and Smith (1992) note that 'where established firms enter young industries, they do not pursue the new product aggressively, and they continue to make substantial commitments to their old product even after its sales begin to decline' (Imparato and Harari, 1994, p. 104).

MP4: Marketing or Adopting a Technological Innovation Tends to be Tumultuous

Among industrial participants in the marketing and adopting or rejecting of new industrial technologies, tumult is likely to occur in two ways: inside the customer firm in discussions among advocates of the new versus the old technologies and between marketing, customer and third party firms who present conflicting 'facts' and a continual series of revised proposals to attempt to switch the customer firm to the new form of technology or to keep it with the current form. In the scholarly and popular business literature, very little has been written to describe these tumults, or to build theories useful for predicting or explaining outcomes of such unsettling processes (for an exception, see Yoder, 1994).

We do know that champions of the older technology product forms do not go quietly into the good night; they fight. And we know that customer firms successfully making 'the chasm leap' from old to new technologies (see Starr, 1991) often involve third party firms to verify, help test the new technology on site, and recommend such transformations (see Biemans, 1990; Herbig and Kramer, 1993).

MP5: Innovation Marketing or Adopting Processes Tend to be Nonlinear

This micro proposition implies that push only marketing strategies for innovations are doomed; marketers of innovations need to work patiently with customers who are 'lead users' (von Hippel, 1988) to help pull innovations through distribution channels. Often such pulling strategies involve using new distribution linkages that were not planned originally by the marketer. Consequently, marketers of innovations need to plan two actions which are often overlooked: (1) initiating direct contacts and working closely with potential lead users of customers' customers located in multiple industries, and (2) opening up new distribution linkages that are preferred by lead users in customer categories previously unrecognised by the marketers (see Lynch, 1994).

For example, such strategies were used by Hewlett–Packard in the firm's successful relaunch strategy for inkjet printers: towards the end of a two-day meeting to discuss strategy retreat in 1988, the H–P inkjet product development team identified a new target market, a new distribution channel and a different competitor to overcome to gain market acceptance for the failing innovation. In late 1994, six years later, the new strategy appeared to be a major cause of both the dramatic increase in sales of inkjet printers and the substantial decline in sales of dot matrix printers. The new Hewlett–Packard strategy included concentrating on small-firm customers currently buying dot matrix printers who were most sensitive to a combination of better performance and quality and low purchase price. This was instead of the previous strategy of aiming at large-firm customers currently buying laser printers, demanding the best performance and quality and who were less sensitive to purchase price. The new marketing strategy included considerable effort by Hewlett–Packard to gain store channel distributions of its inkjet printers and the demand that these stores place these printers alongside Epson's dot matrix printers (for additional details, see Yoder, 1994).

The details of this example are given to imply that a 'shift of mind, seeing the world anew' (Senge, 1990) is often a necessity for overcoming the environmental blocks that greet innovations that are technically superior in performance and priced competitively. The Hewlett–Packard case is presented to suggest that, while the details may vary, the problems and solutions described can be found in the realised strategies of most successful innovations. Senge (1990, p. 71) develops a compelling case that systems thinking is part of the antidote 'when doing the obvious thing does not produce the obvious, desired outcome'. Systems thinking is the discipline for seeing the 'structures' that underlie complex situations, and for discerning effective versus ineffective (high versus low) leverage points for improving system performance.

'Reality is made up of circles but we see in straight lines' (Senge, 1990, p. 73). In thinking about marketing and distributing the initial focus of the marketing strategists of the firm manufacturing the innovation is on the existing distribution structure because it is most attractive and/or visible. It is also most likely to be dominated by distribution and 'end' customers who will reject the innovation. The strategists in the manufacturing firm will focus most often on the biggest customers currently buying the older, proven technology that the innovation is designed to replace. Given the powers of customer inertia and the relationship marketing programmes of manufacturers of the older technology, such a focused marketing effort for the innovation will almost always fail initially (or result in very slow or delayed customer adoptions: see Herbig and Kramer, 1993; Herbig *et al.*, 1995).

Often, other (that is, smaller) customers in different industries than those intended initially need to be identified for successful market entry *somewhere* for the technological innovation. This focus–failure–refocus–success in marketing and adopting might be shortened if dynamic complexity of such systems were recognised by all the parties in the distribution channels, including manufacturers, within channel members, third parties, and large and small customers.

Elg and Johansson (1994) report a case study of a network of manufacturers, wholesalers and retailers in the Swedish food industry. It deals with the way in which large wholesalers were successful in blocking a new, superior technology (a computer-based data information system). These researchers concluded, 'The success of the more powerful organisations [of wholesalers] suggests interorganisational inertia as a major factor in cooperation and strategic change [prevention] in industrial networks' (Elg and Johansson, 1994, p. 2).

P2: With Few Exceptions, New Channel Connections with New Customers are Required to Achieve Marketing Success for New Superior Product Technologies

This proposition follows directly from the work of Herbig and his colleagues, as well as field studies by Biemans (1989) in the medical equipment industry, Elg and Johansson (1994) in the Swedish food industry and Woodside (1994) in industrial manufacturing.

While new users are not shackled by a commitment to an old standard, current users frequently are (Farrell and Saloner, 1985). This inertia leads directly to the Installed Base Effect. Consequently, since old users are usually hesitant to switch immediately to the new technology, most of the growth of a new product must come from new, previously uncommitted users. (Herbig *et al.*, 1995, p. 393)

P3: Rejection of a New Superior Technology by Heavy Users of the Installed Base Technology is Associated with Lack of Familiarity or Experience in Buying From the Manufacturer of the New Technology Compared with High Familiarity, Experience, Trust, Comfort and Efficiency in Buying from Known Suppliers Providing the Installed Base Technology

Given that new superior technologies are often not developed by manufacturers of the dominant installed base technologies, customer adoption of the new technologies requires the customer to move outside his or her comfort zone. Thus the new superior technology suffers from a triple effect: the customer is unfamiliar with the new technology applied to his or her manufacturing process; the customer is unfamiliar with the manufacturer of the technology; the installed base technology is up and running. Consequently, high relative advantage of a new manufacturing technology over the installed base technology is not enough to ensure changeover. A combination of additional forces probably need to be present to force customers to install the new superior technology. Such additional forces are likely to include requests (that is, pressure) by important customers of the prospective buyer of the new technology to provide the performance benefits and lower prices associated with the new technology. Also third-party technical expertise endorsement, and on-site installation, of the new superior technology may be required. Third, additional third-party participation in financing the purchase and installation of the new technology may be required (for example, see Woodside, 1994).

A corollary to P3 is the lack of standards in engineering and purchasing specifications of the new technology coupled with the in-place and operating standards of the installed base technology. 'Failure to meet standards' is often used as a primary reason for rejecting proven, better performing new technologies by users of the installed base technology. This corollary holds especially when: (1) the current standards include materials and design features related to the installed base technology only rather than standards which focus exclusively on the performance requirements of the product; (2) important network externalities relate to purchases of the installed base technology that need to be changed or eliminated if the new technology is adopted; and (3) much effort, time and risk is associated with testing, approving and writing new standards associated with buying the new technology.

A new manufacturing firm (firm X) considering the purchase of alternative technologies is more likely to consider the purchase of the new technology than an on-line manufacturing firm operating with standards related to the installed base technology. Herbig *et al.* (1995, p. 393) conclude, 'since old users are usually hesitant to switch immediately to the new technology, most of the growth of a new product must come from new, previously uncommitted users'. This proposition holds true for purchases of MRO (maintenance, repair and operating) items and component parts.

P4: Defensive Marketing Tactics by Marketers of the Installed Base Technology Occur to Block the Adoption of a New, Superior Technology

Though often overlooked in planning the launch of new, superior technologies, the marketers of installed base technologies do not often fade away without fighting. Substantial evidence supports the proposition that supplier firms that sustain long term relationships with customers are more able to retain and improve their own profitability than firms with high customer turnover (see Kalwani and Narayandas, 1995).

Marketers of new, superior technologies should expect counter-attacks from marketers of the installed base technologies (see Kotler, 1994, pp. 384–90). Given the continuing working relationships with suppliers of the current technologies, the odds are strongly in favour of the installed base technologies winning such battles. In fact, some industrial customers have been found to review specifications and proposals of marketers of new technologies with their current suppliers of the installed base technology. This process results in the conclusion that 'the new, superior technology might work elsewhere but it can't work here' (see Woodside, 1992).

Systems thinking that includes such status quo forces and counters to such counterattacks is rarely described, and rarely done, by marketers of new, superior technologies. In fact, the most notable finding on the marketing strategies of small high-technology firms is the (1) lack of formal marketing planning of any sort; (2) lack of knowledge about customer applications of the new, superior technology; (3) the general lack of expertise in implementing marketing strategies (see Oakey *et al.*, 1990; Oakey, 1991).

P5: Third-Party Involvement in the Marketing and Purchasing Process is Necessary to Achieve Adoption of the New, Superior Technology

Substantial empirical evidence from case research studies supports this fifth proposition especially from European scholars (see Biemans, 1989; Gemunden, 1985; Gemunden *et al.*, 1992; Gemunden and Walter, 1994). In Europe, Biemans' (1989, 1990) in-depth case research reports of third-party involvement in the adoption of proven, superior new technologies provide strong support for propositions. Biemans concludes from his research in The Netherlands that third parties contribute substantially both in developing working prototypes of new technologies and in commercially launching superior new technologies; and that most manufacturers of the new, superior technology are focused 'insufficiently' on customers compared with their first true love, the new technology. This second conclusion fits perfectly with a central conclusion on innovation and marketing of new technologies by British firms reported by Oakey (1991) and his colleagues (1990).

In North America, Wilson and Woodside (1992) and Woodside (1994) report on third-party activities in creating, sponsoring and sustaining new inter-firm organisational associations to stimulate marketing and purchasing of a new technology. Wilson and Woodside (1992) report on the strategy implementation of an electric utility company in designing and financially sponsoring an association of industrial distributors to market new heating and cooling technology equipment (heat pumps) for commercial and residential customers. Both the manufacturers of the new technology and most industrial distributors tended to be in active in marketing the new technology. The third-party organisation and its electric utility sponsor provided both training and financial support to distributors and their customers to obtain replacement of the installed base technology and adoption of the new technology.

Woodside (1994) reports on the strategy implementation work of a 'network champion' to gain adoption of superior new technologies in manufacturing. Network champions are those firms and individuals bringing about new relationships among firms at multiple channel levels to support and sustain the marketing and purchasing of new, superior technologies (see Woodside and Wilson, 1994; and Woodside, 1994).

P6: Within the Customer Firm, the Appearance of an Innovation Buying Champion is Necessary for Overcoming Resistance, Gaining Acceptance and Purchasing a Superior New Technology that Replaces an Installed Base Technology

Ridicule and scepticism may be the initial (and long-term) reactions to superior new technologies by some members of the buying centre in the customer firm. One or more persons in the buying centre may need to champion the idea by seriously evaluating the innovation in terms of its performance capabilities and its impact on revenues, costs and profits. Most likely, someone with substantial organisational power has to be won over to advocate the new technology; the innovation-buying champion (IBC) has to be able to handle the personal criticism he or she is likely to receive about causing problems (for example, 'extra work for us in testing something that we don't need and does not meet our specs').

The IBC concept for a superior new technology is analogous to the product champion concept in developing and marketing a new technology (Burgleman, 1983; Madique, 1980; Schon, 1967). Peters and Waterman (1982) propose that product champions are found for almost all successful innovations. This proposal probably holds true for several organisations developing, marketing and buying a superior new technology: manufacturing firms including suppliers to the new technology firm; third parties; and lead users. If the IBC concept is viable, research is needed to identify such persons and the streams of interactions, decisions and events included in their support of the adoption of the superior new technology and in overcoming resistance to change.

INITIAL THEORY OF CUSTOMER REJECTION OF SUPERIOR NEW MANUFACTURING TECHNOLOGIES AND NEW PRODUCT SERVICE INNOVATIONS

Figure 7.1 is a summary of some of the propositions described in the previous section. The model shown in the figure is intended as a rudimentary expert system (see Harmon and Sawyer, 1990) of acceptance or rejection of new superior technologies. The model represents a general framework of the set of heuristics and events operating through time that lead an enterprise to embrace or reject a new superior technology. Thus the attempt is to respond to Sheth's (1996) call for theory development beyond case study description to reach abstract theories, laws and principles.

The new technology evaluation and adoption/rejection model in Figure 7.1 represents a simplified binary decision process model intended to reflect buyer information processing and decision processes often implemented in evaluating new, superior manufacturing technologies. Certainly, not all persons responsible for buying the installed base technology or evaluating new, superior technologies follow the decision routes shown in Figure 7.1. However, the model is a simplified summary of the reality often faced by marketers and buyers of new superior technologies.

The model is based on intensive interviews of channel members, including customers and third parties, involved in marketing and adopting or rejecting a new industrial technology. Details of this empirical study are reported in the next section. This new technology evaluation model was developed using a 'think aloud' (van Someren *et al.*, 1994) methodology as well as a summary 'gatekeeping' (Montgomery, 1975) analysis of key questions raised and answered by buyers considering information about new technologies. Montgomery (1975) developed a similar gatekeeper model from interviews with three supermarket channel buyers evaluating 124 new product proposals. Gatekeeper modelling includes hierarchy threshold analysis. With this, the researcher searches for a variable and for a value of that variable that enables him or her to reach a classification decision for all or a part of his or her sample while making very few errors. Following this initial classification, the researcher searches for additional variables for further classification until a classification is reached that indicates acceptance or rejection of the alternative of which the research is focused (for example, adoption or rejection of a new technology).

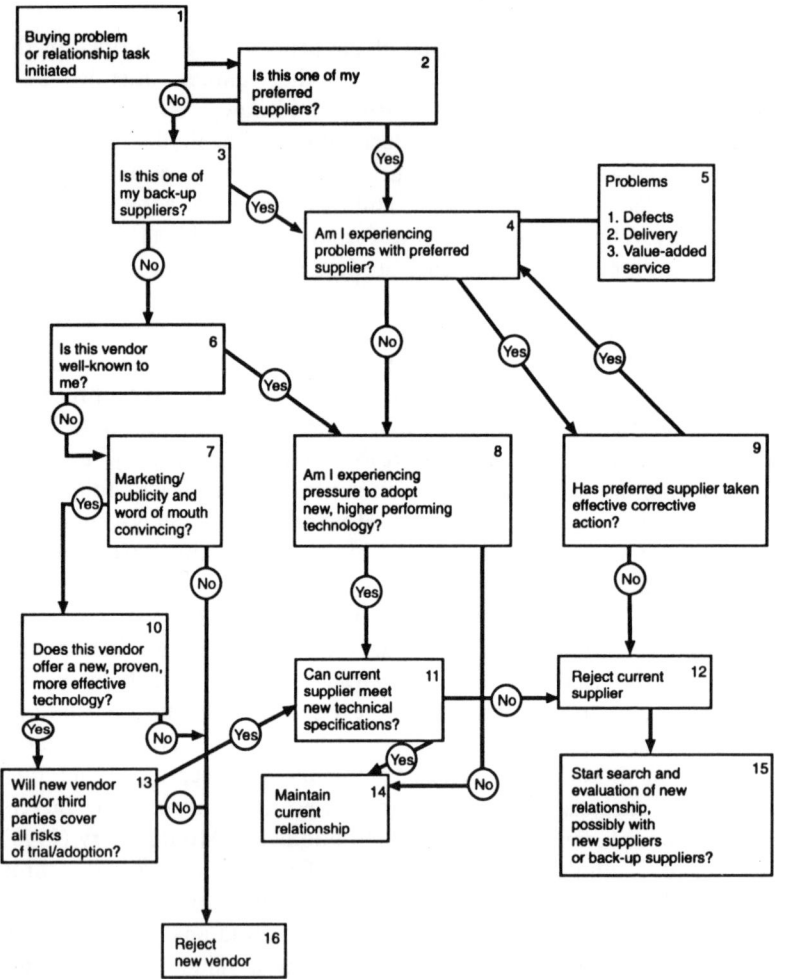

Figure 7.1   Buyer model of industrial supplier rejection, relationship
continuation and search for new supplier relationships

Among the advantages of Montgomery's modelling approach is that it appears to be a less labour-intensive way of developing a process model than more traditional methods. On the other hand, there is no assurance that the resulting model has any descriptive validity. Rather, the approach provides a heuristic for developing an 'optimal' node sequence, 'optimal' in the sense that it appears to minimise the amount of information processing necessary to arrive at a decision. Such an approach offers a means to attain parsimony, and a criterion by which to evaluate and perhaps to attempt to modify descriptively valid information-processing models (Hulbert, 1981, pp. 35, 39). Wind (1967a, 1967b, pp. 106–9) used a similar 'think aloud' research method to collect data for buyers' evaluation of a hypothetical new part needed by an R&D engineer. While several similarities exist in both the methodologies and findings, Wind's model does not consider the issue of a new technology replacing an installed base technology.

While the model summarised in Figure 7.1 appears to be a micro analysis of information search and decision making, the description included offers only a broad outline of the way buyers address related issues in evaluating superior new technologies against installed base technologies. Marketers and scholars interested in the way a new technology overcomes the installed base effect would want to learn the detailed, individual and group, mental steps involved in going from box 10 to box 13 in Figure 7.1. In response to this issue, research findings reported here and elsewhere (Woodside and Sherrell, 1980; Woodside and Wilson, 1994) indicate that buyers prefer to include a period of local, in plant testing of the new technology whenever possible, before adopting the new technology.

The Starting Point of the Model: Prior Experience with the Vendor

Note in Figure 7.1 that, in response to being asked to consider a new technology (box 1), a buyer asks himself/herself if this is one of their preferred suppliers (box 2). Typical questions include the following: 'Do I know this guy? Am I buying from him/her now? Do I trust him/her? Do I know for sure that the manufacturer he or she represents produces high-quality workpieces that meet my firm's engineering standards at a price I can live with?'

Because the innovation process often comes through manufacturers and lead users outside the existing channel manufacturing, marketing and purchasing the installed base technology, the buyer is often unfamiliar with the industrial manufacturing representative, the manufacturer and the new technology itself. Consequently, for new superior technologies the route most often taken from box 2 is to box 3 and from boxes 3 to 6. The need to create new relationships among new channel members is a central requirement in gaining adoptions of new superior technologies and the lack of buyer knowledge and working relationships in such new channels is a primary cause of early rejection of new technologies.

The Customer Considers the New Superior Technology: Getting in and out of Boxes 7 and 10

To achieve consideration and further evaluation, the information about the performance characteristics of the new superior technology needs to be overwhelming, supported by third party sources judged by the customer to be reliable, and able to withstand the immediate attack by sources loyal to the installed base technology. Most superior new technologies fail to meet all three of these requirements among current buyers or users of the installed base technology. Consequently, for most current customers of the installed base technology, the answer to box 7 in Figure 7.1 is negative. Thus, box 16 is reached: both the new vendor and the new technology are rejected.

Offering Overwhelming Relative Advantages

To overcome the installed base effect, the relative advantages (Rogers and Shoemaker, 1971; Soete, 1985) of adopting the new superior technology have to be overwhelming compared to the installed base technology with regard to three dimensions of quality: (1) a combination of better or greater numbers of performance features in the workpiece, (2) more consistent quality (for example, greater than sixth sigma defect free performance), and (3) higher fitness in use and customer satisfaction. Also this combination of relative advantages should be offered at a lower, total operating life cost to the customer for the new as compared to the installed technology. In the 1990s, the replacement of natural fuel based technologies by electronic technologies in manufacturing are examples of such combinations of higher quality (performance, consistency and fitness-in-use quality) with lower total operating life cost (see Woodside, 1994; Gross *et al.*, 1995).

Support by Third Party Sources

A second necessity is for third-party sources to provide testimonial support concerning the relative advantages and lower cost of the new technology. Such endorsements help to counter the argument offered by members of the customer firm that, 'our local situation [industry, company, operating site] is unique and it would not work here'. Herbig *et al.* (1995, p. 391) also stress this negative view towards the new technology. 'While potential adopters know about the innovation, many do not know enough about its actual performance within their own specific economic environment. This uncertainty (risk) often leads to the inertia inherent in the installed base effect.'

A localised on-site test of the new technology may be required by the customer firm to overcome the 'it can't work here' objection. Examples of such field tests of new technologies have been reported for MRO items (Woodside and Sherrell, 1980) and potable water treatment plants (Woodside and Wilson, 1994).

Withstanding Attacks from People Loyal to the Installed Base Technology

Several types of argument against serious evaluation of a new superior technology are likely to arise: (1) we have no time or budget to evaluate the new technology; (2) why fix something that is not broken; (3) the new technology has a serious operating flaw that prevents our adoption; (4) our situation is unique; (5) its physical and performance features do not meet our engineering standards; (6) the risks of operating with the new technology are too great because of the financial risks and the possible harmful impact on relationships with our customers, (7) we have no funds available to test the new technology locally; (8) the suppliers of the installed base technology are also our customers and we will harm these relationships if we replace the installed technology with the new one. Consequently, negative responses to box 10 often occur for most users of installed base technologies.

Providing convincing additional evidence in favour of a new superior technology to meet these counterattacks usually involves a multi-party, network marketing strategy of the manufacturer of the new technology and their close working with channel members and third-parties. Gaining the support of customers' customers (CCs) for the new technology by demonstrating its relative advantages and having CCs champion the new technology has been found to help overcome the inertia inherent in the installed base effect (see discussion in Woodside, 1994).

In addition, at some point in the adoption process a new technology champion inside the customer needs to emerge at the customer's site. An example of such a new-tech champion is found in case study research reports in industrial marketing and purchasing (for example, Woodside, 1981a). This level of detail in the adoption process is not included in Figure 7.1.

Covering All Risks of Trial and Adoption (Box 13)

Given the multiple reasons for not adopting the new, superior technology and the lack of marketing and customer knowledge and financial resources of many new technology manufacturers (see Oakey, 1991), involvement by third parties often becomes a necessity in providing the technical and financial resources required by customer firms to install, test and adopt the new technologies. For several new electronic technologies used in manufacturing, starting in the 1980s in the USA some electric utility companies served this third-party role to provide technical and financial support for their commercial customers.

Examples of such marketing programmes include the new technology marketing programmes offered by Duke Power in North and South Carolina and Entergy Corporation in Louisiana, Arkansas and Mississippi; such programmes include paying for all testing costs and, in some cases, for the new technology manufacturing equipment as well as guaranteeing that the new technology will surpass the performance of the installed base technology (see Woodside, 1994). Biemans (1989) reports details of third party support for both marketers and customers in adoptions of new medical equipment in hospitals in The Netherlands. More complex networks of firms supporting the adoption of new technologies in extensive case studies are reported by Hakansson and Snehota (1995).

Suppliers of the Installed Base Technology Meeting the New Technology Challenge (Box 11)

After effectively holding back the adoption of a new superior technology, almost all manufacturers and marketers of the installed base technology fail to change in time. Cooper (1986) reports that, in 56 of 58 cases of major innovations studied, the established or dominant firm failed to make the necessary transition to the next generation of superior technology. Imparato and Harari (1994) offer useful heuristics for practising the necessary creative destruction to 'jump the technology curve'.

Note that box 11 in Figure 7.1 emphasises the status quo benefits of the supplier of the installed base technology. Most customers would prefer to be able to buy the new technology from trusted suppliers; industrial customers are supportive of long term relationships with their suppliers (see Kalwani and Narayandas, 1995). However, if supporters of the new technology are able to reach box 11 in Figure 7.1, they are less likely to be thwarted from gaining a share of a customer's requirements by actions of suppliers of the installed base technology. Similar to manufacturers of new technologies not planning on counterattacks by suppliers of the installed base technology, most suppliers of the installed base never believe box 11 can be reached by suppliers of new technologies until it is too late.

EMPIRICALLY TESTING THE MODEL

The model of rejection of superior new industrial technologies was developed from a review of relevant literature and from one set of data on channel and customer evaluations of a new technology. Adequate testing of such a model requires the use of an additional set of data (see Howard and Morgenroth, 1968; Morgenroth, 1964; Gladwin, 1989). Thus two sets of data were collected and used; both sets were interviews with channel members and buyers involved in marketing or purchasing the installed base and new technologies.

The New Technology and the Installed Base Technology

Fibreglass reinforced poles (FRPs) for lighting (lamp posts) were the new technological innovation selected for study for several reasons. First, in a pretest of six industrial buyers responsible for buying (lamp posts), all six reported that FRPs were representative of a new technology competing with installed base technologies. Second, at the time of the study some knowledge of FRPs was widely held by marketing firms and customers with some customers having completed evaluation processes leading to rejection or adoption of the new technology. In the USA, FRPs were marketed commercially for the first time in the mid 1970s. In the late 1990s the total market share of this new technology was less than 4 per cent, even though several independent tests confirmed superior operating performance and lower lifetime costs for the new technologies (see, for example, Woodside, 1980).

Third, widespread co-operation was available for interviews from marketing channel members and customers on the topic of adopting or rejecting new technologies. Fourth, one of the six US manufacturers of the new technology funded the study to learn 'why the new technology was not being adopted by customers and what could be done about it': what strategy could be implemented that would be effective in gaining adoptions and reaching profitable levels of sales. The researcher was given a free hand in designing and implementing the study and in examining the manufacturer's financial and marketing documents and customer files. After some initial hesitation, senior managers in the manufacturing firm agreed to a 12-month time-table for the study and a multiple approach to data collection.

Lamp posts represent a MRO (maintenance, repair, and operating) purchase in most buying tasks. Total purchases in the USA were estimated to range from $85 to $120 million through the 1980s, with about 55 per cent of purchases for street and highway lighting and 45 per cent for area, sports and other off-street use (such as parking lots). At the time of the study, and after several years of marketing the new technology and gaining repeat business from some customers, executives of the holding company owning the FRP manufacturing firm were considering terminating FRP production because of continual low returns on the investment compared to the returns of other firms owned by the holding company.

Within Sheth's (1981) typology of innovation resistance, FRPs represent dual high resistance innovations: high perceived risk for the adopter and an attempt to change an existing practice (using the installed base technologies of steel and aluminium poles). The perceived risk of buying FRPs is high, for several reasons. Some members of the buying centre, as well as suppliers of the installed base technology, argue against buying FRPs. For example, 'Fibreglass is so limber, it tends to whip around in the wind,' says David O'Brien, president of Hapco, a producer of aluminium poles (Pierson, 1990, B4). Social risk and possibly job loss risk may be associated with FRPs; for example, the following argument summarises one engineer's comments about FRPs to a buyer of lighting standards: 'Why take up my time and take me away from other projects to test FRPs, when we already have approved suppliers meeting company standards?' Also, if FRPs do fail more than the installed base technology in wind storms, or in other circumstances, the innovation-buying champion may be blamed for the economic loss and related customer complaints.

Table 7.1 summarises the features and benefits considered most often in rejection or adoption of FRPs to replace steel poles. As is shown, FRPs have several substantial advantages over steel standards that translate into lower total life cycle costs (see Thompson *et al.*, 1994) and greater safety in installation and operation. The bottom two rows of Table 7.1 are the issues particularly critical for success and failure for FRPs. Rejectors of FRPs emphasised the dangers of operating failure of the new technology in wind storms 'unique to our operating system', while adopters used broader comparisons which included other systems.

For some (not all) customer industries, new written engineering standards were required if they were to adopt FRPs. Some people, most often engineers in the department testing and approving product standards, resisted the new technology and emphasised that FRPs did not meet the written specifications for lighting standards and, therefore, could not be purchased. If the question then arose about changing the specifications, resistance would be expressed: for example, 'Why should we go through the cost, time and effort when we have suppliers that meet the specs?'

Sampling and Procedure

The method used face-to-face and telephone interviews of 'key informant' decision makers within organisations to learn who did what,

Table 7.1 Comparisons of principal current and new technologies

Attribute	Steel	Fibreglass
Painting/coating required?	yes	no
Corrosion/moisture a problem?	yes	no
Electrical grounding required?	yes	no
Price volatility a problem?	yes	no
Question of availability?	yes	no
Total installed costs in comparisons to steel	100%	78%
Estimated average lifetime costs (base: steel)	100%	72%
Meets rigidity wind requirements?	yes	yes
Meets existing, written, engineering specs?	yes	no

when, why, how and what happened next. Respondents were asked to participate in a study to learn how people in a number of different companies interact with each other when selling and buying standard and new MRO items. The purpose of the study was to learn about all the people and companies involved in selling, buying and servicing major purchases of an MRO and what functions each performed.

Each person in each organisation contacted was asked the name of the person involved directly in marketing, buying and using light poles. In each organisation attempts were made to interview additional staff involved in marketing and buying the product category by asking, 'Who else might it be helpful for me to speak with about buying [selling, installing, using] light poles in your company [organisation]?' Interviews of random samples of customer firms and a survey of the majority ($n = 22$) of manufacturing sales agents (MSAs) of one manufacturer of the new technology were undertaken. A 'snowballing' interview procedure was used to interview industrial distributors, other channel members (for example, additional types of sales agents and electrical contractors), and third parties involved in marketing and buying the new technology.

In total, 137 interviews were completed over a 14-month period; the co-operation rate for completed interviews was greater than 95 per cent. The high degree of co-operation was achieved as the result of several factors. First, field work began with a participant observation (Reason, 1994; Whyte, 1984) study of behaviour and interactions of the sales manager with MSAs, and MSAs with customers; and analysis of the customer files of the FRP manufacturer funding the study. Specific names, addresses and telephone numbers of all customers (prospects and buyers) from the start of their relationships with MSAs and/or the manufacturer were examined. Open ended questions were asked in person and by telephone.

Telephone interviews with MSAs assigned sales territories for selling the manufacturer's FRPs followed initial contact by letter. Two letters were sent in the same envelope. One letter was written by the sales manager of the manufacturing firm, and described the purpose of the study in general terms, requesting co-operation when contacted by the researcher. The second letter was written by the researcher: This letter expressed gratitude to the person participating in the study and mentioned that the researcher would telephone and request a face-to-face meeting. A total of six such interviews were completed in six different sales regions and 16 telephone interviews were completed in 16 additional sales regions.

The face to face interviews were completed in four to seven hours; more than half-a-day per interview was necessary when these interviews included one or two sales visits to a customer's location (four interviews included such sales calls). Each telephone interview was 30 to 45 minutes in length; a 23-item, three-page, open-ended interview form was used for the telephone interviews.

Interviews were completed in person and by telephone with one to four people in 37 electric utility companies and 17 governmental units (mostly municipalities). Personal, on-site interviews were completed with one to four persons in six utility companies, five installation contractors, 11 industrial distributors, four construction contractors, six alternative type MSAs (explained below), nine electrical contractors and 17 site location users (for example, subdivision developers, home-owner organisations, shopping mall developers and tenants). Also multiple individual and group interviews were held over 10 months with executives, engineers and the sales manager of the FRP manufacturer co-operating in the study.

Attempts to interview by telephone some channel member participants in marketing or buying light poles were both successful and unsuccessful, depending upon industry sector. Telephone interviews were most successful with buyers, engineers and branch managers of electric utility companies (all those contacted by phone participated in the telephone interviews and/or face to face interviews); telephone interviews were highly unsuccessful with electric contractors (none of these respondents was willing to talk on the phone for more than five minutes).

However, co-operation and completion rates were very high (above 90 per cent) for all persons when face-to-face interviews were requested. For the majority (70) of all on site interviews, initial contacts were made by letter, followed by telephone contact, and finally by face-to-face interview.

Additional Instruments

Individual customer files kept by the co-operating FRP manufacturer were analysed to learn about the customers' relationships with this manufacturer. Many of the analyses described by Cardozo *et al.* (1988) were completed to learn customer segments, by heavy and light users, as well as non-buyers; industry categories; years of relationship; frequency of orders; specific types of FRPs purchased; and annual buying trends for individual accounts.

FINDINGS

Key Findings from the FRP Manufacturer's Files on Customers and from Interviews with the FRP Manufacturing Firm and its Manufacturing Agents

Sales and customer documents of the FRP manufacturer matched a key finding from the personal interviews: about 90 per cent of poles were purchased by buyers placing orders with local area industrial distributors. Thus industrial distributors were the largest number of customers appearing in the FRP manufacturer's customer file: over 50 percent of all buyers are industrial distributors. Most industrial distributors (IDs) purchased one to 15 poles annually from the FRP manufacturer. In most cases the IDs' customers were unknown to the FRP manufacturer before the study was started. Senior managers and the sales manager of the FRP manufacturing firm assumed that most FRPs were being purchased by electrical utility companies from IDs.

The majority of prospects (that is, known buyers of lighting poles but non-buyers of the FRP manufacturer's products) in the customer file were electric utility companies. A large electrical utility company's (EUC's) annual lighting pole requirements range from 500 to 2000 poles per month (for example, Woodside, 1981a). At the time of the study and still today (1996) almost all electrical utility companies have formal engineering standards for lighting poles which specify steel or aluminium poles. Thus EUCs were a particularly attractive customer target for the FRP manufacturer for several years before the start of the study. Becoming a sole source supplier for one large EUC would increase the FRP manufacturer's annual sales by more than 1000 per cent. Thus the FRP manufacturer concentrated its marketing strategy exclusively on gaining EUC and municipality customers. Local government municipalities often purchased poles for street lighting from EUCs, with the local EUCs buying the poles from local industrial distributors.

However, this manufacturer has only ever made one major sale of FRPs to a major EUC. In 1979, after a successful installation (a field test) of five poles in 1978, a total of 300 FRPs were purchased from the manufacturer by Houston Power & Light Company (HP&L). In this case, a facilities engineer (Bobby Burgess), formerly in HP&L's engineering standards department, recommended a large scale test of FRPs; Mr Burgess had enough influence at HP&L to overcome the objections of other members of the informal buying centre.

In search of an alternative, in 1979, Burgess recommended a test installation of 1000 FRP poles after a successful installation of five of these poles in 1978. The recommendation was based on a lower installed cost of the FRP poles due to lower labour cost and handling charges, compared to costs for installing steel and concrete [poles]. The purchasing and civil engineering departments suggested testing fewer FRP poles because of the company's limited experience with the poles and because the existing written specifications called for steel octagonal poles.

Accordingly, a total of 300 30-ft FRP poles have been installed in residential areas in downtown Houston. These poles serve a lighting system powered by a street-side located, underground cable system. All the poles were direct buried to a depth of 5 ft, and set atop a 10 × 10 × 2-in. concrete pad to prevent settling. One yard of stabilizer sand was placed in the hole with each pole. Unlike steel-pole installations, no copper-wire grounding was necessary because FRP poles are nonconducting. (Woodside, 1981a)

The successful marketing and buying of 300 FRPs in HP&L's operating area indicated to the FRP manufacturer that a marketing strategy could be designed successfully to market such poles to EUCs. However, for the next five years, no other EUC placed a similar order for FRP poles and HP&L did not become a repeat customer. The manufacturing sales agents contracted to sell the FRPs made sales calls on several different people in different EUC departments. These MSA carried product lines of 20 to 40 manufacturers; they worked almost exclusively with EUCs as their customers. The MSAs also sometimes called on government municipalities and local industrial distributors.

Details of the main participants and their relationships are indicated in Figure 7.2, where boxes 1 and 2 represent competing manufacturers of FRPs and poles made of competing materials, respectively. Both of these manufacturers hire the same type of MSAs to call on EUCs. The sales managers in the manufacturing firms often made joint sales calls with the MSAs. In some cases, a government municipality hires a construction contractor to buy lighting poles. The contractors then contact the EUC to order the poles. In the majority of cases the EUC buys lighting poles from a local industrial distributor. Also the EUC usually hires a separate firm, a local installation contractor, to actually install the poles.

The participants and principal communication flows summarised in Figure 7.2 represent the single view-of-reality offered by the FRP

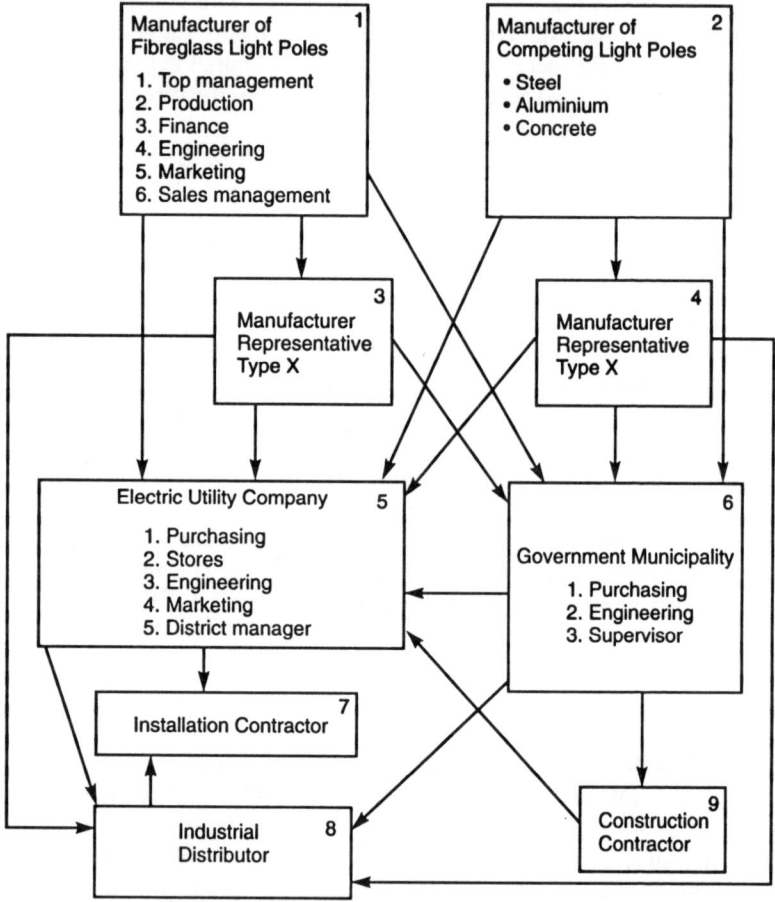

Figure 7.2 'Current reality' and principal communication flows in the marketing channel rejecting the new technology

manufacturer and the firm's MSAs participating in the study. When asked about other customer categories, the MSAs admitted that FRPs were sometimes made for electrical contractors and other types of customers, but such sales represented 'small potatoes compared to purchases made by any medium to large size EUC'.

Examining the Buyer Model of Rejection Applied to FRPs

Table 7.2 is a summary of the frequencies of use of paths found in the buyer model of rejection of FRPs. This summary is based on interviews with buyers and staff in other departments in the 37 EUCs. Data from 24 EUCs were used to build the model summarised in Figure 7.l; the resulting model was tested on a sample of 13 EUC interviews. The model is based on responses to a series of awareness and information-processing questions, and 'what if' scenarios, presented to respondents to learn what their firms do, and would do, when buying lighting poles and innovations in lighting poles.

In building and testing ethnographic decision tree models as shown in Figure 7.1 and Table 7.2, Gladwin (1989) recommends sample sizes of 40-plus cases, each for developing and testing the model. Thus the model summarised in Figure 7.1 and the results shown in Table 7.2 are exploratory and highly limited by small sample sizes. The sample of ten EUC case interviews was selected randomly from the total set of 37 EUC firms studied.

Table 7.2 Use of model paths in original and test samples of electrical utility companies

Path											Model development sample	Test sample
(A)	1	2	4	8	14						7	6
(B)	1	2	3	4	8	14					3	1
(C)	1	2	3	4	9	4	8	14			3	1
(D)	1	2	3	6	7	16					5	2
(E)	1	2	3	6	7	10	16				3	0
(F)	1	2	3	6	7	10	13	11	12	15	1	0
(G)	1	2	3	6	7	10	13	16			2	3
Total											24	13

Path A shown in Table 7.2 occurred most frequently in both samples of EUC firms. This path was explained by EUC buyers and other EUC decision makers as the one by which lighting poles were often purchased. This buying strategy can be summarised by the following statement, 'I buy from my preferred supplier, unless there is a problem with this supplier, and problems rarely occur.' 'Problem' might include defects, inability to deliver when needed and inability to provide value added services (such as bracket-arms to mount on top of the poles).

Path B indicates that a back up supplier is the vendor being considered. Such a back up supplier offers products and services that meet current specifications. Back up suppliers are used infrequently, mainly when a problem is being experienced with a preferred supplier.

Path C indicates that a problem is being experienced with a preferred supplier. Usually, if box 9 is reached, the problem is solved to the complete satisfaction of the EUC executive requesting the preferred supplier to solve the problem. Consequently, going from box 9 to box 12 occurs rarely; no case of such an event was found, but several EUC executives reported such events for other MRO items.

Path D indicates that the suppliers who are not used are little known to the EUC decision makers who are not convinced by the information provided by this vendor. Note, in Table 7.2, that no cases were found connecting box 6 to box 8: 'I've never heard of the company/manufacturer' usually reflects no buying experience with the manufacturer.

Path E indicates that a new product champion is being found or created in the customer firm: the connection between box 7 and 10 indicates that a decision maker in the EUC has requested other decision makers 'to look at' the new product being offered by the vendor. Reach box 10 occurred in 24 per cent of the 37 cases.

Path F represents some agreement in the customer firm that the innovation offers substantial advantages over the installed based technology *and* that somehow risks of testing and adopting the innovation and new vendor relationship can be reduced to an acceptable level (box 13). The one case found described by path F is the HP&L case. However, even this did not result in FRPs replacing the installed base technology for this customer.

Path G occurred more often than path F: the decision was made by the EUC that the risk was too great to test the innovation. The sales manager and senior executives of the FRP manufacturing firm had no strategies for handling customer risk-related issues.

An Alternative Marketing Channel

Given that sales of the FRPs were increasing annually at a slow rate and the product was not being bought by EUCs, somebody else had to be buying them. Who were these customers? In what ways were the poles being used? What marketing channels were being utilised to reach these customers? Additional interviews in the field work uncovered customers other than EUCs who were willing to consider innovative materials for their lighting pole requirements. A representative marketing channel and third party participants of these customers are summarised in Figure 7.3. Commercial developers and their electrical contractors are the customers in this second market channel. Most lighting pole requirements are for off street (for example, parking lot) use by these customers. Most applications involve small purchases: (one to ten poles). In the USA, type X MSAs calling on EUCs do not call on commercial developers and electrical contractors; they specialise in calling on EUCs (see Figure 7.2). However, type Y MSAs specialise in calling on commercial developers, electrical contractors and other parties involved in buying MRO items, for example, architects and site users (see Figure 7.3). Types X and Y MSAs are familiar with each other but rarely have contact with each other; both have national trade organisations.

Because most sales of the FRPs were made through industrial distributors, the FRP manufacturer was unaware that the majority of the innovative poles were being purchased by commercial developers via electrical contractors. In fact, the sales manager and senior executives were unaware that type Y MSAs existed. When the availability of type Y MSAs was mentioned to a sample of five X MSAs, all five explained that such MSAs were 'small potatoes' and calling on electrical contractors would be unprofitable for them (X MSAs). All the product lines carried by X MSAs focused on EUC requirements only. Also the following statement was made by X MSAs, 'Don't go mentioning these [Y] reps to the [FRP manufacturer] because it will create problems in getting credit for orders.' Given that most orders from both electrical contractors and EUCs were made from their local industrial distributors, tracking purchases to customers of the industrial distributors would result in conflicts as to whether X or Y MSAs should receive sales commissions.

The following abstract is representative of a case study example of the several firms interviewed that includes a Y MSA.

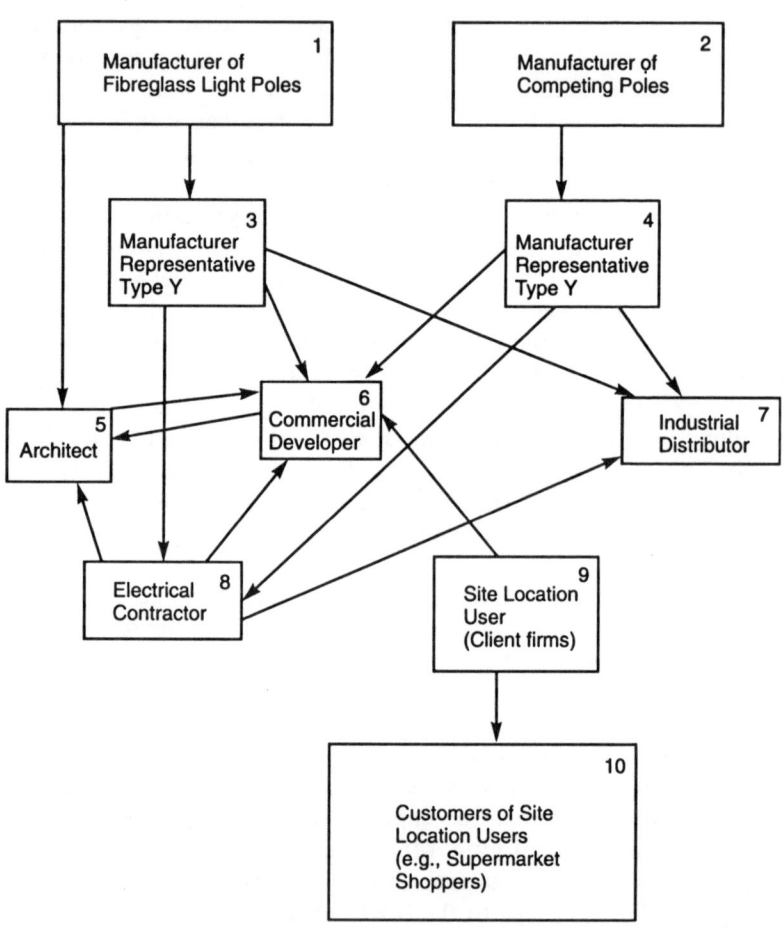

Figure 7.3   'Alternative reality' and principal communication flows in the marketing channel accepting the new technology

In Greenville, South Carolina, First Carolina Developer's Skip
Snedigar [commercial developer] stated that the quotes received on
purchasing and installing two 35–ft steel poles in the parking lot of a
new Winn Dixie supermarket were 'completely out of budget'. He
asked architect David Narramore to help find a solution. [Narra-
more asked an electrical contractor to recommend a solution.] The
electrical contractor, West Electrical Contractor of Newbury, Inc.,
recommended using fiberglass reinforced poles (FRPs) instead of
metal poles. The total cost of using the FRP was 43 percent less than
the lowest bid received for metal poles. (Woodside, 1981b)

Electrical contractors were central contacts in this alternative marketing channel. Reaching electrical contractors effectively required the
development of a new marketing channel, with Y MSAs, for the
fibreglass reinforcement pole manufacturer. Consequently, a hybrid
marketing channel was designed over the objections of X MSAs. This
hybrid channel and its principal relationships are summarised in Figure
7.4. Two channels to two different sets of customers are included in this
hybrid design, resulting in co-ordination difficulties and MSA X versus
Y conflicts. As described by Moriarty and Moran (1990, p. 146), such
'hybrid systems are hard to manage – and an important way to increase
sales and decrease costs'.

The industrial marketing channel on the right-hand side of Figure
7.4 represents the system designed by the manufacturer; this channel
focuses on EUCs as the principal customers and site users. The
marketing channel on the left-hand side of Figure 7.4 represents the
unplanned system that developed on its own; that is, the system was
not designed by the FRP manufacturer but generated by interest in the
new product by a principal party in the network (that is, the electrical
contractors). The ultimate use of lighting poles in this alternative
channel was in off-street (for example, parking lot) applications. These
electrical contractors were lead users (von Hippel, 1988) of the innovation. They were not customers identified by the FRP manufacturer or
its X MSAs. However, the majority of sales of FRPs involved electrical
contractors via industrial distributors and not EUCs.

Successful resolutions of MSA channel conflicts involved direct
participation in customer relationships by the FRP manufacturer,
including direct sales calls with both X and Y MSAs and their
customers by the FRP manufacturing firm's sales manager. Hiring
and training assistant sales managers were necessary to develop the
number of contacts to accomplish this objective. Also the customer

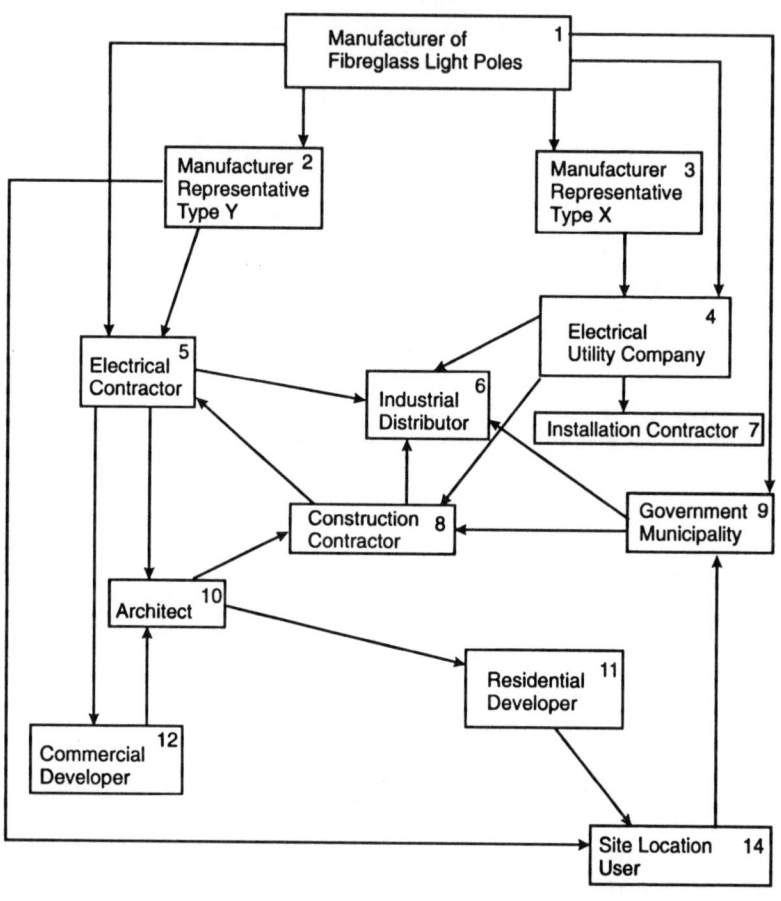

Figure 7.4   Revised parallel/overlapping realities leading to successful market introduction of new technology

database needed to be extended and deepened to account for layers of customers (the customer of the customer's customer) in order to plan and implement effective marketing strategies. The results of the study served to refocus the manufacturer's marketing strategy on 'small potato customers' as opposed to the customers the manufacturer found most attractive (the EUCs). The study ended before results were learned on the profitability of the firm's revised marketing strategy.

EXAMINING THE THEORETICAL PROPOSITIONS

Chaos in Successful Innovations

The first proposition is supported by the findings in the FRP study: managing technological innovation marketing and adoption is controlled chaos. Certainly the more controlled, initial channel design was less chaotic than the revised, more complex design.

The micro propositions were supported by the field study. MPI: the innovation was individually motivated; a buying champion emerged in an unplanned marketing channel. MP2: marketing and adopting the technological innovation was opportunistic and required interactive learning; the FRP manufacturer learned that X MSAs were distinct from Y MSAs and Y MSAs were needed to reach customers who would buy the innovation. MP3: successful marketing and adopting of the technological innovation was customer-responsive; in fact, the manufacturer had to change the firm's selected customer on the basis of the lower or higher responsiveness to the new product of different customer segments. MP4: marketing and adopting the technological innovation was tumultuous; tumult was found in marketing the FRPs successfully, in that the manufacturer had to create a new channel design over the objections of currently used X MSAs. MP5: innovation marketing and adopting processes were nonlinear; the FRPs were pulled through an unplanned marketing channel by customers unknown, and only indirectly linked to the manufacturer.

Support Found for P2: New Channel Connections with New Customers were Required

The FRP field study resulted in learning about new customers who were not mentioned by executives of the FRP manufacturing firm during the first few months of the study. The product would probably have been cancelled without the development of the new relationships shown in Figures 7.3 and 7.4, compared with Figure 7.2.

P3 Supported: Rejection of New Superior Technology by Heavy Users of the Installed Based Technology is Associated with Lack of Familiarity and Experience in Buying from the Manufacturer of the New Technology

The FRPs and their manufacturer represented two unknowns for customers. EUC customers were uncomfortable in starting relationships with new, unknown vendors. Consequently, as noted by Beard and Easingwood (1992, p. 18), 'the credibility of the producer is highly important', and rejection of both the innovation and the new vendor is the likely outcome among heavy users of the installed based technology.

P4 Supported: Defensive Marketing Tactics Observed

Marketers of the installed based technology attacked the FRPs on the basis of performance risk: the claim was often made by manufacturers of metal poles that FRPs would whip around, break, fall down and/or bend and stay down in a wind storm. Posing this fear was enough to persuade nearly all EUCs not to consider buying FRPs.

Support Found for P5: Third-party Involvement Necessary for Adoption

Several parties had to be convinced before purchase. The electrical contractor's role was one of recommending the purchase of the FRPs to the commercial developer; the electrical contractor thus served as a third-party buying champion for the new technology in a new network of relationships previously unknown by the FRP manufacturer.

Support Found for P6: Appearance of Innovation-buying Champion Necessary to Overcome Resistance if the Innovation is to Replace the Installed Base Technology

Innovation-buying champions (IBCs) were found among both EUC customers and electrical contractors. Within EUCs, the IBCs were unsuccessful in overcoming the resistance of other members of informal buying centres involved in changing lighting pole purchases from routine purchases to modified rebuys. Engineers in EUCs argued that the FRPs 'did not meet the specs' (engineering specifications). When asked who set the specs, these engineers would respond, 'I do.' When asked about testing the FRPs and writing new specs, frequent responses included the following: There's no need, the poles we buy now work well.' 'It's a lot of work.' 'Why should I?' 'I have lots of things to do now.'

However, purchases of the installed base technologies by electrical contractors did not involve written specifications other than specifying a lighting pole requirement. Such purchases were not a monthly requirement. When such purchases did occur, they did not involve using well-established supplier–customer relationships. An individual order was often one to ten poles not 500 to 1000 poles. Among electrical contractors, little resistance was found in their learning.

CENTRAL CONCLUSIONS AND SUGGESTIONS FOR FUTURE RESEARCH

The focus in this chapter has been on the seemingly unexpected: market failure of proven, superior, new industrial technologies. The central conclusions of the reported field study include the following points. Overcoming resistance in the marketing channel and among heavy users of the installed base technology is a task more formidable than was probably realised by manufacturers of superior new technologies. Finding and serving customers responsive to the benefits of adopting the superior new technologies probably requires developing hybrid marketing channel relationships.

Theories of customer rejection and acceptance of new superior technologies would benefit from comprehensive descriptions of the streams of behaviour, decisions and networks of relationships that occur through several months of marketing and evaluating the technologies. To do such work involves a triangulation of data collection methods (Denzin, 1978; Jick, 1979), getting face-to-face with some respondents, and considerable time. Mail surveys do not permit learning about the unknown relationships and third-party participation that we can identify by getting out into the field.

References

Arabie, P. and Y. Wind (1994) 'Marketing and Social Networks', in S. Wasserman and J. Galaskiewicz (eds), *Advances in Social Network Analysis* (Thousand Oaks, CA.: Sage).

Argyris, C. (1985) *Strategy, Change and Defensive Routines* (Boston: Pitman).

Associated Press (1994) 'GAO Says Billions Spent, Little Done at Nuclear Sites', *The Advocate*, 1 September, D1.

Baker, M. J. and S. J. Hart (1989) *Marketing and Competitive Success* (London: Philip Allen).

Beard, C. and C. Easingwood (1992) 'Sources of Competitive Advantage in the Marketing of Technology Intensive Products and Services', *European Journal of Marketing*, 26 (12), 5–18.

Benedetto, C. A. di (1994) 'Defining Markets and Users for New Technologies', in W. E. Souder and J. D. Shemlan (eds), *Managing New Technology Development* (New York: McGraw-Hill), 73–115.

Biemans, W. G. (1989) *Developing Innovations within Networks* (Eindhoven: Technische Universiteit).

Biemans, W. G. (1990) 'The Managerial Implications of Networking', *European Management Journal*, 8 (4), December, 529–40.

Burgleman, R. A. (1983) 'A Process Model of Internal Corporate Venturing in the Diversified Major Firm', *Administrative Science Quarterly*, 28, (3), 223–44.

Cardozo, R. N., D. K. Smith, Jr. and M. Viswanathan (1988) 'Identifying Key Customers for Novel Industrial Products', *Journal of Product Innovation Management*, 5 (2), 102–13.

Cooper, A. and C. Smith (1992) 'How Established Firms Respond to Threatening Technologies', *The Academy of Management Executives*, 6 (2), 61–9.

Cooper, R. (1986) 'New Product Performance and Product Innovation', *Research Management*, 18, May/June, 17–25.

Denzin, N. K. (1978) *The Research Act* (New York: McGraw-Hill).

Drucker, P. (1994), 'Infoliteracy', *Forbes ASAP*, 29 August, 104–9.

Elg, U. and U. Johansson (1994) 'Cooperative Strategies and Interorganizational Inertia', Working Paper Series, Lund University, Sweden, School of Economics and Management.

Farrell, J. and G. Saloner (1985) 'Standardization, Compatibility and Innovation', *Rand Journal of Economics*, 16 (Spring), 70–83.

Gatignon, H. and T. S. Robertson (1989) 'Technology Diffusion: An Empirical Test of Competitive Effects', *Journal of Marketing*, 53 (January), 3549.

Gemunden, H. G. (1985) 'Promotors. Key Persons for the Development and Marketing of Innovative Industrial Products', in K. Backhaus and D. T. Wilson (eds), *Industrial Marketing: A German–American Perspective* (Berlin: Springer).

Gemunden, H. G. and A. Walter (1994) 'The Relationship Promotor – Key Person for Inter Organisational Innovation Cooperations', in J. N. Sheth and A. Parvatiyar (eds), *Relationship Marketing: Theory, Methods and Applications* (Atlanta: Emory University Center for Relationship Marketing) Section III.

Gemunden, H. G., P. Heydebreck and R. Herden (1992) 'Technological Interweavement: A Means of Achieving Innovation Success', *R & D Management*, 22 (Spring), 359–76.

Gladwin, C. H. (1989) *Ethnographic Decision Tree Modeling* (Newbury Park, CA: Sage).

Granovetter, M. (1973) 'The Strength of Weak Ties', *American Journal of Sociology*, 78, 1360–80.

Gross, N., P. Coy and O. Port (1995) 'The Technology Paradox', *Business Week*, 6 March, 76–81, 84.

Guiltinan, J. P. and G. W. Paul (1991) *Marketing Management: Strategies and Programs* (New York: McGraw-Hill).

Hakansson, H. and I. Snehota (eds) (1995) *Developing Relationships in Business Networks* (London: Routledge).

Harmon, P. and B. Sawyer (1990) *Creating Expert Systems for Business and Industry* (New York: Wiley).

Herbig, P. A. and H. Kramer (1993) 'Innovation Inertia: The Power of the Installed Base', *Journal of Business and Industrial Marketing*, 8 (3), 44–57.

Herbig, P. A., C. A. Howard and H. E. Kramer (1995) 'The Installed Base Effect: Implications for the Management of Innovation', *Journal of Marketing Management*, 11, July, 387–402.

Howard, J. A. and W. M. Morgenroth (1968) 'Information Processing Model of Executive Decisions', *Management Science*, 14, March, 416–28.

Hulbert, J. M. (1981) 'Descriptive Models of Marketing Decisions', in R. L. Schultz and A. A. Zoltners (eds), *Marketing Decision Models* (New York: North Holland) 19–53.

Hutt, M., P. H. Reingen and J. R. Ronchetto, Jr. (1988) 'Tracing Emergent Strategy Formation', *Journal of Marketing*, 52, January, 4–19.

Imparato, N., and O. Harari (1994) *Jumping the Curve* (San Francisco: Jossey Bass).

Jick, T. D. (1979) 'Mixing Qualitative and Quantitative Methods: Triangulation in Action', *Administrative Science Quarterly*, 24, December, 602–11.

Kalwani, M. and N. Narayandas (1995) 'Long Term Manufacturer–Supplier Relationships: Do They Pay Off for Supplier Firms?', *Journal of Marketing*, 59, January, 1–16.

Kotler, P. (1994) *Marketing Management* (Englewood Cliffs, NJ: Prentice-Hall).

Linestone, H. A., and D. Sahal (1976) *Technological Substitution* (New York: American Elsevier).

Lynch, J. E. (1994) 'Only Connect: The Role of Marketing and Strategic Management in the Modern Organisation', *Journal of Marketing Management*, 10, August, 527–42.

Madique, M. A. (1980) 'Entrepreneurs, Champions and Technological Innovations', *Sloan Management Review*, 21, Spring, 59–76.

Martino, J. P., K. L. Chen and R. C. Lenz, Jr. (1978) 'Predicting the Diffusion Rate of Industrial Innovation', *NTIS*, PS, 286–693, March.

Mintzberg, H. and J. A. Waters (1985) 'Of Strategies, Deliberate and Emergent', *Strategic Management Journal*, 6, April, 257–72.

Montgomery, D. B. (1975) 'New Product Distribution – An Analysis of Supermarket Buyer Decisions', *Journal of Marketing Research*, 12, August, 255–64.

Moore, W. L. and E. A. Pessemier (1993) *Product Planning and Management* (New York: McGraw-Hill).

Morgenroth, W. A. (1964) 'A Method for Understanding Price Determinants', *Journal of Marketing Research*, 1, August, 255–64.

Moriarty, R. and U. Moran (1990) 'Managing Hybrid Marketing Systems', *Harvard Business Review,* 68, November–December, 146–55.

Narasimhan, R., S. Ghosh and D. Mendez (1993) 'A Dynamic Model of Product Quality and Pricing Decisions', *Decision Sciences,* 24 (5), 893–908.

Nicosia, F. M. and Y. Wind (1977) 'Behavioural Models of Organisational Buying Processes', in F. M. Nicosia and Y. Wind (eds), *Behavioural Models for Market Analysis: Foundations for Marketing Action* (Hinsdale, Ill.: Dryden Press) 96–120.

Oakey, R. (1991) 'Innovation and the Management of Marketing in High Technology Firms', *Journal of Marketing Management,* 7 (4), 343–56.

Oakey, R., P. R. Tothwell and S. Y. Cooper (1990) *The Management of Innovation in High Technology Small Firms* (London: Pinter).

Peters, T. J. and R. H. Waterman, Jr. (1982) *In Search of Excellence* (New York: Harper & Row).

Pierson, L. (1990) 'Trying to Steal Market for Highway Light Poles', *Wall Street Journal,* 15 January, B4.

Quinn, J. B. (1985) 'Managing Innovation: Controlled Chaos', *Harvard Business Review,* May–June, 73–84.

Ram, S. (1987) 'A Model of Innovation Resistance', in M. Wallendorf and P. Anderson, (eds) *Advances in Consumer Research,* Vol. 14 (Provo, UT: Association for Consumer Research).

Reason, P. (1994) 'Three Approaches to Participative Inquiry', in N. K. Denzin and Y. S. Lincoln (eds), *Handbook of Qualitative Research* (Thousand Oaks, CA: Sage) 324–39.

Rogers, E. M., and F. F. Shoemaker (1971) *Communications of Innovations: A Cross Cultural Approach* (New York: Free Press).

Schon, D. A. (1967) *Technology and Change* (New York: Delacotte Press).

Senge, P. M. (1990) *The Fifth Discipline: The Art and Practice of the Learning Organisation* (New York: Doubleday Currency).

Sheth, J. N. (1981) 'Psychology of Innovation Resistance: The Less Developed Concept (LDC) in Diffusion Research', in J. N. Sheth (ed.), *Research in Marketing* (Greenwich, CT: JAI Press) 273–82.

Sheth, J. N. (1996) 'Organisational Behaviour: Past Performance and Future Expectations', *Journal of Business and Industrial Marketing,* forthcoming.

Soete, L. (1985) 'International Diffusion of Technology, Industrial Development and Technological Leapfrogging', *World Development,* 13, 17–25.

Starr, M. A. (1991) *Global Corporate Alliances and the Competitive Edge* (New York: Quorum Books).

Taylor, L. A. and J. B. Kaufmann (1990) 'Technology Driven Strategic Alliances; The Impact of Technological Risk and Potential on Strategic Alliance Form', unpublished working paper, Chapel Hill, NC, Kenan-Flagler School of Business, University of North Carolina.

Thompson, K. N., B. J. Coe and J. R. Lewis (1944) 'Gauging the Value of Suppliers' Products', *Journal of Business and Industrial Marketing, 9, (2),* 29–40.

van Someren, M. W., Y. F. Barnard and J. A. C. Sandberg (1994) *The Think Aloud Method* (London: Academic Press).

von Hippel, E. (1988) *The Sources of Innovation* (New York: Oxford University Press).

Whyte, W. F. (1984) *Learning from the Field* (Newbury Park, CA: Sage).
Wilson, E. J. and A. G. Woodside (1992) 'Marketing New Products with Distributors', *Industrial Marketing Management*, 21, Summer, 15–21.
Wind, Y. (1967a) 'Industrial Buying Behaviour: Source Loyalty in the Purchase of Industrial Components', unpublished PhD dissertation, Stanford University.
Wind, Y. (1967b) 'A Case Study of the Purchase of Industrial Components', in P. J. Robinson, C. W. Faris, and Y. Wind (eds), *Industrial Buying and Creative Marketing* (Boston: Allyn & Bacon) 86–109.
Wisnieski, J. M. (1991) 'Strategic Alliances for Commercializing Technology: Beauty or the Beast', unpublished working paper, Athens, Georgia: College of Business Administration, University of Georgia.
Woodside, A. G. (1980) 'Fiberglass Pitted Against Steel and Aluminium in Residential Light Pole Contest', *CEE*, August, 17.
Woodside, AG. (1981a) 'Fiberglass Poles May Offer Alternative Choice', *Electric World*, March, 126.
Woodside, A. G. (1981b) 'Fiberglass Reinforced Poles Installed in S. Carolina Parking Lot', *Lighting Design & Application*, January 1981, 60.
Woodside, A. G. (1992) *Mapping How Industry Buys*, vol.6 in *Advances in Business Marketing and Purchasing* (Stamford, CT: JAI Press).
Woodside, A. G. (1994) 'Network Anatomy of Industrial Marketing and Purchasing of New Manufacturing Technologies', *Journal of Business and Industrial Marketing*, 9, (3), 52–63.
Woodside, A. G. and D. L. Sherrell (1980) 'New Replacement Part Buying', *Industrial Marketing Management*, 9 (2), 123–32.
Woodside, A. G. and E. J. Wilson (1994) 'Tracing Emergent Networks in Adoptions of New Manufacturing Technologies', in J. N. Sheth and A. Parvatiyar (eds), *Relationship Marketing: Theory, Methods and Applications* (Atlanta: Emory University Centre for Relationship Marketing) Section III.
Yoder, S. (1994) 'Shoving Back: How H–P Used Tactics of the Japanese to Beat Them at Their Game', *Wall Street Journal*, 8 September, 1 and 6.

8 The Evolution of International Business and International Marketing Thought

Neil Hood and Stephen Young

INTRODUCTION

As the contributions to this volume reveal, Michael J. Baker's studies have spanned virtually all subject areas within the marketing discipline. It is, therefore, unsurprising that he has made an influential contribution within the international marketing and international business areas. His most notable contribution perhaps was his article on 'Export Myopia' (Baker, 1979) which was awarded first prize and the Gold Medal by the Institute of Marketing for their 1978 Marketing Writers of the Year competition. Drawing upon Levitt's (1960) 'Marketing Myopia', Michael Baker argued the case for a much greater marketing awareness by British exporters, and distinguished between the short-termist export selling activity which was characteristic of many British companies and long-term international marketing – 'a distinction,' as he puts it, 'which goes far beyond semantic quibbles or academic debating points' (Baker, 1979, p. 1).

Looking back over 25 years, the world of international business has changed enormously. Multinational enterprises (MNEs) have been a major influence upon and beneficiary of the historical tendency for the world economy to become more closely integrated. With regionalisation and globalisation, national economies, especially in the industrialised world, have become mutually interconnected through cross-border flows of goods, services and factors of production. The sales of foreign affiliates have overtaken exports as the principal method of servicing foreign markets (United Nations, 1994).

The purpose of this essay in honour of Michael Baker is to review the evolution of theories and concepts in international business and international marketing within this increasingly complex global business environment; to evaluate the contribution of academic researchers; and to reflect upon the questions which still remain. Four separate but interrelated themes are discussed: explanations for international production, the internationalisation of the firm, managing across borders and, finally, marketing across borders.

EXPLANATIONS FOR INTERNATIONAL PRODUCTION AND MULTINATIONAL ENTERPRISES

Despite the rapid growth of foreign direct investment (FDI) in the early post-war years, prior to the 1960s there was no established theory of international production or of the MNE. From the work of Hymer in 1960 (eventually published in 1976), however, a continuing thrust in the international business literature has related to explanations for the emergence and growth of the multinational enterprise. The principal question being asked was 'What are the factors explaining multinationality and for choosing international production as opposed to exporting?' The present authors (Hood and Young, 1979; see also Dunning, 1993) traced a variety of themes in the early literature, most of which had their roots in market imperfections and the sources of ownership advantages which MNEs acquired within this imperfectly competitive environment. The work of Hymer (1976), Kindleberger (1969) and Caves (1971) initiated explanations for the MNE in the industrial organisation tradition, revolving around structure, conduct and performance (following Bain, 1956). Others focused more specifically on technological advantage and technological accumulation, a theme pursued most recently within a competitive international industry context by Cantwell (1989).[1] And there were a number of contributions by financial economists, most notably Aliber (1970).

In the mid-1970s, efforts were directed at more holistic explanations of the activities of MNEs. On the basis of Coase's (1937) work, Buckley and Casson (1976) presented an internalisation theory to explain why cross-border transactions were organised by hierarchies rather than by the market. Essentially, firms undertake FDI when the transaction costs of an administered exchange are lower than those of a market exchange. The authors' major contribution included the identification of situations in which the markets for intermediate products were likely to be internalised, including government intervention, inequalities between buyers and sellers with respect to knowledge, the inability of the market to ensure sufficient control over the quality of the final products and so on. It is fair to comment that much of the subsequent orthodox economics literature on explanations for international production has followed this internalisation/transaction costs tradition, including the work of Williamson (1985), Teece (1986) and others. Dunning's eclectic (or OLI) paradigm[2] (1988) has taken a somewhat different path but has probably had more influence through its clarity for teaching purposes and value for empirical research. Dunning includes ownership-specific advantages (such as technology, marketing and finance know-how, advantages of common governance), internalisation incentive advantages (such as avoidance of search and negotiation costs, buyer uncertainty, quality protection) and location-specific variables (for example, input prices, quality and productivity, transport and communication costs, tariff and non-tariff barriers) as the constituents of his framework. The level and form of FDI will depend upon the possession of ownership-specific advantages, the advantages gained from internalising these, and the extent to which the global interests of the MNE are served by creating or utilising its ownership advantages in a foreign location (Dunning, 1993). By comparison with other theorists, Dunning does not indicate that internalisation is a general theory of international production, and recent discussion (for example, Kogut and Zander, 1993) has raised important questions about whether market failure is either a necessary or sufficient condition for the existence of MNEs and about the place of ownership advantages in multinational theory (Love, 1995).

Much of the above work has focused upon the discrete investment decisions of MNEs, within a rationalist, profit-maximising framework. Attempts are being made to provide explanations for joint ventures, strategic alliances and other kinds of cross-border relationships between and within firms, and for the choice between greenfield ventures and acquisitions. The even greater challenge is to incorporate globalisation and systems of transactions as opposed to individual transactions within the analysis, where strategic variables have a major influence (Dunning, 1993). The theoretical approaches reviewed above have also been criticised for their static nature, and there is in consequence some revival of interest in an evolutionary theory of the MNE. In reality this is bringing back to centre-stage the early work of scholars such as Penrose (1959), Vernon (1966), Burenstam Linder (1961) and Aharoni (1966).

From the perspective of this chapter, there is particular interest in Vernon's (1966) product cycle model of international trade and investment, given its roots in marketing as opposed to economics. Using the product cycle concept, Vernon explained the evolution from trade to market-seeking FDI and then to efficiency-seeking (low labour cost) FDI as the product progressed through its new, mature and standardised phases. The model was strongly rooted in its 1960s context and thus provided a framework within which the early post-war expansion of US investment into Europe, much of this in consumer goods, could be interpreted. Because of the widespread attention attracted to the critique of the model by Giddy (1978) and perhaps a recognition of criticisms of the product life cycle as a marketing concept, the framework became sidelined from core international business theory. In supporting its revival, however, Buckley and Ghauri (1993) argue that the model provided new thinking on the emergence of innovations: firms are strongly stimulated by their local environment which may be conducive to the creation of potential new techniques and products; and this idea is recognised in technological development in developing economies, which in turn, together with the notion of 'cycles', was incorporated into Dunning's (1981) investment development cycle framework. The present authors (Hood and Young, 1979) also commented that the sequential development process assumed in Vernon's product cycle model could have applicability for firms which are expanding abroad for the first time and for MNE activity associated with final product type. In that sense it was one forerunner of a second major body of literature in international business theory, namely, that of the internationalisation of the firm − if not (as Buckley and Ghauri, 1993, claim) spawning much of the empirical literature in international marketing.

THE INTERNATIONALISATION OF THE FIRM

As economists' interest in an evolutionary theory of the MNE has revived (see, for example, Kogut and Zander, 1993), so the literature on explanations for international production and on the internationalisation of the firm has begun to converge. The antecedents are also similar as the internationalisation literature is rooted in Vernon (1966) and especially, perhaps, Aharoni (1966); but, whereas Vernon assumed profit-maximising decisions, Aharoni stressed behaviouralist principles in internationalisation, rejecting the notion that firms scan the environment in search of profit opportunities. For Aharoni the decision process was regarded as a series of steps: the decision to look abroad, the investigation process, the commitment to invest and, finally, follow-up reviews and refinement. In this process the strength of commitment to proceed depends less on market growth and profit prospects than on the strength of internal or external stimuli.

Despite common roots and current signs of convergence, the literature on the internationalisation of the firm has between-times developed rather separately from that on explanations for multinationality. 'Internationalisation' has been defined as the developmental process of increasing involvement in international business, but the term is used more generally to describe firms' international market entry and market development activities (Young *et al.*, 1989). The principal questions asked include: Do firms internationalise in an evolutionary, step-by-step process, and what forms does the internationalisation take? Is foreign country market choice an important constituent of this internationalisation? Are any such processes applicable to established MNEs?

Much of the research into the internationalisation of the firm has been influenced by the behavioural conceptualisations which emanated from the 'Uppsala School' in the mid to late 1970s. The 'establishment chain' theory was initially proposed by Johanson and Wiedersheim-Paul (1975) and subsequently developed by Johanson and Valhne (1977). It postulated an internationalisation process which develops in four stages: no regular export activities; exports via agents; exports via sales subsidiary; and production via foreign subsidiary. This sequence of 'stages' indicated increased commitment in the market as a result of greater knowledge and experience. A further component of the stages approach was the idea that firms initially concentrate on nearby countries and subsequently enter foreign markets with successively greater 'psychic distance' in terms of cultural, economic and political differences. The limited empirical research underlying this model (based on a study of four Swedish firms: Johanson and Wiedersheim-Paul, 1975) was strongly rooted in the Nordic experience and its chief interest was the emergence of the multinational enterprise.

Other behavioural models also emerged from North America in the late 1970s and early 1980s, with less emphasis being placed on the evolution to multinationality. Rather the approaches highlight firms' growing dependence on exports and commitment to an increasing number of foreign markets, with authors in the marketing area being principally involved. Some of the models considered the development of export activities as an innovation–adaption cycle, based on Rogers' (1962) diffusion of innovation theory (Lee and Brasch, 1978). Others postulated an export development 'learning curve', influenced by external 'attention-evoking' stimuli (for example, unsolicited orders or enquiries) and/or internal factors (for example, managerial ambitions or excess capacity) (Bilkey and Tesar, 1977; Cavusgil, 1980; Czinkota, 1982). All of the models propose an incremental 'stages' approach – from being unwilling to export, firms proceed through various stages to become experienced, highly committed exporters – and generally support the notion of psychic distance. As with some of the developments in internalisation theory discussed earlier, the differences between the models (Crick, 1995, reviews seven such models, of which that of Bilkey and Tesar, 1977, is probably best known) reflect semantic rather than real differences (Andersen, 1993).

There has been a substantial amount of empirical literature around the themes of internationalisation stages and psychic distance. The theories have gained considerable support while also attracting significant criticism and a number of empirical studies have challenged their basic proposition. Bell and Young (1996) largely reject the five basic tenets of most models: first, firms develop in their domestic market before initiating exports; second, there is some initial resistance to becoming involved in export activities; third, firms begin by exporting to psychologically close countries before moving to more distant markets; fourth, there is a logical, linear sequence whereby firms begin by exporting, before progressing to the establishment of sales subsidiaries, or manufacturing facilities which require greater levels of commitment and investment of resources; and, fifth, the process is unidirectional and to some extent inevitable once the first tentative steps have been taken. While there is some evidence to support each of these propositions, there is also mounting counterevidence from mature and industrial markets as well as high-technology sectors. Companies may (or may not) proceed through stages; and a major problem in most quantitative research studies is that the classification criteria on stages may predetermine the findings. Psychic distance has become much less relevant as global communications and transport infrastructure improve. Rather than being undirectional and inevitable, firms may continue, for example, in the export mode indefinitely, and reversal of mode is not uncommon. For recent reviews and new evidence, see Bell and Young (1996), Young (1995) and Bell (1995).

A further major stream of work on the subject of internationalisation has developed from international industrial marketing, focusing upon interactions, relationships and networks (see Turnbull and Valla, 1986, and the work of Industrial Marketing and Purchasing group generally). The interaction approach (Håkansson, 1982) draws on a range of existing streams of thought including interorganisational theory and institutional economics. It applies concepts such as risk reduction, power and dependence, distribution channel behaviour and industrial buying behaviour. The approach is fundamentally descriptive, pragmatic and flexible in its analysis. The interaction approach may be encompassed within the broader concept of network theory (again largely developed at Uppsala), with co-operation, bonding and complementarity of objectives being stressed, and internationalisation occurring as other firms in companies' domestic networks internationalise (Johanson and Mattsson, 1988; Nordstrom, 1990; Blankenberg and Johanson, 1992). Johanson and Valhne (1990) have attempted to extend their establishment chain theory by linking it to industrial networks. The authors accept the evidence that the establishment chain model is less appropriate in turbulent, high-technology industries. Their explanation is that entrepreneurs in such firms have international networks of colleagues who influence internationalisation behaviour and facilitate the rapid establishment of subsidiaries. More recently, these same authors (Johanson and Valhne, 1992) have argued that many firms enter new markets almost blindly, with market entry emerging out of the interplay between actors in the foreign market and the local firm, including social exchange processes.

The interaction and network approaches essentially confirm the complexity of internationalisation. There is growing interest, therefore, in new conceptualisations, drawing on a variety of frameworks and stressing contingency theory (as argued initially by Reid, 1983). Thus Bell and Young (1996) have highlighted the importance of linking external environmental variables to internal characteristics of firm behaviour, and modelling the effects of rational (transaction cost) versus behavioural frameworks. There is still implicit in this model, perhaps, the notion of internationalisation as a series of independent, albeit linked, decisions; and network theory may have particular value in explaining the activities of global MNEs. There is evidence of heterarchical development in some (but perhaps not many?) MNEs (Hedlund, 1986; Forsgren, 1989; Forsgren et al., 1992), a trend which is compatible with the predictions of network theory. In networks, MNEs are transformed into loosely coupled political systems, in which subsidiaries may develop as independent power centres and decision making becomes vague (Sharma, 1992). Others (Buckley and Ghauri, 1993), however, argue that for larger, diversified multinationals, a global planning horizon is now much nearer.[3] The controversy continues, but marketing, as an eclectic discipline itself, undoubtedly has a role to play in the search for explanations (as opposed to knowledge, which is already extensive).

MANAGING ACROSS BORDERS

It is difficult to do justice to the range of issues encompassed within 'managing across borders' in the limited space available here. This is so even if the scope is restricted to international management, with an emphasis on general and strategic management. Topics covered, therefore, include global strategic planning, organising strategy (organisation design and structure) and functional management strategies in production, marketing, human resource management and finance (see, for example, Rugman and Hodgetts, 1995) – in essence managing international assets and resources (Ghauri and Prasad, 1995). The principal question being asked is: 'How does the firm, at different stages of development, manage itself for international or global competitiveness?' In large part because of the dominance of American thinking, based on an American corporate context, the focus is management of the multinational enterprise.

In reviewing the development of theories, models and frameworks in international management, what is apparent is that little of the early work provides insights which still have applicability today: this is very different, for example, from studies on the theory of the MNE, as discussed earlier. As part of their twenty-fifth and thirtieth year issues, the *Journal of International Business Studies* (Wright and Ricks, 1994) and *Management International Review* (Schöllhammer, 1994) respectively reviewed the state of research at the time when these leading journals were first launched. Schöllhammer (1994, p. 10) commenting in 1973 states that: 'Conceptualizing studies in international business and comparative management are few in number [and] . . . never became the nucleus for systematic and extensive empirical research', primarily because of difficulties in operationalising them. (A similar comment might still be appropriate today). The one conceptual framework from the early days which is still widely cited is Perlmutter's (1969) typology of management orientations (ethnocentric, polycentric and geocentric, later extended to include regiocentric). Perlmutter advocated geocentrism, meaning a global approach in both headquarters and subsidiaries, as the ideal for MNEs. The Perlmutter model was based on the prevailing culture of the company and its chief executive. While this would be seen as only one of a series of determinants of MNEs' strategic approach today, there are undoubtedly links between Perlmutter and, for example, the work of Bartlett and Ghoshal (1989) on global strategies and that of Hedlund (1986) on the heterarchical MNE. A recent study which tests for a relationship between a geocentric mind-set and multinational strategy is Kobrin (1994).

It is arguable that the most consistent themes in the international management literature have related to the strategy and structure of the multinational enterprise. Evolving from Chandler's (1962) classic environment–structure–strategy paradigm, there have been a series of theoretical and empirical contributions concerning the organisation of the MNE. Within the latter category is the work of Stopford and Wells (1972) (updated by Egelhoff, 1988) on American MNEs, who developed a 'stages' model of international organisational structures. Some recent studies have continued to stress the need for 'fit' between environment, strategy and structure, while recognising that great differences exist within the same multinational across the world in terms of environments and resources. Bartlett and Ghoshal's (1989) conceptualisation of the 'transnational organisation' as opposed to the 'international', 'multinational' or 'global' categories has received considerable attention. The transnational is seen as an integrated network organisation with some resources centralised in the home country, others distributed among national operations and all integrated through strong interdependencies. Other authors have rejected the strategy–structure paradigm and emphasised instead the role of ambiguity and chaos within organisations (Mintzberg, 1973; Nonaka, 1988). Yet other writers discuss the emergence of hybrid organisational arrangements, represented by strategic partnerships, networking and alliances (Ohmae, 1990): the environmental circumstances of the 1990s require rapid responsiveness and these are best handled by small or flat, decentralised firms or by co-operative arrangements.

The most formal approach to the development of an alternative model is contained in Hedlund's (1986) concept of the 'heterarchical MNE', which rejects the deterministic conclusions of the strategy–structure paradigm in favour of an approach which does not necessarily start with the environment but, rather, recognises multiple interactions. The view of structure is thus as a complex heterarchy of geographically diffused but globally co-ordinated core functions (Hedlund and Rolander, 1990, p.41). The heterarchical MNE may have many centres, with notions such as 'headquarters', 'home country' and 'corporate-level' disappearing. Clearly there are very close links to the network theory concepts reviewed earlier, and to the work of Forsgren and colleagues (Forsgren, 1989; Forsgren *et al.*, 1992) – a further review is found in Young *et al.*, 1994) – as well as to sociological theory and transaction cost economics.

Multinational strategy frameworks have been developed by Porter (1986) amongst others. Porter's major contributions, however, derive from his work on competitive advantage and competitive strategy (Porter, 1980, 1985) and, at least from a Western perspective, the model of the forces driving industry competition, and the concepts of the value chain and generic competitive strategies are powerful and have been extremely influential: they are also applicable in both domestic and international contexts. In understanding the constituents of MNE strategy, insightful contributions have been made by Doz (1986), Prahalad and Doz (1987) and Ghoshal (1987); Bartlett and Ghoshal (1989) and earlier White and Poynter (1984) and other Canadian authors have recognised the potential contribution of MNE subsidiaries and the role of world product mandates. There is still ambiguity about what a global strategy really means, in relation, for example, to dimensions such as co-ordination and integration across a range of value chain activities and encompassing both head-quarters and subsidiaries. Nevertheless, the distinction between multi-domestic or national responsiveness and global strategies is an important one. An understanding of the concept of 'globalisation' itself is also critical for large and small, national and multinational firms alike. There are problems in terminology which need to be addressed: for instance, the term 'multinational' (or 'transnational', the terminology preferred by the UN) may be used to describe firms with income-generating assets across borders, but is also applied in the international management literature to depict particular forms of strategy or structure ('multinational' equates to 'multidomestic'; 'transnational' is used by Bartlett and Ghoshal, 1989, to represent an organisational form). In addition, the common 'two by two matrix' frameworks are open to considerable criticism as part of an over-simplistic, 'recipe book' approach to international management.

A recent reader on international management (Ghauri and Prasad, 1995) presents three other main themes in the literature: co-operative international competition, understanding non-Western structures and developing global managers. Strategic alliances have, without question, become a major feature of global competition in the world economy. Definitional advances have primarily come from international business economists, as have the limited attempts at modelling alliances and collaborations (Buckley and Casson, 1995; Parkhe, 1991; and see also Sheth and Parvatiyar, 1992); but there have been efforts to incorporate collaboration within the context of global strategy formulation (Hamel *et al.*, 1989). As Ghauri and Prasad (1995) point out, following the emphasis in the 1960s and 1970s on comparative management studies using the US context as a norm, in the 1980s Japanese management and an understanding of non-Western structures became a major focus for comparative research. This work developed separately from that on cross-cultural management (and indeed from that on cross-cultural or intercultural marketing). And the common core, namely that of culture, has not been utilised to provide a unifying framework in the international management field. Hofstede (1994) claimed in a recent article that 'The business of international business is culture.' His own work on identifying five dimensions of national cultural differences (power distance, individualism versus collectivism, masculinity versus femininity, uncertainty avoidance, and long-term versus short-term orientation) has had a major impact (Hofstede, 1980, 1991). However, because of the fact that it concerned organisational cultures and derived from anthropological roots, it has not stimulated the wider discussion and research which it undoubtedly deserves.

MARKETING ACROSS BORDERS

In 'marketing across borders', research is directed at the central question: 'How does the exporting or international marketing firm market its products and services competitively to international and global markets?' The export decision process model of Rosson and Seringhaus (1991), suggests that there are five underlying questions to be answered in the export marketing field:

1. Should expansion be achieved through domestic or export markets?
2. If through exporting, which markets should be aimed at?
3. How should these markets be entered?
4. How should marketing and selling operations in these markets be managed?
5. What export performance level is achieved in these markets?

For the international marketing enterprise, similar questions apply, although the foreign market entry choice process is also relevant, and the co-ordination or integration of marketing programmes in the context of the regionalisation and globalisation of markets is of major importance.

In introducing this section, it is necessary to record the criticism which has been levelled at much of the prior work in, for example, the export field. Despite an extensive body of literature over more than three decades, Aaby and Slater (1989, p. 23) bemoan the fact that 'so few solid conclusions are available'. Criticism relates to the very different contexts within which research has been undertaken, leading in turn to inconsistencies in findings across studies. The literature is also criticised for its lack of conceptual frameworks, weaknesses in methodology and an emphasis on investigating simplistic research questions. Li and Cavusgil (1995) take a more optimistic view (in fact only a different interpretation) in their review of research in international marketing in the 1980s. The authors conclude that international marketing has evolved into an integrated and systematic field of study, with an identifiable series of research streams providing a general framework for researchers. However, a number of question marks remain, relating to the academic identity of international marketing and to the relationship between academic research and managerial practice. In regard to the former, some authors argue that the subject area is 'impoverished' since it lacks a theoretical base, that is a general theory of international marketing. From this perspective, it is difficult to find 'a consistent and defensible explanation of the roles, differences and similarities of international marketing to domestic marketing and international business' (Li and Cavusgil,1995, p. 271). The contrary viewpoint is that the subject area is enriched by theories drawn from other disciplines and applied and adopted in international marketing. A second question mark refers to the connection between academic research and management practice. Although management relevance has been adopted as an important criterion in research in international marketing, Li and Cavusgil rightly query whether academic work really has an impact upon practitioners. These issues go to the very heart of the dilemma concerning research in the international marketing field (and more generally in marketing and management research).

In reviewing the early literature in the international marketing area, it is interesting to observe contributions by Perlmutter applying his (by then) EPRG framework[4] to international marketing strategies (Wind *et al.*, 1973). Prominent contributions were also made by Keegan (1979) in providing a conceptual framework for multinational marketing, and Sheth (1972) who developed a model of long range multinational marketing planning. Li and Cavusgil (1995) identified the following research streams in international marketing : environmental studies, comparative studies of market systems, international marketing management (including issues of export and entry strategies as well as segmentation, product and pricing decisions and so on), internationalisation process perspectives, international marketing research, buyer behaviour studies, interaction approach (relationships of networks, cooperative ventures or alliances) and market globalisation perspectives. Environmental and comparative marketing along with internationalisation studies were pre-eminent in research up to the 1970s, while through the 1980s international marketing management was by far the most important research stream.

Of more significance than the streams of research, however, are the issues investigated. Reflecting the Li and Cavusgil (1995) observation that international marketing continues to draw heavily on other disciplines, studies of international marketing strategy commonly utilise Ansoff's (1988) growth strategies, the work of Porter (1980, 1985), Ghoshal (1987) and others (for illustrations, see Lim *et al.*, 1993; Douglas and Craig, 1995). The distinction between 'international' and 'global' also derives from the general management literature; although, in fact, there are instances of international or multinational marketing texts being reincarnated as global marketing textbooks without much, if any, change in content (Young, 1990)! What is encouraging is the growing cross-fertilisation of notions and concepts, with marketing ideas, for example, being applied in multidisciplinary research in the relatively new field of global sourcing (Levy, 1995; Cavusgil *et al.*, 1995).

Since the 1960s perhaps the most consistent interest has been in the topic of standardisation versus adaptation in international marketing programmes. Early work, mainly of a conceptual nature, focused upon the advertising function (for example, Elinder, 1961; Roostal, 1963; Fatt, 1964). Among the first authors to investigate standardisation of marketing activities were Bartels (1968) and Buzzell (1968). Bartels' (1968) starting-point (undoubtedly music to the ears of Michael Baker!) was that marketing principles are essentially the same everywhere and that the major differentiating factor is the environmental characteristics of markets. Hence, for products minimally influenced by environmental factors, a standardisation strategy was possible. Buzzell (1968) observed the benefits of and barriers to marketing standardisation and discussed which elements of the marketing mix should be standardised, to what extent and under what conditions.

This standardisation theme was popularised by Levitt's (1983) essay on the globalisation of markets. The simple but powerful argument was that companies were evolving towards global product standardisation, with advances in transport and communication technologies driving the world 'towards a converging commonality'. Standardisation of marketing programmes was regarded as an essential means by which a firm could achieve a low cost competitive position in global markets, through the realisation of scale economies in all value adding activities.

Research in this standardisation/adaptation area, however, has been bedevilled by the same problems facing much of international management and international marketing study. Differing methodologies, frameworks for analysis, research question and contexts (country, industry, product, company and type of marketing programme) have meant, unsurprisingly, widely differing results. The solution, probably correctly, is seen in terms of contingency perspectives. From this standpoint, standardisation and adaptation are viewed as extremes of a continuum, with the degree of standardisation/adaptation being contingent upon a variety of internal and external factors. A conceptual framework for determining the degree of marketing programme standardisation was developed by Jain (1989) and a revised version together with empirical evidence is contained in Cavusgil *et al.* (1993). Researchers are thus moving in this area, as in others (for example, see Yeoh and Yeong, 1995) towards a series of common contingencies which may yet facilitate a generic organising framework for, if not a theory of, international marketing.

The role of culture was suggested earlier as an under-researched topic in international management. The same conclusion is true in the field of international marketing. However, significant progress has been made with the publication of Jean-Claude Usunier's (1993) text, *International Marketing. A Cultural Approach*. Although far from an easy read, the research on culture and consumer behaviour provides concepts and insights which are applied to marketing programmes and processes around the options of global marketing or intercultural marketing approaches. Apart from reviewing and synthesising much of the earlier research on standardisation or adaptation from a cultural perspective, Usunier also highlights the significant developments which have taken place in studies on country of origin factors. Consumers' evaluations of the relationships between product and nationality were first studied with respect to the 'made-in' label (Nagashima, 1970, 1977; Cattin *et al.*, 1982; for a recent contribution, see Samiee, 1994). But there are other elements which contribute to consumer perceptions of product nationality including the image of imported products compared to national products, or the image of national versus international products; national images of generic products; the national image of the manufacturing company; and the image associated with the brand name. The research on these issues is reviewed in Usunier (1993, ch. 9). Consumer behaviour research in an international context has much to offer international marketing.

This review of some of the themes, concepts and research in the international marketing area has been brief and very selective. However, the lessons and dilemmas are clear, as pointed out earlier in the summary of Li and Cavusgil's (1995) review paper.

SOME CONCLUDING OBSERVATIONS

This partial and perhaps idiosyncratic review of the evolution of theories and models in international business over the past 25 years has highlighted significant progress in providing explanations for international production and for the internationalisation of the firm. But the explanatory power of the relevant models is being stretched by the pace of change in the international business field, and the introduction of new concepts (such as those derived from network theory, for example), while presenting helpful insights and greater realism, also removes some of the conceptual simplicity apparent in earlier work. This may, however, have to be accepted if progress is to be made. Efforts to promote, say, internalisation theory as a general theory of the multinational firm, including a theory of management direction, face major constraints (but see Buckley, 1991). Internationalisation theory, while heavily criticised, has led to the accumulation of a considerable body of empirical evidence.

In the international management and international marketing fields, the relative absence of useful, theoretical contributions is recognised fairly generally. The nature of the articles in a recent (excellent) reader on global marketing (Czinkota and Ronkainen, 1995) illustrates this conclusion very clearly. As Andersen (1993, p. 209) notes:

> academics have been too preoccupied with describing international marketing problems. As a result, little endeavour has been devoted to theory construction and evaluation. This, if true, is a phenomenon that international marketing shares with other sciences that have not reached the level of maturity in their theory development.

Despite these facts, there do seem to be ample opportunities to make progress in deriving robust organisational frameworks for problem solving in the areas of management and marketing across borders. The use of contingency approaches and the application of multidisciplinary perspectives should provide the foundations for a route ahead. What is now required is sufficient interest on behalf of academics – a case undoubtedly for intensive academic interchange, perhaps through the forum of one or a series of workshops. If this could be made to happen, it would indeed be the best tribute possible to the contribution of Michael Baker.

Notes

1. In his review of theories of international production, Cantwell (1991) regards the industrial organisation tradition as developing in two different ways: first, the market power approach in which MNE activity is not so much an independent response to competition as a means of further extending collusive networks, raising barriers to entry and reducing efficiency; and, second, competitive international industry approaches in which rivalry sustains the process of technological competition among MNEs. Like the present authors (Hood and Young, 1979), Cantwell also recognises a macroeconomic approach to understanding MNE activity: this has been excluded from the present chapter for reasons of space.
2. Dunning (1993) terms his model a 'paradigm' and also cites Buckley (1990), who indicates that internalisation is better described as a paradigm than a theory because 'the tenets of market failure that determine one form of foreign added value activity may be quite different from that of another' (Dunning, 1993, p.75). OLI refers to ownership, location, and internalisation factors.
3. Young *et al.* have presented a 'business strategy' approach to internationalisation which is consistent with the idea of global planning horizons. It is, of course, an organising framework, not a theory. In a critique of this approach, Johanson and Valhne (1992, p.25) comment that: 'the conclusions we reach concerning management of foreign market entry depends on our departure from a very different theoretical assumption about the nature of business than do competing approaches [cf. Young *et al.*, 1989]. Our business world is dynamic and invisible in a way that makes received rationality assumptions fundamentally superficial.'
4. EPRG means ethnocentric, polycentric, regiocentric and geocentric.

References

Aaby, N. E. and S. F. Slater (1989) 'Management Influences on Export Performance: A Review of the Empirical Literature 1978–88', *International Marketing Review*, 6 (4), 7–26.

Aharoni, Y. (1966) *The Foreign Investment Decision Process* (Boston, Mass.: Division of Research, Graduate School of Business Administration, Harvard University).

Aliber, R. Z. (1970) 'A Theory of Direct Foreign Investment', in C. P. Kindleberger (ed.), *The International Corporation* (Cambridge, Mass.: MIT Press).

Andersen, D. (1993) 'On the Internationalization Process of Firms: A Critical Analysis', *Journal of International Business Studies*, 24 (2), 209–31.

Ansoff, H. J. (1980) *The New Corporate Strategy* (New York: John Wiley).

Bain, J. S. (1956) *Barriers to New Competition* (Cambridge, Mass.: Harvard University Press).

Baker, M. J. (1979) 'Export Myopia', *Quarterly Review of Marketing*, 4, 1–10.

Bartels, R. (1968) 'Are Domestic and International Marketing Dissimilar?', *Journal of Marketing*, 32 (July), 56–61.

Bartlett, C. A. and S. Ghoshal (1989) *Managing Across Borders* (Boston, Mass.: Harvard Business School Press).

Bell, J. (1995) 'The Internationalization of Small Computer Software Firms. A Further Challenge to "Stage" Theories', *European Journal of Marketing*, 29 (8), 60–75.

Bell, J. and S. Young (1996), 'Towards an Integrative Framework of the Internationalisation of the Firm', paper presented at the Annual Meeting of the Academy of International Business, UK Chapter (Birmingham, Aston Business School).

Bilkey, W. J. and G. Tesar (1977) 'The Export Behavior of Smaller Sized Wisconsin Manufacturing Firms', *Journal of International Business Studies*, 8, 93–8.

Blankenberg, D. and J. Johanson (1992) 'Managing Network Connections in International Business', *Scandinavian International Business Review*, 1 (1), 5–19.

Buckley, P. J. (1990) 'Problems and Developments in the Core Theory of International Business', *Journal of International Business Studies*, 21, 657–66.

Buckley, P. J. (1991) 'Developments in International Business Theory in the 1990s', *Journal of Marketing Management*, 7 (1), 15–24.

Buckley, P. J. and M. Casson (1976) *The Future of the Multinational Enterprise* (London: Macmillan).

Buckley, P. J. and M. Casson (1995) 'A Theory of Cooperation in International Business', in P. N. Ghauri and S. B. Prasad (eds), *International Management. A Reader* (London: The Dryden Press) 126–45; reprinted from F. J. Contractor and P. Lorange (eds), *Cooperative Strategies in International Business* (New York: Lexington Books).

Buckley, P. J. and P. N. Ghauri (1993) 'Introduction and Overview' in P. J. Buckley and P. N. Ghauri (eds), *The Internationalization of the Firm : A Reader* (London: Academic Press) ix–xxi.

Burenstam Linder, S. (1961) *An Essay on Trade and Transformation* (New York: Wiley).

Buzzell, R. (1968) 'Can You Standardize Multinational Marketing?', *Harvard Business Review*, 49 (November–December), 102–13.

Cantwell, J. A. (1989) *Technological Innovation and Multinational Corporations* (Oxford: Basil Blackwell).

Cantwell, J. A. (1991) 'A Survey of Theories of International Production' in C. N. Pitelis and R. Sugden (eds), *The Nature of the Transnational Firm* (London: Routledge) 16–63.

Cattin, P., A. Jolibert and C. Lohnes (1982) 'A Cross-Cultural Study of 'Made-in' Concepts', *Journal of International Business Studies*, 13 (4), 131–41.

Caves, R. E. (1971) 'International Corporations: The Industrial Economics of Foreign Investment', *Economica*, 38, 1–27.

Cavusgil, S. T. (1980) 'On the Internationalization Process of the Firm', *European Research*, 8 (6), 273–81.

Cavusgil, S. T., A. Yaprak and P.-L. Yeoh (1995), 'A Decision-making Framework for Global Sourcing', *International Business Review*, 2 (2), 143–56.

Cavusgil, S. T., S. Zou and G. M. Naidu (1993) 'Product and Promotion Adaptation in Export Ventures : An Empirical Investigation', *Journal of International Business Studies*, 24 (3), 479–506.

Chandler, A. D. Jr. (1962) *Strategy and Structure* (Boston, Mass.: MIT Press).

Coase, R. H. (1937) 'The Nature of the Firm', *Economica*, 4, November, 386–405.

Crick, D. (1995) 'An Investigation into the Targeting of UK Export Assistance', *European Journal of Marketing*, 29 (8), 76–94.

Czinkota, M. R. (1982) *Export Development Strategies: US Promotion Policies* (New York: Praeger).

Czinkota, M. R. and I. A. Ronkainen (1995) *Readings in Global Marketing* (London: The Dryden Press).

Douglas, S. P. and C. S. Craig (1995) *Global Marketing Strategy* (New York: McGraw-Hill).

Doz, Y. (1986) *Strategic Management in Multinational Companies* (Oxford: Pergamon Press).

Dunning, J. H. (1981) 'Explaining Outward Direct Investment of Developing Countries: In Support of the Eclectic Theory of International Production', in K. Kumar and M. G. McLeod (eds), *Multinationals from Developing Countries* (Lexington, Mass.: D. C. Heath and Company) 1–21.

Dunning, J. H. (1988) 'The Eclectic Paradigm of International Production', *Journal of International Business Studies*, 19, 1–31.

Dunning, J.H. (1993) Multinational Enterprises and the Global Economy (Wokingham, Berks: Addison-Wesley).

Egelhoff, W. E. (1988) 'Strategy and Structure in Multinational Corporations: A Review of the Stopford and Wells Model', *Strategic Management Journal*, 9, 1–14.

Elinder, E. (1964) 'How International Can Advertising Be?', in S. W. Dunn (ed.) *International Handbook of Advertising* (New York: McGraw-Hill) 59–71.

Fatt, A. C. (1964) 'A Multinational Approach to International Advertising', *International Advertiser*, September, 17–19.

Forsgren, M. (1989) *Managing the Internationalization Process: The Swedish Case* (London: Routledge).

Forsgren, M., U. Holm and J. Johanson (1992) 'Internationalization of the Second Degree: The Emergence of European-based Centres in Swedish Firms' in S. Young and J. Hamill (eds), *Europe and the Multinationals* (Aldershot, Hants: Edward Elgar) 235–53.

Ghauri, P. N. and S. B. Prasad (1995) *International Management. A Reader* (London: The Dryden Press).

Ghoshal, S. (1987) 'Global Strategy: An Organising Framework', *Strategic Management Journal*, 8, 425–40.

Giddy, I. H. (1978) 'The Demise of the Product Cycle in International Business Theory', *Columbia Journal of World Business*, 13, 90–7.

Håkansson, H. (1982) *International Marketing and Purchasing of Industrial Goods: An Interaction Approach* (Chichester: John Wiley).

Hamel, G., Y. L. Doz and C. K. Prahalad (1989) 'Collaborate with Your Competitors – and Win', *Harvard Business Review*, January–February, 133–9.

Hedlund, G. (1986) 'The Hypermodern MNC – A Heterarchy?', *Human Resource Management*, 25 (1), 9–35.

Hedlund, G. and D. Rolander (1990) 'Actions in Heterarchies: New Approaches to Managing the MNC', in C. Bartlett, Y. Doz and G. Hedlund (eds), *Managing the Global Firm* (London: Routledge) 15–46.

Hofstede, G. (1980) *Culture's Consequences: International Differences in Work Related Values* (Beverly Hills: Sage Publications).

Hofstede, G. (1991) *Cultures and Organisations: Software of the Mind* (London: McGraw-Hill).

Hofstede, G. (1994) 'The Business of International Business in Culture', *International Business Review*, 3 (1), 1–14.

Hood, N. and S. Young (1979) *The Economics of Multinational Enterprise* (London: Longman).

Hymer, S. H. (1976) *The International Operations of National Firms: A Study of Direct Investment* (Cambridge, Mass.: MIT Press).

Jain, S. C. (1989) 'Standardization of International Marketing Strategy: Some Research Hypotheses', *Journal of Marketing*, 53 (January), 70–9.

Johanson, J. and L.-G. Mattson (1988) 'Internationalisation in Industrial Systems – A Network Approach', in N. Hood and J.-E. Valhne (eds), *Strategies in Global Competition* (Beckenham, Kent, Croom Helm) 287–314.

Johanson, J. and J.-E. Valhne (1977) 'The Internationalization Process of the Firm – A Model of Knowledge Development and Increasing Foreign Commitments', *Journal of International Business Studies*, 8, 23–32.

Johanson, J. and J.-E. Valhne (1990) 'The Mechanism of Internationalisation', *International Marketing Review*, 7 (4), 11–24.

Johanson, J. and J.-E. Valhne (1992) 'Management of Foreign Market Entry', *Scandinavian International Business Review*, 1 (3), 9–27.

Johanson, J. and F. Wiedersheim-Paul (1975) 'The Internationalization of the Firm – Four Swedish Case Studies', *Journal of Management Studies*, 12, 305–22.

Keegan, W. J. (1979) 'A Conceptual Framework for Multinational Marketing', in S. C. Jain and L. R. Tucker, Jr (eds), *International Marketing: Managerial Perspectives* (Boston, Mass.: CBI Publishing Company) 25–36.

Kindleberger, C. P. (1969) *American Business Abroad: Six Lectures on Direct Investment* (New Haven, Conn.: Yale University Press).

Kobrin, S. J. (1994) 'Is There a Relationship between a Geocentric Mind-Set and Multinational Strategy?', *Journal of International Business Studies*, 25 (3), 493–511.

Kogut, B. and U. Zander (1993) 'Knowledge of the Firm and the Evolutionary Theory of the Multinational Corporation', *Journal of International Business Studies*, 24, 625–45.

Lee W. Y. and J. J. Brasch (1978) 'The Adoption of Export as an Innovation Strategy', *Journal of International Business Studies*, 9, 85–93.

Levitt, T. (1960) 'Marketing Myopia', Harvard Business Review, 38 (July–August), 45–6.

Levitt, T. (1983) 'The Globalization of Markets', *Harvard Business Review*, 61 (May–June), 92–102.

Levy, D. L. (1995) 'International Sourcing and Supply Chain Strategy', *Journal of International Business Studies*, 26 (2), 343–60.

Li, T. and S. T. Cavusgil (1995) 'A Classification and Assessment of Research Streams in International Marketing', *International Business Review*, 4 (3), 251–77.

Lim, J.-S., T. W. Sharkey and K. I. Kim (1993) 'Determinants of International Marketing Strategy', *Management International Review*, 33 (2), 103–20.

Love, J. H. (1995) 'Knowledge, Market Failure and the Multinational Enterprise. A Theoretical Note', *Journal of International Business Studies*, 26, 399–407.

Mintzberg, H. (1973) *The Nature of Management Work* (New York: Harper & Row).

Nagashima, A. (1970) 'A Comparison of Japanese and US Attitudes towards Foreign Products' *Journal of Marketing*, 34 (January), 68–74.

Nagashima, A. (1977) 'A Comparative "Made-in" Produce Image Survey Among Japanese Businessmen', *Journal of Marketing*, 41 (July), 95–100.

Nonaka, I. (1988) 'Creating Organisational Order out of Chaos: Self-Renewal in Japanese Firms', *California Management* Review, 30 (3), 57–73.

Nordstrom, K. A. (1990) *The Internationalization Process of the Firm – Searching for New Patterns and Explanations* (Stockholm: Stockholm School of Economics).

Ohmae, K. (1990) *The Borderless World* (London: Collins).

Parkhe, A. (1991) 'Interfirm Diversity, Organisational Learning and Longevity in Global Strategic Alliances', *Journal of International Business Studies*, 22 (4), 579–601.

Penrose, E. T. (1959) *The Theory of the Growth of the Firm* (Oxford: Basil Blackwell).

Perlmutter, H. V. (1969) 'The Tortuous Evolution of the Multinational Corporation', *Columbia Journal of World Business*, 4, 9–18.

Porter, M. E. (1980) *Competitive Strategy* (New York: The Free Press).

Porter, M. E. (1985) *Competitive Advantage* (New York: The Free Press).

Porter, M. E. (1986) 'Competition in Global Industries: A Conceptual Framework', in M. E. Porter (ed.), *Competition in Global Industries* (Boston, Mass.: Harvard Business School Press) 15–60.

Prahalad, C. K. and Y. L. Doz (1987) *The Multinational Mission: Balancing Local Demands and Global Vision* (New York: The Free Press).

Reid, S. (1983) 'Firm Internationalization, Transaction Costs and Strategic Choice', *International Marketing Review* 1 (2) 44–56.

Rogers, E. M. (1962) *Diffusion of Innovations* (New York: The Free Press).

Roostal, I. (1963) 'Standardization of Advertising for Western Europe', *Journal of Marketing*, 27 (October), 15–20.

Rosson, P. J. and F. H. R. Seringhaus (1991) 'Export Promotion and Public Organisation : Present and Future Research' in F. H. R. Seringhaus and P. J. Rosson (eds), *Export Development and Promotion: The Role of Public Organisations* (Boston, Mass.: Kluwer Academic Publishers) 319–39.

Rugman, A. M. and R. M. Hodgetts (1995) *International Business* (New York: McGraw-Hill).

Samiee, S. (1994) 'Customer Evaluation of Products in a Global Market', *Journal of International Business Studies*, 25 (3), 579–604.

Schöllhammer, H. (1994) 'Strategies and Methodologies in International Business and Comparative Management Research', *Management International Review*, 34 (1), 5–20 (reprinted from MIR, vol. 13, no. 6, 1973).

Sharma, D. (1992) 'International Business Research: Issues and Trends', *Scandinavian International Business Review*, 1 (3), 3–8.

Sheth, J. N. (1972) 'A Conceptual Model of Long-Range Multinational Planning', *Management International Review*, No. 4–5.

Sheth, J. N. and A. Parvatiyar (1992) 'Towards a Theory of Business Alliance Formation', *Scandinavian International Business Review*, 1 (3), 71–87.

Stopford, J. and L. T. Wells Jr. (1972) *Managing the Multinational Enterprise* (New York: Basic Books).

Teece, D. J. (1986) 'Transaction Cost Economics and the Multinational Enterprise', *Journal of Economic Behavior and Organisation*, 7, 21–45.

Turnbull, P. W. and J. P. Valla (1986) *Strategies for International Industrial Marketing* (London: Croom Helm).

United Nations (1994) *World Investment Report 1994* (New York and Geneva: UN).

Usunier, J.-C. (1993) *International Marketing: A Cultural Approach* (New York: Prentice-Hall).

Vernon, R. (1966) 'International Investment and International Trade in the Product Cycle', *Quarterly Journal of Economics*, 80, 190–207.

White, R. E. and T. A. Poynter (1984) 'Strategies for Foreign Owned Subsidiaries in Canada', *Business Quarterly*, Summer, 59–69.

Williamson, O. E. (1985) *The Economic Institutions of Capitalism* (New York: The Free Press).

Wind, Y., S. P. Douglas and H. V. Perlmutter (1973) 'Guidelines for Developing International Marketing Strategies', *Journal of Marketing*, 37 (April), 14–23.

Wright, R. W. and D. A. Ricks (1994) 'Trends in International Business Research: Twenty Five Years Later', *Journal of International Business Studies*, 25 (4), 687–701.

Yeoh, P.-L. and I. Yeong (1995) 'Contingency Relationships Between Entrepreneurship, Export Channel Structure and Environment', *European Journal of Marketing*, 29 (8), 95–115.

Young, S. (1990) 'Special Issue on International Marketing: Spotlight on Europe', *Journal of Marketing Management*, 6 (3), iii–xi.

Young, S. (1995) 'Export Marketing: Conceptual and Empirical Developments', *European Journal of Marketing*, 29 (8), 7–16.

Young, S., N. Hood and E. Peters (1994) 'Multinational Enterprises and Regional Economic Development' *Regional Studies*, 28 (7), 657–77.

Young, S., J. Hamill, C. Wheeler and J. R. Davies (1989) *International Market Entry and Development* (Hemel Hempstead, Hants: Harvester Wheatsheaf/ Prentice-Hall).

9 The Changing Nature of the Marketing Profession and the Implications for Requirements in Marketing Education

Michael J. Thomas

INTRODUCTION

In 1985, my colleague Michael Baker was the national chairman of the (as it was then designated) Institute of Marketing. This year (1995) I have had the honour of becoming only the second professor in the history of the body to be chairman of the Chartered Institute of Marketing, the Royal Charter having been granted in 1989. As in many other matters, I have trodden a path pioneered by Michael Baker. That the two professors who have held the post should both be from Strathclyde University is itself remarkable since the chairman is elected by the Institute membership, which consists of professional marketing managers and directors (26 000 of them). That members have supported both of us suggests that we are both credible in the eyes of practitioners, and that they have been prepared to listen to both of us as we have played a role in directing the profession towards the future, at the level of students and at the practitioner level.

In this chapter, I would like to say something about my view of the world of marketing and business. These views will not be entirely foreign and strange, but the emphasis may differ. I would like to begin by identifying the points of emphasis that I will attempt to communicate:

1. The world of business is changing very rapidly. The world of information technology is a catalyst transforming that world.
2. The world of marketing is changing from one based on function and transactions to one based on relationships.

3. These relationships are, themselves, intercontinental and global rather than national and local, at least as far as market leaders are concerned. To understand these relationships, we have to recognise the diversity of capitalism – something that is difficult for Anglo-Americans.
4. This dynamic and changing environment has profound implications for the future of the marketing profession.
5. In this, the last decade of the twentieth century, capitalism is triumphant, but which type of capitalism? Anglo-American? Rhineland? Japanese? Brussels? Nordic? – yes, I should include oxymoronic Chinese capitalism – each offers a different vision of the way society functions but each is affected by the forces of 'global' capitalism, particularly by global financial markets.

The future of marketing and the marketing profession is the subject of fairly intense debate, as the quotation below illustrates. Marketing as a specialist function is under scrutiny. If a company embraces the marketing concept, does it need a marketing department? And if the marketing department becomes one without walls, where does the marketing profession go from here?

AGENDA FOR DISCUSSION

As the following quotation demonstrates, marketing has been coming under scrutiny, both as a concept and as a technology:

Whatever the reality behind marketing's vaunted contribution to corporate success, the large budgets it has enjoyed for decades are finally beginning to attract attention – even criticism. So much so, in fact, that doubts are surfacing about the very basis of contemporary marketing: the value of ever more costly brand advertising, which often dwells on seemingly irrelevant points of difference; of promotions, which are often just a fancy name for price cutting; and of large marketing departments, which, far from being an asset, are often a millstone around an organisation's neck. . . . why does marketing lack direction today? One answer is that the environment has changed so dramatically that marketers are simply not picking up the right signals any more. Past experience is no longer a reliable guide to what today's concerns should be. Marketing has been struggling to respond to several environmental forces that have been at work since the mid-1970s. Of these, none has been more powerful than the rise of retailers. Marketing departments have become tremendously averse to risk. Despite the accelerating rate of product launches, few genuinely new products are emerging. Of the top 50 brands in the United Kingdom, for example, only nine have been introduced in the past 18 years. Fairly or unfairly, many consumer goods CEOs are beginning to think that marketing is no longer delivering. Marketers need also to develop a deeper understanding of the details of the consumer goods value chain. This involves purchasing, logistics, and key features of the buying process, where new technologies (such as EPOS systems) and new market research techniques (such as product attribute trade-off analysis) can be used to great effect. In future, what will matter will be the ability to understand the behaviour of consumers both at the moment of purchase and during consumption; the flexibility to make trade-offs within a company's business system; and the determination to make a proactive response to retailers' strategies. Among others, Procter and Gamble has introduced the concept of category management, which combines the management of all brands in the same segment to ensure greater coherence in strategy. In the era of marketing now emerging, new divisions may be needed to separate tactical from strategic activities, just as there is likely to be a rethink about which aspects of marketing are best handled from the centre, and which on a devolved or local basis. (Brady and Davis, 1993)

This quotation, mirrored in a number of works (see, for example, Cranfield School of Management, 1994, University of Bradford Management Centre, 1995) leads me to ask a number of questions about the future: about customers (broadly defined), about markets, about technology, about communications and about marketing organisations. These questions themselves set an agenda for the discussion that follows.

Customers

1. How do customers define value and satisfaction? Do we have access to any methodology that really explores these issues?
2. From what base do we build customer loyalty?
3. How do customers trade off quality and price?
4. Can we any longer reach customers by mass advertising?

5. What implications does globalisation have for local identity: does local identity have any meaning in a world of global brands?

Markets

1. Have we begun to understand the implications for markets of the information based, post-industrial society?
2. Market saturation is a common characteristic of Western developed economies, with too many goods and services chasing too few discretionary spending customers; can marketers find solutions to this problem?
3. There are too few discretionary spending customers: is this the beginnings of bipolar society, with high-income, highly educated workers as a small minority, surrounded by a low-income proletariat, a development with radical consequences for market segmentation?
4. If markets are dominated by global producers and/or distributors, will there be any space for small and medium-sized enterprises?

Technology

1. Will the convergence of computing and telecommunications lead to the dominance of direct marketing at the expense of national advertising?
2. Real time productivity analysis in producing companies will expose unprofitable products, customers and outlets. Will outlets quickly delist unprofitable brands?
3. Customer-based market analysis brings with it risk of redundancy for data based analysis (based on aggregate Census data). Will lifestyle analysis come to dominate consumer market analysis?
4. The distance is reduced between suppliers and their customers by way of electronic data interchange, electronic mail, voice mail, video conferencing and video phone. Who will become the communicators?
5. Cable makes interaction possible: interactive marketing, voting, home shopping and game playing will touch a significant proportion of all householders. Who will be the interaction managers?
6. New product development and testing will have new interactive/response mechanisms. What are the implications for co-designing and co-makership? Where does marketing fit in?

Communications

1. Technology is already revolutionising both information access and communications. What are the marketing implications of interactive marketing: dealing directly with the human face of the customer. Multimedia are the human face of electronic information!
2. The advertising industry is showing the same globalising tendencies as manufacturing. What are the implications for marketing of a global oligopoly in advertising: eight or ten world conglomerate communications companies?

Marketing Organisation

Is the current criticism of marketing due to all (or some) of the following factors?

1. A failure to distinguish between the marketing concept and marketing function.
2. A failure to decide whether marketing is a holistic concept or a specialist subject.
3. A failure to see that the only thing that really matters is that strategic thinking is dominated by marketing imperatives.
4. A failure to match the claims of finance and manufacturing / engineering/research and development in respect of sovereignty over boardroom decision making.
5. A failure to discern that marketing and sales are inseparable.
6. A failure to understand that internal marketing must precede external marketing.
7. A failure to realise/understand that the marketing concept is the only strategic vision that can forge value added relationships with customers, employees and suppliers.

A CHANGED FOCUS

The above questions suggest that marketing as a function is going through a period of challenge and change. A recent article (Kashani, 1995) based on extensive research among international business executives concludes:

The marketing function in companies may appear to be under threat from 'own label' products, re-engineering, and advances in information technology. But it is alive and well and has undergone important shifts in recent years so as to provide a better service for top management. It has frequently become more of a line than a staff responsibility, it has developed a strategic bias, and it has become diffused throughout the organisation.

Increasing price competition, more (general) competition and the growing role of customer service are among the most important changes facing marketers generally, according to a recent study. Four key management tasks stand out: improving product quality, developing new products, keeping up with customers and improving customer service. The three most relevant competencies for marketeers are: strategic thinking, communication capability and sensitivity to customers. Specialist marketing skills appear to be among the least important.

The conclusion from this analysis is that the traditional functional approach to marketing management, emphasising the manipulation of the four Ps, must be replaced by relationship marketing because in the exchange relationship the demand side has much more power than heretofore, reducing substantially the power of the supplier, hence limiting the supplier's ability to manipulate the four Ps. We must learn to live with the death of deference, caveat vendor replacing caveat emptor.

The following quotation, from Regis McKenna's *Relationship Marketing* (1991), begins to explore the new agenda:

not a 'do more' marketing that simply turns up the volume on the sales spiels of the past but a knowledge- and experience-based marketing that represents the once-and-for-all death of the salesman. . . These two fundamentals, knowledge-based and experience-based marketing, will increasingly define the capabilities of a successful marketing organisation . . . Knowledge-based marketing requires a company to master a scale of knowledge: of the technology in which it competes, of its competition, of its customers; of new sources of technology that can alter its competitive environment; and of its own organisation, capabilities, plans, and way of doing business. Armed with this mastery, companies can put knowledge-based marketing to work in three essential ways: integrating the customer into the design process to guarantee a product that is tailored not only to the customers' needs and desires but also to the customers' strategies; generating niche thinking to use the company's knowledge of channels and markets to identify segments of the market the company can own; and developing the infrastructure of suppliers, vendors, partners, and users whose relations help sustain the company's reputation and technological edge. The other half of this new marketing paradigm is experience-based marketing, which emphasizes interactivity, connectivity, and creativity. With this approach, companies spend time with their customers, constantly monitor their competitors, and develop a feedback-analysis system that turns this information about the market and the competition into important new product intelligence. . . It is a fundamental shift in the role and purpose of marketing: from manipulation of the customer to genuine customer involvement; from telling and selling to communicating and sharing knowledge; from last-in-line function to corporate-credibility champion. . . Successful companies realize that marketing is like quality, integral to the organisation. Like quality, marketing is an intangible that the customer must experience to appreciate.

It may be concluded that, if 'do more' marketing is unsuitable to the present market condition, with knowledge-based and experience-based marketing replacing the macho, manipulative 'do more' approach, then what we are defining is relationship marketing. I have never believed that the traditional 4 Ps approach to marketing, the manipulation of the 4 Ps, so long an article of marketing faith, is in any way defensible as a theory of marketing. Interactivity, connectivity and creativity constitute at least the basis of a philosophy of dealing with the customer and the market place. Relationship building and management are the cornerstones of our future success.

What does the replacement of functional marketing by relationship marketing portend for the marketing professional? Table 9.1 summarises the contrast between the two approaches. The major conclusion that can be drawn from this analysis is that marketing is or should be an organisational orientation which transcends narrow functional activities and informs and illuminates every aspect of organisational strategy and operations. The crucial fact is that the most significant contribution which marketing brings to an organisation is not functional, but attitudinal.

At this point I want briefly to touch upon an issue that must inform our thinking about the future of the profession. Before Michael Baker

Table 9.1 The marketing strategy continuum: some implications

Strategic emphasis	Functional marketing	Relationship marketing
Measurement of customer satisfaction	Monitoring market share (indirect approach)	Managing the customer base (direct approach)
Customer information system	Ad hoc customer satisfaction surveys	Real-time customer feedback system
Interdependency between marketing, operations and personnel	Interface of no or limited strategic importance	Interface of substantial strategic importance
The role of internal marketing	Internal marketing of no or limited importance to success	Internal marketing of substantial strategic importance to success
The product continuum	Consumer packaged goods	Consumer durables, industrial goods, services
Time perspective	Short-term focus	Long-term focus
Dominating marketing function	Marketing mix	Interactive marketing (supported by marketing mix activities)
Price elasticity	Customers tend to be more sensitive to price	Customers tend to be less sensitive to price
Dominating quality dimension	Quality of output (technical quality dimension) is dominating	Quality of interactions (functional quality dimension) grows in importance and may become dominating

Source: Grönroos (1994).

began his writing career, the quality literature on marketing originated in the USA. We are to some extent still in the thrall of America. It is still reasonable to talk about Anglo-American capitalism, indicating a degree of shared heritage of values. Michael Baker, as one of the most prolific of British writers on marketing has of course made a major contribution to the British literature, and generations of students are grateful for that. We must, however, be aware of the new reality. The UK is part of the European Union and we must increasingly be informed about the differences between the Anglo-American attitude towards marketing and, for example, the German and, indeed, the

Nordic view, which has long embraced the relationship view of the marketing concept.

Let me dramatise the point that I wish to communicate by comparing certain dimensions of capitalism in the USA and the UK with capitalism in Germany and Japan, which are in many ways different from one another. Table 9.2 shows that German and Japanese attitudes towards capitalism differ significantly from Anglo-American attitudes. It is not hard to see how those differences affect marketing and marketing management.

The focus is upon the dynamics of particular industries and sectors, the emphasis on the social benefits of effective wealth creation, the emphasis on quality, the understanding of the concept of both obligation (to customers) and reciprocity, and the availability of long-term low-finance enabling both investment in people and product development, and time to develop market share and strength, rather than the tendency in Anglo-American capitalism to respond to the short term demands for profit and dividends (Thomas, 1994).

In a global marketing environment, for we all live in one global village now, we must as marketing professionals be informed about the complexity of the environment in which we operate. The challenge facing the marketing profession is to come out of the marketing silo, to interact closely with other business functions and to demonstrate that we do think globally: that, as the motto of the Chartered Institute of Marketing states, the world is our market. We must demonstrate that we are best informed with respect to the changing market-place and that we really have a strategic competence based upon the marketing concept. Do we have informed news about all of the questions raised at the start of this chapter? Will the corporation be informed at the highest level about the relationship view of marketing? If our views are not heard, understood and embraced, will we be ruled for another generation by accountants?

THE PROFESSONAL ISSUE

The dynamic and changing environment must have an impact on our profession and the way we prepare students for entry into the profession. What do professions profess?

1. That they have mastered an esoteric body of knowledge based on systematic theory.

Table 9.2 Attitudes towards capitalism

	UK and USA	Germany and Japan
Time factor	Early industrialisers	Late industrialisers
Development strategy	Innovate across a broad front of entrepreneurship and management	Catch up in technological sectors seen as the most valuable
Historical role of governments	Generally ignorant of new business developments. Interfere after the fact to 'reform' wealth creators, who have adversarial roles to regulators	Generally informed about strengths of leading economies. Co-operate before the fact to facilitate industrialisation, playing a constructive role
Education	Extremely broad and generalist, with stress on pure science and management studies	More focused on successful technologies and science applied to key sectors
Economies	Divided between macroeconomics (the whole economy) and microeconomics (the individual firm)	Organised around mesoeconomics (the dynamics of particular industries and sectors)
Social Policies	Left behind in the lead to innovate. Government may seek to reimpose social 'burdens' on business retroactively	Included in concerted efforts to industrialise, Government sees social benefits as key to winning popular consent
Development philosophy	Laissez-faire, free-trade and Anglo-American empiricism towards what markets demand, eschewing grand designs or 'picked winners'	Managed competition, early protection, and teleology – a logic of ends – already accomplished by leading economies. Target key niches, 'picked teachers'.
Transition from feudalism	Slow and largely complete. Industry built on middle-class values of individualism and self-interest	Rapid and partly unfinished. Industry built on collective concepts of feudal obligations and reciprocities
Approach to financing industry	Domination by shorter-term equity markets and risk-taking profit-oriented individuals with high uncertainty, limited knowledge, fleeting relations	Domination by longer-term bank financing and lower-risk industry-oriented institutions with lower uncertainty, deeper knowledge, closer relations

Source: Hampden-Turner, C, and A. Trompenaars (1993).

2. Its acquisition is by way of formal advanced education.
3. That that knowledge is useful and valuable in solving clients' problems.
4. By virtue of superior knowledge, professionals can, if they choose to, exercise power over their clients.
5. Because of this potential power, professionals are governed by a code of ethics.
6. It is the responsibility of professionals to avoid conflicts of interest in serving their clients.
7. In exchange for status, authority and autonomy (reinforced by self regulation), a social contract must exist between society and a profession.
8. The ultimate client for a profession is society and its need.

The accounting profession has constituted around itself what might be described as a professional ideology, and one of the questions that we in the marketing profession must address is whether we have such an ideology. I shall argue that we have. It should, however, be noted that, in addition to claiming distinctive knowledge, and responsible qualities (common sense, diligence, respectability, honesty, independence), the accounting profession over the years has well understood that the setting of accounting principles is a political process. The accounting professional institutes have been successful, in fact, as a result of their claims to possess special knowledge, and because they consistently press their claim (a political activity) that their knowledge is a strategic resource.

The knowledge base of accounting represents a mix of technology (codified knowledge) and myth (uncertainty) which has developed to manage the profession's legitimacy in the face of competing institutional demands. It is not without irony that the great myth makers of our profession, the advertising agencies, have heretofore gained such a high profile that many members of the public believe that marketing is advertising! Myth has become dissociated from codified knowledge.

THE CHALLENGES AHEAD: THE CHANGING MARKETING ENVIRONMENT

We marketers have in some respects become the victims of our own success. If we differentiate between the marketing concept and the function of marketing, there is evidence that senior management in most British and American companies have at last absorbed the concept. Companies have understood that they must be market-driven, hence everyone in the company (or organisation) must be market-driven. Thus the ownership of the ideological resource known as marketing knowledge now extends beyond our specialism and threatens to dissolve its distinctiveness and its identity. I believe that too much of the myth and not enough of the codified knowledge is being claimed by non-marketing specialists. I believe that corporate management, though claiming to understand the marketing concept, still confuses trappings with substance. I would cite three examples. Accountants will rarely admit that the marketing function is the primary revenue generator and cash flow provider to the company. If you do not market your products or services effectively and efficiently, wealth does not flow back into the organisation to underwrite costs already incurred. The operations function tends to be preoccupied with production (the Japanese have taught us all why production must be focused on the market place and market place acceptance), research and development frequently held marketing in low esteem. Few human resources managers are to be found who understand why the company telephone operators are part of the marketing team.

Thus the challenge facing the marketing profession is to demonstrate, both within the corporation and at the highest political levels, that not only are we masters of our information-based technology, but that the precise skills of marketing, namely planning, logistics and creativity, based on superior understanding of the market-place, of market forces and the need to deliver superior value, are the crucial foundation for future corporate survival and success.

What is it that we need to do to become more professional?

1. We need to come to terms with finance, we need to be able to argue effectively with the accountancy profession, to persuade them that profit is not merely the bottom line, but the residual effect of successful dealing with customers, and that most marketing activities are an investment, not a cost.
2. We need to demonstrate that we are the professional experts in respect of marketing information and as a consequence we must come to terms with information technology, since we are the people best equipped to exploit the facilities that IT capability provides.
3. We must play an active role in driving total quality management, since TQM can only work in a customer driven culture if it is

clearly understood that the customer's assessment of value added is frequently coterminous with quality.

4. We must think strategically, from the top, and recognise that in the future companies will be constructed according to customers (and perhaps customers' customers), not to product, geography or function, as has been the tradition. The marketing silo will be dismantled, but our professional skills will be in demand at the top of the organisation and at all interfaces with the customer.

We will not become more professional until we address these issues. Our critics will argue that markets are organised for purposes of exploitation, not fulfilment, that marketing as a function does not possess a monopoly of understanding human wants and values, that 'marketing's rapacious orientation to consumer needs is more plausibly attributed to the dynamics of capitalism than it is to the development and application of marketing expertise' (McKenna, 1991).

As a profession we have an unparalleled opportunity. We must demonstrate by our professionalism that we are crucial to the survival of the organisation. We must be much more forceful in transmitting our professional knowledge. Marketing professionals should become *primus inter pares* in the new environment, but this will not happen if we fail to demonstrate our superior insights.

Marketing as a culture means that marketing professionals have a critical role to play as advocates for customers and for the value system that puts the customer first. The customer is not defined as only the ultimate purchaser – the concept of internal and external marketing defines the customer as any downstream contact. Marketing relationships are becoming much more complex, and mutual dependency relationships, strategic alliances and network organisations require insights well beyond those traditionally associated with the marketing function: the management of promotion and distribution, the management of the sales force and some opportunities to influence pricing and product policy. The new insights will derive from such diverse disciplines as political economy, organisation psychology and cultural anthropology, to name but three.

The most important asset a business has is its continuing relationships with customers. We, marketing professionals, have a legitimate claim to a profound understanding of the development and nurturing of those relationships. Though increasingly it is claimed that everyone in the corporation must be charged with this responsibility, understanding it and interpreting it is the domain of the marketing professional. Marketing has a powerful rhetoric, we do not lack ideological materials. It is more than a set of techniques for the management of external markets. Our flexible ideology, our disposition to accept change as the inevitable consequence of the interplay of market forces could, however, be hijacked by others, for quite different purposes. We must therefore market marketing, certainly as a culture, and more effectively as strategy, since it is surely no longer possible to differentiate corporate strategy from market strategy. We must improve our reputation as a knowledge generator, through strategic linkages and alliances with 'leading-edge' knowledge generators. We must demonstrate, perhaps by benchmarking, that the most successful companies are those that are truly market-driven.

THE BRIDGE TO THE FUTURE

For the company, advanced marketing capability, wedded to R&D management, is the bridge to the future. We need to move from today's business to a position where we can pre-empt the future. Marketing professionals can and should play a critical role as bridge builders, indeed as innovations managers, as integrators in cross-functional project teams. I say this because I believe that the marketing professional should be the company's window onto the changing global market place, that marketing professionals can and should be able to provide those insights that are a bridge to the future. We, as marketing professionals, and as marketing educators, must be developing insights that pre-empt the future (see Table 9.3).

More urgently, perhaps, we must recognise that, in addition to high standards of objectivity, integrity and technical competence, we must, in responding to the changing environment, demonstrate that we can and will serve society in general. This requires a clear and articulate demonstration of our ability to be relevant in the political sense. Accountants have been successful in part because they have been so obviously servants of Anglo-American capitalism, with its historical focus on finance. Though this is not the correct forum to discuss this, we could develop an argument that this historic focus has served us poorly in competition with the Japanese. In the global economy, and in the face of the competitive forces within it, it is the company and the country that delivers value to the market-place that will survive. If we remain tied to the forces of manipulation and hype, if we are seen

Table 9.3   Advanced marketing capability: the bridge to the future

	Today's Business	Pre-Empting the Future
1. Intelligence gathering	Collect data about existing markets and competitors	Create insights about emerging markets and competitors; develop 'early warning signals' capability
2. Strategy formulation	Employ technology for today's competitive advantage	Exploit technology for reformulating the strategic vision of the business paradigm shift
3. Idea creation	Screen new ideas to fit to existing business	Nurture ideas for creating new business opportunities
4. Innovation	Reduce time to market	Create new products and new markets
5. Technology development	Boost performance of today's technology	Exploit the potential for leapfrogging into new technologies.
6. Technology sources	Tap and enrich the existing network	Set up new networks

merely to be the servants of our capitalist masters, we will remain marginal and untrustworthy. If we can demonstrate that we have the keys to the knowledge base that will benefit society as a whole then we may prosper.

References

Brady, J. and I. Davis (1993) 'Marketing's Mid-Life Crisis', *McKinsey Quarterly No.2*, 17–28.

Cranfield School of Management (1994) *Marketing – the Challenge of Change*; research undertaken on behalf of the Chartered Institute of Marketing.

Grönroos, C. (1994) 'From Marketing Mix to Relationship Marketing: Towards a Paradigm Shift in Marketing', *Management Decision*, 32 (2), 4–20.

Hampden-Turner, C. and A. Trompenaars (1993) *The Seven Cultures of Capitalism* (New York: Doubleday).

Kashani, K. (1995) 'Marketing Future: Priorities for a Turbulent Environment', *Journal of Long Range Planning*, 28 (4), 87–98.

McKenna, R. (1991) *Relationship Marketing* (Reading, Mass.: Addison-Wesley).

Thomas, M. J. (1994) 'Marketing – In Chaos or Transition', *European Journal of Marketing*, 28(3), 55–62.

University of Bradford Management Centre (1995), *Manufacturing – the Marketing Solution: Benchmarking marketing's contribution to competitive manufacturing*, research undertaken on behalf of the Chartered Institute of Marketing.

10 Star of Marketing Academe: the Person, the Place, the Nation, the World, the Universe and Everything

John Saunders

the real source of the depression, as the conference gathered for the sherry, and squinted at the little white cardboard badges on which each person's name and university were neatly printed, was the paucity and, it must be said, the general undistinguished quality of their numbers. Within a very short time they had established that none of the stars of the profession was in residence – no one, indeed, whom it was worth travelling ten miles to meet, let alone the hundreds that many had covered. But they were stuck with each other for three days. (David Lodge, 1984, p. 4)

Then Morris Zap, a star, flies in and David Lodge's *Small World* is in motion.

Although universities often put the academic secondary to the university, that is only appropriate in the great universities, such as Cambridge, Harvard, the Sorbonne or Tokyo. Elsewhere stars outshine the institution. On an early trip to the USA, I met a distinguished American academic in an airport. He asked who I was; of course he had never heard of me. I mentioned what was then my university. 'Never heard of it,' he said. I then mentioned a colleague. This time he responded: 'Oh! So Bradford *is* Peter Doyle. Is there anyone else in England besides Peter Doyle and Michael Baker?' Crestfallen, I decided not to tell him that Michael Baker *is* Scotland, not England. Sometimes the star is bigger than the institution, the town or even the country.

This chapter asks what makes a star in our academic firmament? We use exploratory research to seek the essence of stardom. First, qualitative research techniques identify stars and non-stars and then triads of these are compared to measure stardom. Next, a natural analogy produces a classification of stars and their birth. The conclusion defines stars.

METHODOLOGY

Methodology usually follows a literature review and a theoretical framework. Here we do not follow that tradition since no one has written about what makes a marketing academic a star, beyond Boorstin's (1962) observation that 'A celebrity is a person who is known for their well-knowness.' Or maybe, in academic life, stars are the people who write a best seller: 'a book which somehow sold well simply because it is selling well' (Boorstin, 1962). We search for more substance than these tautologies.

Since we know little about the problem in question, we use qualitative research (Sampson 1986). First, a series of non-directive interviews with a small sample of academics gave a list of 20 marketing academics they thought were stars and 20 people who were not. Repertory grid interviews then tested a random triad of the stimuli (the 40 academics) asking a second sample of academics to explain how two out of the three were alike and how they differed from the third (Riley and Pulmer, 1975). The basis for the similarity became the emergent pole and the difference, the implicit pole. With the poles from the first triad exhausted, respondents commented on other triads until no more poles emerged.

Most marketing researchers now prefer elicitation interviews to the repertory grid approach, but this method was dropped after people could not stop laughing when asked questions such as: 'You are at a bar at a MEG conference and David Jobber walks up towards you. What do you think?'

ACADEMIC POLES

As is usual with the repertory grid, many of the responses were unusable, being either too descriptive or too evaluative: for example, 'Baker and Saunders are fat and Mark Uncles is not', or 'he's an absolute ****.' After analysing the results and combining similar poles, several pairs predominated. We look at them.

Clear or Weighty

Some stars are clarifiers; others are weighty. David Aaker's, George Day's and Malcolm McDonald's articles sometimes cover complex subjects but they are usually interesting and clear. Lord Chesterfield (1750) advised his son to read such writers: 'The easiest books are generally the best for whenever the author is obscure and difficult in his language, he certainly does not think clearly.' Although virtuous, this does not differentiate stars from non-stars. Some writers, such as Igor Ansoff and Robin Wensley, write in a weighty style that has gravity and that shows they are grappling complex problems. Maybe Colton (1821) is more wise than Chesterfield: 'Many books require no thought from the people who read them, and for a very simple reason – they made no such demand on those that wrote them.'

Clarity comes from both content and style. Many of the clarifiers write in plain English but others of their breed use long sentences with complex structures. The lesson is: unless you can do it well, keep it simple. Alternatively, make things complicated if your case is poor. George Orwell fell foul of this. He always strove to write clearly (Orwell, 1946) so it is obvious when he writes piffle (Orwell 1947). In Orwell's case, clear writing does not mean clear thinking. Recently I overheard a weighty author explain why his papers were so difficult to understand: 'My papers are deliberately confusing because that way I make people think.' Think what? People similarly defend bad lecturing: a bad lecture is good for students because it makes them work harder outside the class. Weighty writers and lecturers are frustrating to work with. One great artist of confusion always leaves people thinking that he is too clever for them; when I confuse people, they think they are too clever for me! Most stars strive to make their work factual, entertaining and brief. Only a few master the art of acquiring the right reputation by being judiciously boring (Maugham, 1930).

Focused or Opportunistic

Leslie de Chernatony and Malcolm McDonald joined academic life and grew to eminence quickly by focusing on areas of great academic and business interest: branding and marketing planning. Internationally there are so many researchers and so much is being published that concentrating on one or a few research areas is the only way to keep up to date and gain attention. In Britain the competitive pressures are fewer but, by focusing, researchers quickly become *the* authority in their chosen area. It is a seductive strategy. Many of our stars focus and their names are synonymous with their interest: Gordon Foxall with consumer behaviour, Peter Leeflang with aggregate modelling, Paul Green with multi-attribute modelling, Robert Cooper with new product development, Luiz Moutinho with new algorithms, and many others.

Focusing works for many but other stars flit from subject to subject. I learned from Peter Doyle the delight of skipping between modelling and qualitative research. Outside the UK, Gilles Laurent, Shelby Hunt, Philip Kotler and Arch Woodside enrich marketing with their joyful disregard for boundaries. Do not be seduced by these seemingly random walks. Their interests represent concentric diversification around core interests rather than cherry plucking. Although switching interests can give insights that less flexible researchers do not have, switching interests can poorly position an academic career. I learned this at an AMA conference when introduced on consecutive tracks by Susan Douglas as Britain's expert on international marketing and then by Paul Green as Britain's leading modeller. Thank goodness there were no more Brits there!

Intellectual or Pragmatic

Our profession is like Hollywood: there are more intellectuals among the stargazers than among the stars. The comparison is not completely true since many of our stars do show raw intelligence and the ability to think rationally rather than emotionally. What often is lacking is the ability or desire to think abstractly about a wide range of aesthetic or philosophical subjects. They are akin to other high achievers, like the great adversaries Rommel and Montgomery, who only read books about war (Young, 1950). These obsessive characters are hard to beat. Defeated Boris Spassky bleated: 'I have a wife and child, I read Tolstoy. I cannot play with Fischer' (*The Economist*, 1995). At any American conference, go to the sports bar to hear similar groans from the few Brits there.

Not all stars are dull. P. V. Abede, Scott Armstrong, Gilles Laurent and Robin Wensley are intellectual by any measure, but are they a dying breed? Once high achievers balanced their excellence with other lives: authors as civil servants or destitutes, chess players as Shake-

spearean scholars or drunks,[1] athletes as police or carpenters. Mono-
mania matters little in sport but what of those in positions of influence?
A politician staying with the Reagans was not able to sleep so he
looked round their holiday home for a book to read. There were none.
On another occasion a reporter asked Ronald Reagan what he read.
The President replied that he was going to read *Bonfire of the Vanities*.
A year later the reporter asked the same question and got the same
answer. Help!

Compared with the national population, all university academics
must be intelligent and most academic stars are very bright. But even in
our very gifted community some are demonstrably at the extreme end
of the bell-shaped curve. Watch Alain Bultez solve equations on a
board at an international conference and you know you are seeing
something special; working with Michel Wedel through some econo-
metrics is like hanging onto the back of a power boat without the water
skis. These two are not monomaniacs; both were international athletes.

Intelligence helps academic success, yet many business schools house
Oxbridge scholars whose brains never delivered. In Britain, others hide
their intellect, sometimes so successfully that other people think success
comes without effort. The French admire cleverness, Japanese admire
dedication, the Americans admire hard work, but we think some
people are too clever by half. What hope for a country where the
people dislike cleverness and the intellectuals despise business?

Pragmatists in Britain learn not to look too smart, but it takes a
special sort of intelligence to be pragmatic. They see what matters and
go for it. Pragmatism helps academics communicate widely, speak to
practitioners and make money. It is market orientation. Pragmatists
give what people want, be they publishers, industrialists, the Economic
and Social Research Council, journal editors or reviewers.

Team Player or Individualist

Many stars are individualists whose only concern is their own development, although most do work with peers or their junior colleagues
on research projects. They lead by example but act as mentor accidentally. In contrast, Michael Baker, Malcolm Cunningham, Andrew
Ehrenberg and Graham Hooley are team players whose influence
extends beyond their immediate colleagues. Solitary researchers enhance their business school's reputation but not as broadly, or as long
term, as team builders.

Much of academic life is solitary. There are few jobs that have people sitting alone so often. Individuals build research and teaching reputations that stick. When managers change companies they carry their belongings in a briefcase; academics need a Pickford van. Football stars transfer their fame to their new club but, through their research, academics transfer their past goals, too. Gaining tenure, achieving good teaching ratings, having to claim percentages of publications when being put up for promotion – all train young academics to work independently, yet we know that teams win. There is certainly a tension between the early stages of academic development and cultivating stars who can lead.

Are solitary stars enough? If it were just a matter of buying stars, any fool could create a good football team or business school. Individuals can win fame and fortune but research excellence needs depth, not the odd genius.

Extrovert or Introvert; Visible or . . .

After Michael Baker and I cleared the dance floor by dancing a jig together, he explained that doing that sort of thing was important because it showed 'we are only human'. Possibly true, but if so there could be a panic to leave the human race as well as the dance floor. Other explanations for the behaviour are exhibitionism, drunkenness or anti-intellectualism. The British at international conferences are often as conspicuous as British tourists. The event impresses us but by joking and acting about we show we are one of the lads, not really international researchers. At home or in business the British use humour to avoid revealing their true selves, or to have social contact when there is nothing to say. This apparently extrovert behaviour is more conspicuous abroad because other nationalities have other defences.

Extroverts find conferences great fun. They are events that give them a chance to drink a lot, eat (sometimes well) and socialise, all at someone else's expense. They enjoy the networking, performing and heated discussions in sessions. They increase their stardom by showing their skills and by allowing people to put a jolly face to their name. While conferences are the big payoff and joy to some jet setting academics, others find them painful. Many do not bother – for a long time such jaunts were beneath London Business School – or attend them because it is what one has to do. Stars come in both forms. Some extrovert characters are always around, hard to miss or avoid. Other stars rise without ever being seen, shining from paper only.

Qualitative or Quantitative

Neither side of this divide dominates. Some stars, such as Paul Green,
J. D. C. Little, Gary Lilien and Peter Leeflang, are almost wholly
quantitative, while others, Gordon Foxall, Dale Littler and top Scandinavian researchers, are conspicuously not. Butterflies, like Peter
Doyle and myself, flit between the two to no great advantage.
     Although not modellers, most stars are methodologically strong.
Qualitative research does not mean loose or non-rigorous research.
Similarly, quantitative does not mean unimaginative or unpractical
research. Both domains have value and produce excellent and poor
research. Few stars are really modellers, that is, people who solve
problems using mathematics. Many people do, however, use appropriate statistical methods to analyse or validate their results. These
researchers look like modellers to many innumerate academics because
their statistics are as impenetrable as the modeller's algebra. Mathematics is not essential to becoming a star but few rise without being
comfortable in Graham Hooley's (Hooley and Hussey, 1994) multivariate jungle.

Consultant or Academic

There can be few professions where total income is as unrelated to
professional status as it is in business schools. The stars who earn six
figure incomes outside their faculties show that consulting need not do
academic damage. Equally, consulting is not essential to stardom, since
many stars are poor and pure.
     Consulting and academic stardom can mix at the top but can
damage getting there. It takes time and energy to become a star, so
the best sequence is to become a star first and then get rich. Many
people who have tried to do it the other way round often have to make
do with being only rich, although usually charging lower daily rates
than stars. This is true of business schools as well as professors. Schools
dominated by executive teaching, including Ashridge, Cranfield, Hen-
ley and Manchester Business School, find research excellence elusive.
Only the very top schools, Harvard, INSEAD, IMEDE and the
London Business School, have the strength to excel in research,
consulting and management training.
     After the last research selectivity exercise, many people expected that
their experience with the Council for National Academic Awards
(CNAA) would enable the new universities to excel on teaching quality.

Not so: in business and other disciplines there is a high correlation, if not congruence, between the Higher Education Funding Council's teaching and research assessments. All but one of the British business schools rated '5' for research excellence are also excellent at teaching, while over 80 providers of business education are excellent at neither (Saunders and King, 1995). This explodes the myth that researchers ignore teaching. Some do and some do not. While one star gives an inaugural lecture that shows no signs of preparation or consideration for his audience, another preens himself before every encounter with a class: smoothes his jet black hair, checks his well-cut suit and adds an extra dash of *Paco Rabanne*.

Do stars have to excel at research, teaching and consulting? Certainly not, but stars cluster where teaching and research excel, and where consulting opportunities abound. Some stars help create all-round excellence; some are lucky enough to be in the right place; others are smart enough to move there.

The Academic Universe

Like marketing research and co-authors, academic research does not always give what you want. Despite comparing stars with non-stars, the repertory grid does not give dimensions that identify stars. All the poles reported have stars at both ends. They are a mixed bunch. The one feature that marks stars is their individuality, their ability to find their own way through the ambiguous academic world. Stars are original in style as well as thought, or are they?

Qualitative research has many options and one uses analogies to force out new ideas (Crawford, 1991). The one we use here is the celestial star, of which our sun is one. This produces a taxonomy that captures many academic stars.

BIRTHPLACE OF THE STARS

Stars do not occur spontaneously but form in the arms of spiral galaxies or other galaxies where there are the gas, dust and molecular clouds from which young stars are born. These regions also contain old stars, but the new ones one day outshine them.

Great business schools also cultivate stars. A critical ingredient of these are old stars about which the new ones form. The mother of these in Britain is the London Business School, with Andrew Ehrenberg and

Ken Simmonds at the centre of the first star nidus. There grew Paddy Barwise, Peter Doyle, Mark Uncles and Robin Wensley. Peter Doyle soon left to form the second rise of Bradford that nurtured Colin Egan, Jim Lynch, Graham Hooley, David Jobber, Paul Michel, John Saunders and David Shipley. In its first rise under Gordon Wills, Bradford had spun off Martin Christopher and David Midgley. Meanwhile, north of the border, Michael Baker's nest at Strathclyde produced an international line of stars who have chaired the world. Among those who originated there, many of whom started as one of Michael Baker's doctoral students, are George Avlonitis, Adamantios Diamantopoulos, Susan Hart and Steve Parkinson. Not all stars come from these hotbeds. Some rise in other places, but a disproportionate number of senior professors the world over originate from a few universities.

Supernovae

Bradford and Gordon Wills specialise in supernovae: stellar objects that explode, emitting large amounts of energy. When they occur, these rare phenomena scatter debris across the universe. When Gordon Wills left, first Bradford and then Cranfield, he did not go alone. Some people moved with him and changed circumstances caused others to leave. Although cataclysmic for those close to them, these explosions create opportunities where they occur and energise valuable people who otherwise might become too cosy. After Gordon Wills left Bradford, Peter Doyle quickly created another team who grew strong until a second supernova scattered them. With the departure of Peter Buckley and Steve Parkinson from Bradford it looks as though Bradford University Manchester Centre has done it yet again. One is a blip; two is a coincidence; but three looks like a pattern. There must be something in the curry at Emm Lane!

Novae

Novae are stars that suddenly glow brightly. These can occur anywhere, often outside the nidus where most stars are born. By focusing their effort some stars rise quickly, as did Malcolm McDonald and Leslie de Chernatony. Sometimes the rise is not quick but it appears so because of a very significant publication that gains huge attention. Robin Wensley's betas and boxes article did that for him, as did Peter Doyle's early work on multidimensional scaling. So strongly do these early articles position people that the association often remains for decades after their research has changed.

Some novae dull after the sudden bright period. Sometimes this occurs for academic stars when sudden recognition opens consulting opportunities that seduce them away from a threadbare academic life. Others disappear in the UK because they develop an international focus and so concentrate on international journals and conferences. In truth these stars are glowing more brightly than ever before, and will probably help their business schools get a five star rating, but are out of sight of the Marketing Education Group-bound majority. London Business School have gone this way, as have Nigel Piercy and Gordon Foxall.

Blue Giants

Each new wave of academics is more productive than the older, fading ones. Astronomers also believe this of the stars that they observe. These follow a main sequence on a Hertzprung–Russell diagram that plots luminosity against the surface temperature that gives them their colour. Where we have our 4 Ps astronomers use a mnemonic to help them remember the O, B, A, F, G, K and M spectral types of stars: O, Be A Fine Girl; Kiss Me. The youngest, O and B, stars are the blue giants that glow the brightest and consume the most energy. In marketing they dash from conference to conference, writing many articles and books in a way that makes the older lags feel tired. They win many prizes and clearly know their stuff. Adamantios Diamantopoulos, Susan Hart, Luiz Moutinho and Bodo Schlegelmilch are clearly blue giants, but also watch out for rising stars Richard Elliot, Christine Ennew, John Fahy, Jim Saker and Gareth Smith.

Sun

Our sun is a middle-aged star half-way down the main sequence. It has lost some of its energy of youth but still keeps producing. As John Wayne said in *True Grit*: 'She reminds me of me.' Many of the blue giants burn out fast but some of the wily stars in the main sequence gather some planets around them and exchange their energy for the satellite's speed. Malcolm Cunningham was certainly one of these. Solar systems one day run down but in academic life some of these stars create the star beds where new ones grow.

Red Dwarfs

Not all stars rise suddenly. Some stars are less flashy than the blue giants and build great academic strength over time. These K and M stars do not rise without trace but have a steadily evolving career, with a careful accumulation of professional knowledge, contacts and expertise. Count David Carson, Gordon Greenley, Graham Hooley, David Jobber and Peter Turnbull amongst these stalwarts.

Red Giants

A few blue giants do not shrink, but because of their magnitude grow to become red giants – superstars. The strength of these is so great that they shine across the globe. Philip Kotler is probably top of this list that also includes Frank Bass, Robert Cooper, George Day, Paul Green, J. D. C. Little, Gary Lilien and our Peter Doyle and Andrew Ehrenberg.

Cephoids

Millions of years from now our sun will move off the main sequence to become a variable star, such as a cephoid. These do not have a continuous output but pulse. Whereas red dwarfs produce a steady stream of solid material, these yellow cephoids periodically glow as brightly as the giants. J. D. C. Little is one of these. His output is strong, not massive but every few years he produces a paradigm-shifting paper. Robin Wensley's series of noted, and prize-winning, papers in the *Journal of Marketing* makes him one of these. This is the traditional academic model of excellence at which Oxbridge excels, although clearly not in marketing. Sadly, the periodic evaluation of the research selectivity exercise makes this strategy dangerous.

Binary Stars

Hamel and Prahalad, Leeflang and Wittink are binary stars who give off pulsating energy by working together. Occasionally, two people find working together provides synergistic benefits. In academic life these sometimes start with a small solar system with a planet basking in the glow of a star and hoping to be a star themselves one day. I tried for this with Peter Doyle, while Susan Hart and Steve Parkinson achieved it with Michael Baker. Sometimes the binary stars are growing together, as are Jim Saker and Gareth Smith, or even try becoming married: Sally Dibb and Lyndon Simkin and some other couples.

Comets

These are stellar objects that gain momentum and brightness by coming close to a star. The relationship is not as long as a binary star but some academic comets accumulate light in passing. This could include collaborating with a superstar in developing strong papers, as did Robin Wensley and Mary Lambkin with George Day. Although some stars grew into binary stars through long associations with Michael Baker, the successful trajectory of many of his doctoral students was closer to that of a comet.

White Dwarfs

After having fun as a cephoid, our sun will sink to being a white dwarf, hot but not so bright, then probably slowly burn to a cinder, or black dwarf. It sounds a nice way to go.

Black Holes

At the end of their life some stars become flashy supernovae, then collapse to become black holes: large dense masses out of which nothing useful escapes. We all know some of these people and many business schools are like that, too.

STAR QUALITIES

The astronomical analogy, while giving some insights into the life cycle of stars, still leaves us with a fragmented picture but within all this diversity there are features that usually hold true (Figure 10.1). *Intelligence* is not all, but there are few academic stars who are not very bright; but also there are many academics who do not become stars. Besides being intelligent they are also *wise*: they work out how to direct their intelligence. They know themselves and quickly learn how to succeed. They often specialise, get close to other stars, recognise the top people, places and journals and work towards them. The wise and intelligent quickly understand that *knowledge* is critical in the knowledge game. They learn from other people, and often complete a

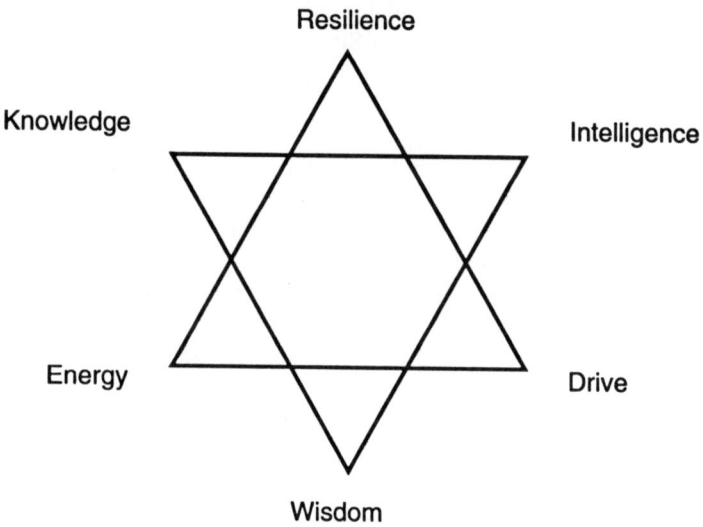

Figure 10.1   The academic star

doctorate early in their career. They learn the methodologies that suit them and how to make the maximum out of the research they do. A few will eventually change the world but, before that, they have the strength of character to change themselves to fit the world they want to change.

Few people succeed accidentally; most succeed because their ability matches their desire to climb their chosen peak. They *drive* to achieve their goals and mostly from a very early age. While many of us were dreaming of being train drivers, one little boy watched Mortimer Wheeler on *Animal, Vegetable or Mineral* and decided to become a professor. Most people will agree that Peter Buckley's early decision paid off. The drive needs *energy* and enthusiasm. In Britain we like to dream of succeeding by flair, without effort. Few people in any profession ever do. Sadly, there is no substitute for hours on the job. The tragedy is that so many people are good at hiding how they worked for their success. Do not be taken in by them. It is just a smart way of keeping the others down. Finally, it takes *resilience*. Resilience because academic success means frequent rejection. Everyone who tries has papers rejected by top journals and the Economic and Social

Research Council proposals turned down. The difference between the stars and the rest is that the stars suffer more rejections.

So, what is a star? Encarta (1995) says a star is 'a large body composed of gravitationally contained hot gasses emitting electromagnetic radiation, especially light'. Not far off what we are seeking. Large body? Yes. Hot gasses? Certainly. Radiating light? That is it! An academic star is a body that gives off more light than it receives. One that sheds light where there was darkness. That influences bodies around it. Has unbounded energy. Cultivates other stars and certainly cannot be ignored. That is Michael Baker: the star's star.

Thank you Michael for all you have done and for all that you will do.

Note

1. The Russian grand master Alexander Alekhine, a doctor of law, was addicted to chess and alcohol. He once was so drunk that he urinated at the chess board in a competition.

References

Boorstin, D. J. (1962) *The Image* (London: Weidenfeld and Nicolson) 3, 8.

Chesterfield, Lord (1750) *Letters to His Son*, February, reprinted Chesterfield Press 1917, 8.

Colton, C. C. (1821, 1922) *Lacon*, printed for the author, Exeter, 2, 248.

Crawford, C. M. (1991) *New Product Management* (Homewood, Ill.: Irwin).

Economist (1995) 'The Grand Masters', 20 May, 120.

Encarta (1995) 'Microsoft'.

Hooley, G. J. and M. K. Hussey (1994) *Quantitative Methods in Marketing* (London: Academic Press).

Lodge, D. (1984) *Small World* (London: Penguin).

Maugham, W. S. (1930) *The Gentleman in the Parlour* (London: Mandarin).

Orwell, G. (1946) 'Politics and the English Language', *Horizon*, April.

Orwell, G. (1947) *The English People* (London: Collins).

Riley, S. and J. Pulmer (1975) 'Of Attitude and Latitude: A Repertory Grid Study of Perceptions', *Journal of Marketing Research Society*, 17(2), 1–23.

Sampson, P. (1986) 'Qualitative Research and Motivational Research', in R. Worcester and John Downham (eds), *Consumer Marketing Research Handbook* 3rd edn (London: McGraw-Hill) 29–55.

Saunders, J. and R. King (1995) Britain's Best Business Schools', *Loughborough University Business School Working Paper*.

Young, D. (1950) *Rommel: The Desert Fox* (Glasgow: William Collins).

Index